AMERICAN NAVAL HEROES

KENNIKAT AMERICAN BICENTENNIAL SERIES

Under the General Editorial Supervision of
Dr. Ralph Adams Brown
Professor of History, State University of New York

ALEXANDER MURRAY ESQ.

Late Senior Officer

of the United States Navy

G. Dawson Printer

BIOGRAPHICAL SKETCHES

OF DISTINGUISHED

AMERICAN NAVAL HEROES

IN THE

WAR OF THE REVOLUTION,

BETWEEN THE

AMERICAN REPUBLIC

AND THE

KINGDOM OF GREAT BRITAIN;

COMPRISING SKETCHES

OF

COM. NICHOLAS BIDDLE,	COM. EDWARD PREBLE, AND
COM. JOHN PAUL JONES,	COM. ALEXANDER MURRAY.

With Incidental Allusions to other Distinguished Characters.

———

" Patriots have toil'd, and in their country's cause
Bled nobly ; and their deeds, as they deserve,
Receive proud recompense."
*   *   *   *   " Th' historic muse,
Proud of the treasure, marches with it down
To latest times."

═══════════

BY S. PUTNAM WALDO, ESQ.

KENNIKAT PRESS
Port Washington, N. Y./London

134337

BIOGRAPHICAL SKETCHES OF DISTINGUISHED
AMERICAN NAVAL HEROES

First published in 1823
Reissued in 1970 by Kennikat Press
Library of Congress Catalog Card No: 73-120897
ISBN 0-8046-1290-0

Manufactured by Taylor Publishing Company   Dallas, Texas

KENNIKAT AMERICAN BICENTENNIAL SERIES

PREFATORY NOTICE

FROM THE WRITER TO THE READER.

———

THE following volume was commenced in consequence of perusing the well known Letter of the venerable Statesman, JOHN ADAMS, to the well known Editor of the Baltimore Weekly Register, in which this unrivalled American Patriot says to that indefatigable American Journalist, "It is greatly to be desired that young gentlemen of letters in all the states, especially in the thirteen original States, would undertake the laborious, but certainly interesting and amusing task, of searching and collecting all the records, pamphlets, newspapers, and even hand-bills, which in any way contributed to change the temper and views of the people and compose them into an independent nation."

Without aspiring to the proud eminence of a "young gentleman of letters," I undertook the "laborious, but certainly interesting and amusing task of searching and collecting all the records, pamphlets, newspapers, and even hand-bills" that came within the scope of my researches.

By the goodness of my parents, a very considerable number of Revolutionary pamphlets, from the scattered library of Maj. Gen. ISRAEL PUTNAM came into my hands. By researches, which would remind a lover of Shakspeare of one of *his* characters, who sought "for two kernels of wheat, in two bushels of chaff," I gathered a file of newspapers, embracing the whole period of the War of the American Revolution; and containing a vast variety of facts relating to NAVAL HEROES, not to be found in voluminous histories of that wonderful war. I also obtained the "Journals of

the Old Congress," the Acts of which were authenticated
by the signature of a man whose *name* and *truth* are synonymous—CHARLES THOMSON.

Before commencing the volume, I made this " Renewed
Request."

Mr. Babcock—

In consequence of a " request," which you obligingly inserted in your useful and interesting paper some weeks
since, and which, no less obligingly, was extracted into
many of the leading Gazettes of the Republic, a very considerable mass of materials has been gathered for an intended publication, to be entitled " Biographical Sketches
of American Naval Heroes in the War of the Revolution."
This subject, for some time past, has occupied much of the
attention of the subscriber. He was induced to commence
the work, not more by his own inclination, than by the so-
licitation of his friends, whose opinions confirmed him in
the propriety of his own. " *Our Fathers ! where are they?*"
was an ejaculation of an ancient patriarch. The members of the " Old Congress"—The signers of the declaration of American Independence—the officers of the Army
and Navy of the Thirteen Colonies, in the gloomy period of
the Revolutionary struggle—" where are they ?" They are,
most of them, reposing in the tombs of a country, the Independence of which they secured by their toil, their blood
or their deaths. Through the medium of the Press, which
is the palladium of our liberties, and the source of our
knowledge, we have learned something of the gigantic
Statesmen and Soldiers of that most important epoch of
American history—but the rising generation, like the writer, must search through the scattered and brief details of
that period, and catch the narrations of the few hoary headed *Seamen* who survive to learn the unsurpassed achieve-

ments of the matchless " Naval Heroes," who then dared,
with means apparently wholly inefficient, to assail the
vaunting " Queen of the ocean," as Britain then called and
still calls herself, upon her favourite element.

Although the writer is aware that "*the half is not told*"
him, yet sufficient has been discovered by research, and
received from obliging correspondents, to have enabled
him to make considerable progress in the work mentioned.
The cotemporaries, sons and grand-sons of the following
catalogue of heroes are most earnestly requested to forward, as soon as possible, brief notices of the birth—early
life—the time they entered the Naval service in the revolution—the ships they commanded—the British ships they
fought and conquered, or to which they were compelled to
strike—incidents of their lives from the conclusion of the
revolutionary war to the times of their death—to wit :

Commodores Whipple—Hopkins—Biddle, the elder—
Jones—Murray—Decatur, the elder—Truxton.

Captains Preble—Manly—Little—Nicholson—Harden
—Tryon, and any others who in a high or minor station
signalized themselves in the revolution.

The task which the writer has undertaken is arduous,
delicate, and interesting—he again solicits aid—he asks
for nothing but the " *raw materials*"—He will *manufacture*
them according to the best of his experience; and if, from the
coarseness of the texture, the *fabric* should be condemned,
he will at least enjoy the satisfaction of having made a laudable attempt to rescue from oblivion the memories of departed patriots which ought to be cherished.

S. PUTNAM WALDO.

In compliance with this " request," I was honoured with
several deeply interesting communications from gentlemen

whose names I should feel proud in mentioning here, were
I not inhibited by injunctions of concealment.

I have listened with rapture and attention to the *oral
narrations* of a few surviving Ocean Warriors of the Revolution, whose frosted locks hung upon bended shoulders,
like shivered sails upon tottering masts—whose furrowed
faces exhibited the stern visage of veterans who had borne
the " peltings of the pitiless storm," but whose trembling
hands would fruitlessly attempt to record their own achievements, or those of their compatriots in ocean warfare. The
subject with them, seemed

> " To raise a *Soul* beneath the ribs of *Death*."

and evinced, that the snow upon their heads, had not
quenched the revolutionary flame in their hearts. These
narrations were noted down with care, when fresh in remembrance.

A recent re-perusal of the productions of MARSHALL,
RAMSAY, GORDON, HUMPHREYS, BOTTA, WILKINSON, LEE,
WIRT, &c. shews that although they have immortalized the
memories of WASHINGTON, PUTNAM, WARREN, MONTGOME-
RY, GATES, GREENE, LINCOLN, HENRY, CLINTON, WAYNE,
and " a long list beside" of ARMY HEROES OF THE REVO-
LUTION, the names of BIDDLE the elder, JONES the elder,
PREBLE, MURRAY, HOPKINS, WHIPPLE, GILLON, NICHOL-
SON, TRUXTON, MANLY, HARDEN, LITTLE, BARRY, DALE,
and the whole of the little peerless band of " NAVAL HE-
ROES OF THE REVOLUTION," are either passed by in silence,
or thrown into the back ground of the sanguinary arena of
the Revolutionary war.

While, in imagination, we can yet hear the reverberation
of the clangor of *Bunker Hill, Trenton, Hœrlem, Monmouth,
Saratoga, Camden,* and *York-Town,* the distant roaring of
our little floating bulwarks, "far away o'er the billow,"

and in the very throat of death upon the coast of Britain and her colonies which dared not resist her, dies away in the roaring of the surges that once echoed them amongst the dismayed subjects of George III.

I had intended to have gathered something like a Register of Naval Heroes of the Revolution. The following extract of a letter from the Secretary of the Navy shows the impossibility of doing it.

" The Records of the Department do not enable me to furnish the information you request, respecting the " Naval Officers who signalized themselves during the War for Independence ;" the correspondence of the Congressional Committee on Marine affairs during the Revolutionary War, does not contain complete lists, even of the Commanders, much less of the several officers attached to the public vessels during that important and interesting period of our history.

" As the work which you contemplate publishing will, it is believed, be one of public utility, it will afford me pleasure to furnish any information connected with the subject that may be found in the archives of the Department."

From such promiscuously scattered materials was the following volume composed. At this remove of time—from the ravages of death, amongst those who survived the revolution, and the diminution and almost destruction of necessary materials for the Biography of Dead Worthies, the difficulty of doing any thing like justice to the memories of the Naval Heroes of the American Revolution, is greatly augmented.

The stain of ingratitude toward our surviving revolutionary fathers is, in some degree, wiped off by the auspicious administration of the FIFTH PRESIDENT of the REPUBLIC. It remains for the PRESS to rescue the memories of the

" Illustrious Dead" from oblivion, and to incorporate their Fame with the archives of the Republic.

The Introduction to these Sketches will be useless to the well versed historian ; but was designed as a mere " birds-eye view" for the young American reader, who has not yet made, as he certainly will endeavour to make himself acquainted with the causes that induced—the astonishing events that accompanied, and the unrivalled characters developed in the Senate, upon the Field, and on the Ocean, in the American Revolution.

As to these " Biographical Sketches," the writer can frankly say that with the materials he had, and the circumstances under which he wrote, he has done the best he could ; and should the first continue to accumulate, and the last be bettered, he hopes his future efforts will be more deserving of the flattering patronage the public has bestowed, not upon the *writer*, but upon the *publishers* of his previous productions.

Eighty Thousand large duodecimo volumes of them published within the four past years, may have increased the *presumption* of the writer, although the sales of them have added nothing to his *pecuniary* means.

This imperfect and unpolished volume is literally " thrust into the world, scarce half made up"—" *in forma pauperis*," without claiming one smile of patronage— one mite of literary aid, one cheering favour from the fortunate sons of academic acquirements. It is all the writer has now to offer—and if this *little all* will have been repulsed, the one who offers it, will feel undisturbed at the sneers of a censorious world, to which he acknowledges but little obligation, as from it, he has hitherto received but a scanty portion of favour.

THE AUTHOR.

Hartford, Conn. September 5th, 1823.

TO

HON. SMITH THOMPSON,

SECRETARY OF THE NAVY.[*]

SIR—

ness of an American, whose ancestors wielded the sword of
Freedom, but never the pen of flattery.
     Avoiding the fulsome eulogy which character-
ises the dedications of mercenary writers, who bask in the
rays of *Royal Favour*—catch the unmeaning smiles of *Lords
Temporal*—the relaxed frowns of *Lords Spiritual*, and whose
language is animated or languid, as their *Pensions* are greater or lesser, I offer this volume to you, Sir, with the frankness of an American, whose ancestors wielded the sword of
Freedom, but never the pen of flattery.

Those acquirements as a Scholar, Statesman, and Jurist,
which once placed you at the head of a great State Court
in the Union, and now sustains you at the head of the Navy
Department of the Confederated Republic, were the well
founded causes of your unsolicited promotion—first, by the
constituted authorities of a leading member of the Union, *which*

---

[*] Since this was written, the Secretary has been appointed a Judge
of the Supreme Court of the United States.

2

knew you best—next, by the government of the whole Republic *which knew and appreciated your merits.*

The voice of your countrymen declares, that while you *derive* honour from the exalted station you fill, you *impart* honour to the station itself.

However much your name may add to the little intrinsic value of these Sketches of " NAVAL HEROES OF THE REVOLUTION," it cannot remove their imperfections. With all these, however, it is offered to you as a small token of the Respect of, Sir, Your Obd't. Serv't. with high consideration.

S. PUTNAM WALDO.

HARTFORD, (Conn.) Sept. 10, 1823.

CONTENTS.

———

ERRATA.

From the rapidity with which this volume was forced through the press, the following errors, amongst others probably undiscovered, have occurred—more justly imputable to the Author than to the Printer.—

Page 16, For *were* read *was*.
    76, For *is* read *was*.
   100, For *gives* read *give*.
   152, For BIDDLE, read PREBLE.
   162, For *Capt. Stewart*, read *Lieut. Stewart*.
   273, For *Charleston* read *Charlestown*.
   276, For *solicited* read *appointed*.
   291, For *controlled* read *constrained*.

INTRODUCTION.

ADDRESSED TO THE ATTENTION OF THE YOUNGER CLASS OF READERS.

Memories of the ancient colonists of America, and heroes of the Army and Navy of the Revolution.—They were always freemen—were always their own defenders.—Presumption and ignorance of British officers in the " French War."—WILLIAM PITT.—The result of the French war in America.—British ambition and cupidity—Her attempts to coerce Americans—their resistance by argument—the eloquence of their statesmen in the senate, and firmness of their soldiers in the Army.—NAVAL HEROES of the REVOLUTION.—Congress, the States, and individuals aid them.—Vandalism of British officers and soldiers.—Firmness of Americans in resistance.

IN the long catalogue of the worthies and benefactors of the human race—amongst the exalted spirits who have rescued MEN from the degradation of ignorance, and stimulated them to manifest their moral and intellectual powers—who have roused them from the humiliated state of bondage to the dignified attitude of Freemen, the Statesmen of the " OLD CONGRESS"—the officers of the American ARMY and NAVY in the WAR OF THE REVOLUTION, are entitled to pre-eminent rank. We might, in retrospect, by the rapid glance of historical recollection, transport the mind to a period still more remote, and contemplate, with solemn admiration, the great champions who laid the foundation of the two grand pillars upon which our REPUBLIC began to rise, and is still rapidly rising—CIVIL LIBERTY and RELIGIOUS FREEDOM. From their toils and unceasing perseverance, our noble cities, charming towns and delightful villages have been rescued from a wilderness. From their

3

science and literature, the *language* and the *arts* of civilization are heard and enjoyed, where yelling savages and
howling beasts poured forth "horrid harmony," and the
arrow and the hook furnished ferocious barbarians with
precarious subsistence.   When the present race of Americans reflect that these blessings were commenced in the
seventeenth—were advanced and secured in the *eighteenth*
—and that in the *nineteenth* century we are in the full fruition of all the enjoyments which the best and freest government on earth can impart, it surely becomes our duty,
and ought to be our pleasure, to render all the grateful
homage to the memories of our unrivalled ancestors which
man may render to man, and all the adoration which man
can render to his Creator.

It is the pastime of the untutored Laplanders to detail
and to chaunt the achievements of their sleeping ancestors;
and the savages of America, still exult in the fame of *Alk-
nomok* and *Ouconnostota*—of *Logan* and *Philip*.   If barbarians thus commemorate the achievements of their progenitors, which, perhaps, were nothing more than encountering and conquering wild beasts, or capturing and torturing a christian or savage enemy, how much more imperious
and obligatory upon us is the injunction—"HONOUR THY
FATHERS."

Our expanded and rapidly expanding Republic, in the
full enjoyment of every blessing which political wisdom
and science—moral and religious principles, and the diffu-
sion of useful knowledge can impart, might now (1823) be
in an humiliated colonial state under George IV.—his vo-
luptuous lords temporal, and his corrupted lords spiritual,
had it not been for the exalted and majestic spirit of freedom and independence which inspired the noble bosoms of

our unrivalled ancestors. Let the free and high-minded people who inhabit that portion of the " WESTERN WORLD" which lies north of the Isthmus of Darien, contrast *their* situation with that of their fellow creatures south of that *natural* division of the American Continent. Although SOUTH America is centuries older in what is called civilization than NORTH America, yet the north is two centuries older in the enjoyment of the Rights of Man than the south. From the days of the blood-glutted *Pizarro*, to this time, South Americans have been the most degraded vassals, to the most tyrannical monarchy, that ever wielded the sceptre of despotic power, and the most subjugated slaves to the most detestable and satanic priesthood, that ever imposed a chain upon the human mind. But from the time that *true Englishmen*, the descendants of *true Saxons*, landed in the North, they have *ever been free;* and their progeny may exclaim with the first of apostles, and one of the first of men "WE WERE BORN FREE." While the Christian world may well exclaim—" *The Sun of Righteousness arose in the East*," and is diffusing his redeeming rays over the earth, an emancipated world will hereafter admit that—*The Sun of Freedom arose in the West :* and that in freedom, there is also a redeeming spirit which will ere long wrest from the hands of tyrants the rod of abused power—convert the chains they have forged for their subjects into ropes of sand, and make their thrones vanish beneath them like the " *baseless fabrick of a vision.*"

The " *Thirteen Colonies of North America*" may at this time be called the *germe* of twenty-four Independent States, confederated together by a voluntary ligament that unites them to the American Republic. These ancient colonies, if the expression is admissible, may be said to be " self-created."—They neither originated from royal favour, nor were fostered by princely munificence. They were not acquired by the resistless arm of a potent monarch, but by the *purchases* of emigrant pilgrims from the oppressed countries of the old world, or by the *voluntary conveyances* of the native, and sole proprietors of the soil. It is inconsistent with the limits of these introductory remarks to the following " Sketches" to discuss the question whether the benefits which Europeans have *gained*, and the original rights which the aborigines have irretrievably *lost*, by the discovery of America, can be justified by the code usually called *" The Law of Nations."* Having had occasion to allude very briefly to this subject in two previous publications,* I hope to be excused for referring the reader to the hasty remarks made in these volumes.

The British monarch and the British nation, as well by intuitive, as by logical deductions, knew well that national wealth was national power, and that both essentially conduced to national glory. They therefore were assiduously engaged in draining from the East and the West Indies, *their* immense wealth into *their own* coffers. They thought little of infant colonies, in an hitherto unexplored region, over a vast expanse of ocean. But France, their natural enemy, were either in actual possession, or had uncontrolled sway, over the whole western and northern boundaries of *" His Britannic Majesty's Colonies in North America"* from the mouth of the Mississippi, to the mouth of the St. Lawrence, two of the most important streams on earth. That aspiring monarchy cast an eye of cupidity upon these growing colonies which had, almost unobserved by East-

* " President's Tour," 3d ed. p. 268, 269. " Memoirs of Jackson," 5th ed. p. 48, 49.

ern potentates, grown up to considerable importance. The British monarchy *then* began to think that their trans-atlantic possessions were worth defending. The king began to profess the most fatherly solicitude for his American subjects; and his ministry most earnestly called upon them to defend themselves, and most graciously condescended to furnish a few British regulars, and a full quota of British officers to command all the American troops.

A sort of predatory warfare was carried on between the *christian* English and French, and the *heathen* Indians, who espoused the cause of that great father, over the great water, who offered the strongest allurements, and gave them the most encouragement for gratifying their insatiable thirst for blood, carnage and plunder.

General Braddock was despatched to America, with a small body of troops, and was joined by that prodigy of a man, designed to begin his splendid military career in aiding the British monarch to secure the colonies from French rapacity, and afterwards to lead his countrymen in wresting them from British tyranny—GEORGE WASHINGTON. Gen. Braddock, as commander in chief, and Col. Washington, the next in command, advanced upon the savage foe. The commander, claiming that importance which a man versed in the science of war—familiar with military tactics, and determined to slay savages *secundem artem*, lost his own life, and much of his force, by rashness and ignorance of savage warfare. The cool courage and consummate judgment of Washington saved the remnant of an army, the whole of which had been exposed to destruction by his superior in command. The American, or what was then called the *provincial* troops, were almost invariably successful when led by their own commanders.*

* Vide English and American histories of the "French War."

In May 1756, war was formally declared by Britain
against France ; and in June following, by France against
Britain.   Another host of British officers arrived from Europe, amongst whom were Lord *Loudon*, Gen. *Abercrombie*,
Gen. *Webb*, Gen. *Hopson*, &c. &c.   One after the other
made his entry and his exit, like actors at a theatre, performing sometimes a comic, sometimes a tragic, and more
frequently a tragi-comic part ; and then retiring behind the
scenes, followed by the hisses of some, the pity of others,
and the contempt of all.   At the close of the year 1758,
by the tardiness, cowardice or ignorance of British generals, the British colonies in America were all but an appen-
dage to the French monarchy.   Americans, although loyal
in the first degree to his Britannic Majesty, formed the
most contemptible opinion of his ministry and his generals.
Even a loyal British historian and biographer, speaking of
the campain of 1758, says, " *That it ended to the eternal
disgrace of those who then commanded the armies, and directed the councils of Great-Britain.*"
    In 1759 the Genius of war and carnage seemed to have
crossed the Atlantic, and to have commenced his terrific
reign in North America.   But that merciful Being, under
whose protecting arm the infant colonies were planted, still
sustained them—" QUI TRANSTULIT SUSTINET."†   A great
and powerful friend of America, as yet but little known,
advanced forward in all the majesty of innate greatness.
A lowering and portentous cloud hung over his king, his
country, and her colonies.   " *He stood alone—modern degeneracy had not reached him—With one hand he smote the
house of Bourbon, and wielded in the other the democracy of
England.*"   The classical reader will immediately call to

† This is the motto of the Arms of Connecticut.

mind the first of orators, the greatest of statesmen, and the noblest of men, WILLIAM PITT, a " name which strikes all human titles dead ;" and which needed not the ennobling title of " Earl of Chatham" to add to his native greatness.

He was the master spirit, under Providence, who directed the storm that was raging in two hemispheres. Profoundly versed in the science of human nature, he selected his officers for the reason, that they would confer more honour upon the station they filled, than they *could* derive from it. Gen. AMHERST and Gen. WOLFE, were made commanders in America. The cool and judicious course pursued by the first, reminds the historian of the Roman *Fabius*, and the fire and energy of the last, of *Scipio*. This wonderful man, WILLIAM PITT, who dared, in youth, to repel manfully an attack from the imperious *Walpole*, dared also, although but a commoner, to expose the effeminacy of a degenerated English nobility. He cared little for the gaudy and evanescent splendour of royalty, but placed his reliance upon the bone and muscle of his country—THE YEOMANRY. His views, like the rapidity of the passage of light, were directed to America. His prescience assured him that Anglo-Americans, who had encountered the dangers of the ocean—the appalling horrors of savage warfare—the dismaying prospects of famine, and all the calamities which " *flesh is heir to*," were the men upon whom his king must place his reliance, to defend his American possessions. He addressed the governours of the several colonies. Although distinct in regard to interest, and different in form of government, he pathetically and energetically appealed to the *interest*, the *pride*, the *patriotism*, the *loyalty*, and, what was paramount, the *religion* of all. His spirit operated upon the despairing Americans, like a shock of electricity upon a morbid system,—it infused life and vigour.

A single paragraph will suffice for the remaining part of this *introduction*, so far as it relates to the war of 1755. The Americans, aided by a few of their English brethren, went on conquering and to conquer, until the *two Canadas* —the *two Floridas*, and *half of the Mississippi*, were added *de facto* to the British crown, but *de jure* to the Americans, by the Peace of Paris in 1763.

The nation now looked upon their immense territory in North America as indefeasibly its own, and rested contented in regard to it. Its views were withdrawn from the *West*, and directed to the *East*. With that avarice and cupidity which reminds the biblical scholar of the daughters of the horse leach, " *crying Give, give,*" its views were extended to India. While *they* were conquering regions which before were conquered by effeminacy, wealth, and luxury, the Americans, without aspiring to conquest or dominion, were unambitiously engaged in the innocent and laudable pursuit of drawing wealth from their own resources, and drawing the wealth of other regions into the bosom of their country.

The " mother country," as Britain was then called, with a rapacity unparralleled in the history of plunder, carnage and bloodshed, was ravishing from the unoffending natives of Asia, the fairest and richest portion of that continent, which may be called the parent of the world. Neither the Law that came by Moses, nor the Grace promulgated by the Gospel, restrained Englishmen from inundating the country in blood, in order to wrest from it its treasures.*

* The language of two British poets,
    " That thieves at *home* must hang; but he that puts

Neither the deleterious effects of the climate, nor agony in the black hole of Calcutta, could restrain these relentless marauders, from accomplishing their diabolical work. As soon may we expect that the grave will say "it is enough," as to see a nation of misers satisfied with gold. But Col. *Clive* was immortalized, and the British treasury was enriched, and that's enough!!

But notwithstanding the immense acquisition of wealth from the East, Great-Britain was in the depth of national bankruptcy, as she fancied she was at the height of national glory. To keep up her sinking credit, and to enable her to prosecute her objects of unhallowed ambition, she resolved to replenish her coffers by draining from her American subjects their hard earned gains.

The British parliament little knew what "stern stuff" it had to deal with upon the west side of the Atlantic. Englishmen, however, *might* have learned, in the war of 1755, that their American brethren had bone and muscle sufficient to conquer the best French generals, and their best troops; Indian sachems and their best warriors. The statesmen of Old England supposed that Americans would not have the temerity to resist the mandates of their European mother. They supposed that they felt grateful for the protection extended to them, not remembering that the colonists had protected themselves by their own men and their own money; and that the wealth acquired by Britain, by monopolizing their trade, very far overbalanced the money expended in aiding them. But that imperious monarchy was determined to show their *power* over the colonies, whether it acquired *wealth* by it or not.

" Into his overgorg'd and bloated purse
" The wealth of *Indian provinces*, escapes !"
" *One murder* makes a villain—millions a hero !"

4

That wonderful statesman, WILLIAM PITT,* was worn
down by incessant service in the cause of his king and
country. But although his majestic frame was tottering to
its fail, his mind retained its native inspiration—

"His soul's dark cottage, batter'd and decay'd,
"Let in new light thro' chinks which time had made."

His knowledge of Americans made him respect them, not

* The following extract from the Speech of William Pitt, (whose
name was *lowered* for that of " *Earl of Chatham*") ought to be committed to memory by every American youth, and admired by every
American Scholar, Statesman and Patriot. It was pronounced the
January before the battle of Bunker Hill, in the British parliament :
   " My Lords,
   " I rise with astonishment to see these papers brought to your table at so late a period of this business ; papers, to tell us what? Why,
what all the world knew before ; that the Americans, irritated by repeated injuries and stripped of their inborn rights and dearest privileges, have resisted, and entered into associations for the preservation of their common liberties.
   Had the early situation of the people of Boston been attended to,
things would not have come to this. But the infant complaints of Boston were *literally* treated like the capricious *squalls of a child*, who,
it was said, did not know whether it was aggrieved or not. But full
well I knew, at that time, that this *child*, if not redressed, would soon
assume the courage and voice of a *man*. Full well I knew, that the
sons of ancestors, born under the same free constitution, and once
breathing the same liberal air as Englishmen, would resist upon the
same principles, and on the same occasions.
   What has government done? They have sent an armed force, consisting of seventeen thousand men, to dragoon the Bostonians into what
is called their duty ; and so far from once turning their eyes to the policy and destructive consequence of this scheme, are constantly sending out more troops. And we are told, in the language of menace,
that if seventeen thousand men won't do, fifty thousand shall. It is
true, my lords, with this force they may ravage the country ; waste
and destroy as they march ; but, in the progress of fifteen hundred
miles, can they occupy the places they have passed? Will not a coun-

as subjugated vassals, but as descendants of English freemen. He warned king, lords, and commons to beware
how they moved in regard to America. His solemn mo-
nitions were like oracles, and his warning voice like a voice

try, which can produce three millions of people, wronged and insulted
as they are, start up like hydras in every corner, and gather fresh
strength from every opposition? Nay, what dependence can you have
upon the soldiery, the unhappy engines of your wrath? They are
Englishmen, who must feel for the privileges of Englishmen. Do
you think that these men can turn their arms against their brethren?
Surely no. A victory must be to them a defeat; and carnage, a sacrifice. But it is not merely three millions of people, the produce of
America, we have to contend with in this unnatural struggle; many
more are on their side, dispersed over the face of this wide empire.
Every whig in this country and in Ireland is with them.

Who, then, let me demand, has given, and continues to give, this
strange and unconstitutional advice? I do not mean to level at one
man, or any particular set of men; but thus much I will venture to
declare, that, if his Majesty continues to hear such counsellors, he
will not only be badly advised, but *undone*. He may continue indeed
to wear his crown; but it will not be worth his wearing. Robbed of so
principal a jewel as America, it will lose its lustre, and no longer beam
that effulgence which should irradiate the brow of majesty.

In this alarming crisis, I come with this paper in my hand to offer
you the best of my experience and advice; which is, that a humble
petition be presented to his Majesty, beseeching him, that in order to
open the way towards a happy setttement of the dangerous troubles in
America, it may graciously please him, that immediate orders be giv-
en to general Gage for removing his majesty's forces from the town of
Boston. And this, my lords, upon the most mature and deliberate
grounds, is the best advice I can give you, at this juncture. Such
conduct will convince America that you mean to try her cause in the
spirit of *freedom* and *inquiry*, and not in *letters of blood*. There is
no time to be lost. Every hour is big with danger. Perhaps, while I
am now speaking, the decisive blow is struck, which may involve
millions in the consequence. And believe me, the very first drop of
blood which is shed, will cause a wound which may never be healed."

from the tomb.* The then young and manly CHARLES JAMES FOX, the eloquent BURKE, and the unyielding BARRE, formed a trio of greatness in favour of America. But that wrong-headed minister, Lord North, was incorrigible. He had an accommodating majority in parliament which would

* It was not far from this period, that Doct. SAMUEL JOHNSON wrote his celebrated pamphlet, " Taxation no Tyranny," in which he sneered at American Rebels ; and, under the influence of a Pension, even frowned at the immortal PITT. He lived just long enough to see George III. ratify the Peace of 1783, and surrender the " AMERICAN JEWEL." " Lord Littleton the Younger" not inaptly styled " the paragon of virtue and of vice," thus expresses himself upon the subject of American Affairs : How such a lord as Littleton, could amalgamate with such a lord as North, is one of the mysteries in " state affairs"——" not to be told."—

" In the great subject of this day's politics, which seems to engulph every other, I am with them. I shall never cease to contend for the universality and unity of the British empire over all its territories and dependencies, in every part of the globe. I have not a doubt of the legislative supremacy of parliament over every part of the British dominions in America, the East and West Indies, in Africa, and over Ireland itself.

I cannot separate the ideas of legislation and taxation ; they seem to be more than twins ; they were not only born but must co-exist and die together. The question of right is heard of no more ; it is now become a question of power ; and it appears to me that the sword will determine the contest. The colonies pretend to be subject to the king alone ; they deny subordination to the state, and, upon this principle, have not only declared against the authority of parliament, but erected a government of their own, independent of British legislation. To support a disobedience to rights which they once acknowledged, they have already formed associations, armed and arrayed themselves, and are preparing to bring the question to the issue of battle. This being the case, it becomes highly necessary for us to arm also ; we must prepare to quench the evil in its infancy, and to extinguish a flame which the natural enemies of England will not fail to feed with unremitting fuel, in order to consume our commerce, and tarnish our glory. If wise measures are taken, this business will be soon comple-

follow, wherever he lead. Their measures would remind
one of the familiar adage—

" Quem Deus, perdere vult, prius dementat."

The parliament imposed a tax upon *tea*, so that the very
matrons of America, while sipping this cheering beverage,
should remember their English mother. Then followed
the *stamp-act*, so that every transaction, evidenced by writing, should carry with it evidence of British supremacy.
Then followed the tax upon *painters' colours*, so that every

ted, to the honour of the mother country, and the welfare of the colonies ; who, in spite of all the assistance given them by the House of
Bourbon, must, unless our government acts like an ideot, be forced to
submission.

For my own part, I have not that high opinion of their Roman spirit, as to suppose that it will influence them contendedly to submit to
all the horrors of war, to resign every comfort in which they have
been bred, to relinguish every hope with which they have been flattered, and retire to the howling wilderness for an habitation : and all for
a dream of liberty, which, were they to possess to-morrow, would not
give them a privilege superior to those which they lately enjoyed ;
and might, I fear, deprive them of many which they experienced beneath the clement legislation of the British government."

COWPER, a *legitimate* British bard, who lived during the " French
War" in America, and who was at the height of poetical fame at the
close of the " War of the American Revolution," thus alludes to the
death of the *first* PITT, (Earl of Chatham) and Gen. WOLFE.-
      " Farewell those honours, and farewell, with them,
      " The hope of such hereafter ! They have fallen,
      " Each in his field of glory ; one in arms,
      " And one in council.—WOLFE upon the lap
      " Of smiling victory, that moment won,
      " And CHATHAM, heartsick of his country's shame ! !"
Speaking of the Independence of America, he says—
      " True we have lost an empire—let it pass—
      " That pick'd the jewel out of England's crown."

ornament upon American buildings should remind the possessor of British power.

If the Parliament of Britian could impose taxes upon the
colonies without their consent, the King of Britain, the
head of the " Holy Catholic Church," could send them
Arch-bishops, Bishops, Priests, Deacons, Curates, &c. &c.
and the whole systematic ramification of a " Church Establishment." *Tythes* might be imposed to support the
gorgeous pageantry of mechanical christianity, and the
Puritans might have been persecuted as *schismatics,* and
their *houses of worship* denounced as *conventicles.*

The stern unyielding men who composed the population of the " Thirteen Colonies" were not of that low-
born, stubborn race of beings who resist the exercise of all
necessary as well as arrogated power, nor were they so
destitute of political science as to deny the right of legitimate rulers to impose salutary restraints, and necessary
contributions. No! amongst them were statesmen who
would have graced the parliament of Britain, either
amongst its Lords or Commons—statesmen who had learned the necessity of obedience, before they aspired to the
arduous duty of commanding. The ADAMSES, JOHN HAN-
COCK, JAMES OTIS, the LIVINGSTONS, BENJAMIN FRANK-
LIN, the CLINTONS, PATRICK HENRY, the RANDOLPHS, HEN-
RY LAURENS, the LEES, PINCKNEYS, and an expanded constellation of exalted patriots like them, knew well how to
manifest a cordial allegiance to a monarch, when in the
exercise of legitimate and constitutional authority. Thanks
to the stubborn resistance against arbitrary prerogatives
and tyrannical power, these peerless and unsurpassed patriots and statesmen knew equally well how to expose the encroachments of tyrants, and to rouse up freemen to resist

them. It would require a "Muse of fire, to ascend the highest heaven of invention" to pen a suitable eulogy upon these Sampsons of the western world. They taught the people that they possessed the right of self-government : and spurned a doctrine since taught by American Aristocrats "that the people are their own worst enemies." Whatever were the nature of the different governments—whether exercised by royal Charters—proprietary governments, or their own municipal regulations, every government in the colonies, emphatically exercised what jurists call the *Jura summa imperii*—the right of supreme power. Their legislative assemblies enacted laws—their judicial forums administered civil and criminal justice. They imposed taxes upon the people, and adopted the incontrovertible axiom—" *That representation and Taxation should be correspondent.*" They viewed the constitution of Britain, and saw an hereditary monarch—an hereditary senate ; and commons, which represented rotten burroughs, rather than a free people.

Notwithstanding the imperious court of Britain seemed to have fixed its course in regard to the colonies, yet their vacillating policy excited the contempt, as well as the indignation of American Statesmen. They imposed taxes, and seeing them resisted, omitted to enforce the collection. They passed acts and repealed them ; but finally resolved " *that the parliament had power to make laws to bind the colonies in all cases whatsoever.*" This was a new species of legislation,—it was a *preamble* without an *act*, an attempt to atone for an offence, and at the same time claiming the power to repeat it. *Fox, Burke* and *Barre*, in the House of Commons, poured forth peals of eloquence and satire, which the imperious *Mansfield* and *North*, and the minis-

ter's dupes, could meet only by dumb legislation, and the
physical power of voting. Said Fox to the minister, " In
your infatuated conduct, *resolutions* and *concession, ever
misplaced*, have equally operated to the disgrace and ruin
of the nation."

But it was *native* eloquence, in the FORUM and from the
PRESS,* that kindled the latent spark of freedom into a

_____

* In presenting to the reader the following extracts from " *A Circu-
lar Letter from the Congress of the United States of America to their
Constituents*,"—" *By the unanimous order of Congress*;" dated 23d
Sept. 1779, I give him a new opportunity of contemplating the native
majesty of the gigantic statesmen, of the members of the " OLD CON-
GRESS ;" and the splendid energy with which their exalted sentiments
are conveyed.

" That the time has been when honest men might, without being
chargeable with timidity, have doubted the success of the present revolution we admit; but that period is passed. The independence of
America is now as fixed as fate, and the petulant efforts of Britain to
break it down, are as vain and fruitless as the raging of the waves
which beat against their cliffs. Let those who are still afflicted with
these doubts consider the character and condition of our enemies. Let
them remember that we are contending against a kingdom crumbling
into pieces; a nation without public virtue; and a people sold to and
betrayed by their own representatives; against a prince governed by
his passions, and a ministry without confidence or wisdom; against armies half paid, and generals half trusted; against a government equal
only to plans of plunder, conflagration and murder; a government by
the most impious violations of the rights of religion, justice, humanity
and mankind, courting the vengeance of Heaven, and revolting from
the protection of Providencce. Against the fury of these enemies,
you made successful resistance, when single, alone, and friendless, in
the days of weakness and infancy, before your hands had been taught
to war or your fingers to fight. And can there be any reason to apprehend that the Divine Disposer of human events, after having separated
us from the house of bondage, and led us safe through a sea of blood,
towards the land of liberty and promise, will leave the work of our political redemption unfinished, and either permit us to perish in a wil-

dame. The impassioned eloquence of the ADAMSES, HAN-
COCK, OTIS, &c. in " Fanueil Hall," in Massachusetts,

derness of difficulties, or suffer us to be carried back in chains to that
country of oppression, from whose tyranny he hath mercifully delivered us with a stretched out arm?"

" What danger have we to fear from Britain? Instead of acquiring
accessions of territory by conquest, the limits of her empire daily con-
tract; her fleets no longer rule the ocean, nor are her armies invincible by land. How many of her standards, wrested from the hands of
her champions, are among your trophies, and have graced the triumphs
of your troops? and how great is the number of those, who, sent to
bind you in fetters, have become your captives, and received their
lives from your hands."

" A sense of common permanent interest, mutual affection (having
been brethren in affliction,) the ties of consanguinity daily extending,
constant reciprocity of good offices, similarity in language, in governments, and therefore in manners, the importance, weight and splendour
of the union, all conspire in forming a strong chain of connexion,
which must for ever bind us together. The United Provinces of the
Netherlands, and the United Cantons of Switzerland became free and
independent under circumstances very like ours : their independence
has been long established, and yet their confederacies continue in full
vigour. What reason can be assigned why our union should be less
lasting ? or why should the people of these states be supposed less wise
than the inhabitants of those ?"

" We should pay an ill compliment to the understanding and honour
of every true American, were we to adduce many arguments to show
the baseness or bad policy of violating our national faith, or omitting to
pursue the measures necessary to preserve it. A bankrupt faithless
republic would be a novelty in the political world, and appear among
reputable nations, like a common prostitute among chaste and respectable matrons."

" The war, though drawing fast to a successful issue, still rages. Be
mindful that the brightest prospects may be clouded, and that prudence
bids us be prepared for every event. Provide therefore for continuing your armies in the field till victory and peace shall lead them home,
and avoid the reproach of permitting the currency to depreciate in
your hands, when by yielding a part to taxes and loans, the whole

reverberated along the shores of the Atlantic, until it reached the "House of Burgesses" in Virginia, where the majestic spirits of PATRICK HENRY, and RICHARD HENRY
LEE, poured forth the thundering and sonorous voice of
indignant freemen, resolved to be free. FRANKLIN, who
had wrested the lightning from the clouds by his philosophy,
led the van of those statesmen in the cabinet, who by the
PEN and the PRESS gave a systematic direction to American Patriotism, which eventuated in the " DECLARATION
OF INDEPENDENCE," and in wresting from the House of
Brunswick the sceptre which she wielded over her American Colonies.   The artillery of the American Press, was
little less potent than the thunder of land and floating batteries, in converting what was denounced as an unnatural
rebellion into the most " GLORIOUS REVOLUTION" of the
eighteenth century.   " *Curses, not only loud, but deep,*"
were uttered forth from the lips of tottering age ; and the
hopes of their country, the rising youth, caught the holy
enthusiasm of liberty.   The massacre at Boston, and the
murders at Lexington, were tocsins of war which echoed

might have been appreciated and preserved. Humanity as well as
justice makes this demand upon you, the complaints of ruined widows,
and cries of fatherless children, whose whole support has been placed
in your hands and melted away, have doubtless reached you; take care
that they ascend no higher. Rouse therefore; strive who shall do
most for his country ; rekindle that flame of patriotism which at the
mention of disgrace and slavery blazed throughout America, and animated all her citizens.   Determine to finish the contest as you began
it, honestly and gloriously. Let it never be said that America had no
sooner became independent than she became insolvent, or that her
infant glories and growing fame were obscured and tarnished by broken contracts and violated faith, in the very hour when all the nations
of the earth were admiring and almost adoring the splendour of her
rising."

from the Atlantic to the Mississippi—from the Canadas to the Floridas.

In the wide range of history, no parallel example of unity of sentiment, and unity of action can be found. Thirteen distinct governments, moved in more perfect unison, than did ever thirteen different dials point to the minutes of the passing hour. From 1765 to 1775, the materials of a dissevering shock, which was forever to dissolve the connexion between the Thirteen Colonies of America and the British monarchy, had been constantly augmenting. A Revolution in public feeling had been effected, before an appeal to arms—the dernier resort—was made.

The immortal WASHINGTON at the head, followed by PUTNAM, GATES, MONTGOMERY, WOOSTER, GREENE, &c. and followed themselves by hosts of true Americans, laid aside the peaceful pursuits of husbandry, and the arts, and repaired to the "tented field," resolved to be

" Fire to fire,—flint to flint, and t' outface the
Brow of bragging horror."*

But a class of Americans was scattered over the bosom

* The following masterly apostrophe to the memories of the Statesmen and Heroes of the Revolution is extracted from an anniversary Oration on 4th July, 1787.

" But what tribute shall we bestow, what sacred pæan shall we raise over the tombs of those who dared, in the face of unrivalled power, and within the reach of majesty, to blow the blast of freedom throughout a subject continent?

Nor did those brave countrymen of ours only *express* the emotions of glory; the nature of their principles inspired them with the power of *practice;* and they offered their bosoms to the shafts of battle. Bunker's awful mount is the capacious urn of their ashes; but the flaming bounds of the universe could not limit the flight of their minds.

They fled to the union of kindred souls; and those who fell at the streights of Thermopylæ, and those who bled on the heights of Charlestown, now reap congenial joys in the fields of the blessed."

of the rising Republic, who are now to be introduced to
the attention, and it is hoped, to the admiration of the reader.   They were the energetic, the daring, the adventurous sons of the ocean,

> "Whose march was on the mountain wave,
> Whose home was on the deep."

It was upon *that element* they wished to display their
courage, and their patriotism.   It was in *floating bulwarks*,
they wished to breast the shock, and hurl the gauntlet of
defiance at the enemies of their country.   Such a desire,
at such a time, with such apparently insuperable obstacles
to surmount, could have originated only from souls, that
were strangers to fear, or have been imbibed in bosoms
glowing with the ardour of patriotism.   The seaboard of
the thirteen colonies, was barricadoed with the " wooden
walls" of Old England, her admirals, post-captains and
seamen, had acquired almost undisputed sway over every
ocean and sea ; and the colonies possessed not a single
armed ship.   In the war of 1755, commonly called by
Americans the " French War," but very few of our ancestors acquired knowledge of naval tactics ; and what they
did acquire, must have been in very humble stations,—for
if the officers of Britain in the army of America, aspired to
supreme command, *a fortiori*, would they in the navy.
What little science in naval tactics was acquired, was lost
by American navigators in the peaceable pursuits of lawful commerce, and drawing from the bosom of the ocean
its inexhaustible treasures.

Thus, in few words, were situated, the ocean-warriors
of the infant Republic, when that awfully unequal contest
commenced, which gave Independence to America, and
wrested from the British diadem, its most brilliant and in-

valuable gem. Merchantmen were suddenly converted into privateers, and British commerce, of immense value, and transport ships, with army and navy stores, were rapidly brought into American ports. The very naval stores indispensably necessary to fit out armed ships, were drawn from the enemy; thus weakening them and strengthening our energetic ancestors. The legislatures of the several colonies, aided the daring sons of the deep in their noble endeavours, and began to build " *state ships.*" The Continental Congress, at the close of 1775, made provision, for building   5 vessels of 32 guns,   160 guns.

$$
\begin{array}{ccccc}
5 & " & 28 & " & 140 \ " \\
3 & " & 24 & " & 72 \ " \\
\hline
13 & & & & 372
\end{array}
$$

None of these were fitted for sea until about the time of the Declaration of American Independence. There were no navy yards—no naval depots—no naval stations—and but few naval architects. But that fecundity of genius which draws the means of action from resources invisible to the eye of despondency, enabled the statesmen and warriors of that portentous period to achieve wonders, bordering upon miracles, with means apparently wholly inefficient. The denominations of vessels at that time were " *Continental Ships,*" " *State Ships,*" " *Letters of Marque,*" and " *Privateers.*"

There was then no *Naval List* of ships, nor Naval Register of Officers ; at least none can be found by the writer. Information upon this subject can be gathered only from the scattered materials of that period,—information from the few surviving veterans of the revolution, and communications from obliging correspondents.

It will excite astonishment in the reader, that the whole

Continental marine force in 1776, was less than four 74's at this time (1823). This diminutive force, with the aid of State ships and privateers, was illy calculated to face the immense naval power of Britain which stretched along the American coast. But it *could* reach the wealthy *commerce* of Britain, if it could not encounter her powerful *marine*. Let the reader run over the following authentic list of Ships of the Line, and add to them more than treble that number of Frigates, Sloops of War, Brigs, Schooners, &c. and he will see what the " Naval Heroes in the War of the Revolution" had to encounter—

" The following is an authentic list of the grand Channel Fleet, which will sail on or before the 21st inst. under the command of Admirals Hardy, Darby, Barrington and Digby :—Victory 100 guns, Britannia 100, Royal George 100, Duke 90, Formidable 90, Namur 90, Ocean 90, Union 90, Barfleur 90, Prince George 90, Queen 90, Foudroyant 90, Princess Amelia 80, Gibraltar 80, Marlborough 74, Alexander 74, Dublin 74, Fortitude 74, Culloden 74, Valiant 74, Courageux 74, Arrogant 74, Alcine 74, Cumberland 74, Bellona 74, Alfred 74, Monarch 74, Diligente, Sp. pr. 70, Princessa, Sp. pr. 70, Monarca, Sp. pr. 70, Inflexible 64, Monmouth 64, Nonsuch 64, Prince William, Sp. 64, Prothee, Fr. pr. 64, St. Alban 64, Buffalo 64, Chatham 55, Isis 50, Jupiter 50, Portland 50, Warwick 50—Total, 41."

Whatever may be the opinion of ethical writers and casuistical declaimers upon the subject of *privateering*, or in any way capturing the property of unoffending merchantmen, let it never be forgotten, that Britain waged a war, not only of vengeance, but of extermination, against her *own children*, in what she vauntingly called, her *own colo-*

nies. Admitting that an affectionate mother is entitled to unceasing gratitude and filial affection; yet, when a mother, with an uplifted hand is about dooming her children to bleed, shall they be called upon to bare their bosoms to the dagger?

The commencement and progress of the first war between Britain and America, was marked on the part of the former, with a ferocity and a barbarism which would have produced compunctions in the breasts, and blushes upon the cheeks of the ancient Vandals and Goths. War was made, not only upon the embattled ranks of our noble ancestors, but upon the humble mansions of unresisting weakness. A cheerless track of desolation, like a flight of locusts through verdant fields, pointed out the path of the vindictive foe; and unappeased wrath and ceaseless rapacity seemed to have converted the once noble Britons into dæmons. Could the hardy sons of Neptune remain inactive spectators of the devastations committed, and committing, upon the cities, towns and villages upon the borders of the ocean,* without ardently wishing to avenge them upon the *bosom* of that element? No! the divine doctrine which enjoins it upon *men* to render to each other "good for evil," may be preached by the "Holy Alliance" of "Legitimate Sovereigns" of Europe, who had waded through blood to their tottering thrones in the 19th century, and still sustain them by blood—it may be echoed

---

* Witness the burning of Falmouth (now Portland) in Maine.— Charlestown, Mass.; the ruin of the island of Rhode-Island; the conflagration of New-London, Fairfield, and Norwalk, Conn.; Esopus, N. Y. Norfolk, Va. and the partial destruction, and plundering of innumerable other places upon the sea-board.

by the Peace Societies* of America. Yet it belongs not to
the code of the Law of Nations, when a powerful sovereign
is waging vindictive war upon unoffending colonies, as Britain did in the War of the Revolution against America, and
as France is now waging war against Spain.

To say more by way of introduction to the following
Sketches, would fatigue the reader—his patience is already exhausted, and yet the "half is not told." This "birds'-
eye view" was deemed necessary to lead the younger class
of readers to contemplate the causes which led to the sanguinary contest, which called forth the unparalleled exertions of the Naval Heroes of the Revolution to achieve
the unsurpassed deeds, imperfectly detailed in the succeeding volume.

* The following is the result of the inquiries of the Massachusetts
Peace Society, formed at about the close of the second war between
the American Republic and the kingdom of Great-Britain ; and of
which the *Autocrat of Russia* is a *peaceable* member. In what class of
wars the War of the Revolution—the naval warfare with France, in
the administration of ADAMS—the war with Tripoli, in the administration of JEFFERSON—the second war between America and Britain in
the administration of MADISON, are included, is not known by the writer of these " Sketches."—

" 44 Wars of ambition to obtain extent of country. 22 Wars for
plunder, tribute, &c. 24 Wars for retaliation or revenge. 8 Wars to
settle some question of war or prerogative· 6 Wars arising from disputed claims to some territory. 41 Wars arising from disputed titles
to crowns. 30 Wars commenced under pretence of assisting an ally.
23 Wars originating in jealousy of rival greatness. 5 Wars which
have grown out of commerce. 55 Civil Wars. 28 Wars on account
of religion, including the crusades against the Turks and heretics."

BIOGRAPHICAL SKETCH

OF

NICHOLAS BIDDLE,

COMMODORE AND POST-CAPTAIN

IN THE

CONTINENTAL NAVY,

IN THE WAR OF THE REVOLUTION

Place and time of his birth—his early propensities and pursuits—his shipwreck and sufferings upon a desolate island—returns to America, and continues in the merchant service—aspires to the service of a warrior under Geo. III.—Falkland Islands—Junius and Johnson. —Expedition to the North Pole—Biddle becomes a coxswain, with Horatio, afterwards Lord Nelson, in that voyage.—Hazard and peril of the voyage.—After Biddle's return to England, he finds that power on the verge of a war with America—Returns to America in 1775—is appointed to a small vessel, the Camden, to defend the Delaware river—is ordered to the Andrew Doria, attached to Com. Hopkins' squadron, destined against New-Providence—Regains two deserters by his consummate courage—Distress of the squadron by the small-pox—Capt. Biddle's humane exertions—he returns to America—Sails alone under orders of Congress—Compels Lord Howe to exchange one of his Lieutenants—Captures many prizes —returns and takes command of the Continental ship Randolph— he suppresses a mutiny—loses all his masts—enters a port, refits and puts to sea—captures the Free Briton and three other vessels, and returns into Charleston, (S. C.) seven days after his departure.— Commodore Biddle is appointed to the command of a squadron, the Randolph, Gen. Moultrie, Fair American, and the Polly—The officers and soldiers of Gen. C. C. Pinckney volunteer on board his squadron—He sails in pursuit of the enemy—Falls in with the Yarmouth British ship of 64 guns, which attacks the Randolph of 32 guns, in the night—Com. Biddle is wounded, and remains upon the deck, until his ship explodes—Reflection—Character of Com. Biddle.

UPON commencing a brief sketch of the life of NICHOLAS BIDDLE, a solicitude is sensibly felt which can be but feebly described. To portray the life and character of an ardent hero, who entered early into the service of a monarch, who swayed the sceptre of dominion over his native country, and who died a Commodore in fighting against the same monarch, to secure the Independence of the land of his birth, at the early age of twenty-seven, requires a volume instead of a sketch,—the hand of a Plutarch, instead of " *such an honest chronicler as Griffith.*"

This gallant and fearless ocean hero was born in the city of Philadelphia, in the year 1750. His ancestry cannot be traced far back by the writer, for the want of materials. Indeed, were materials for such an attempt ever so copiously strewed around, it would be a useless waste of time to trace the genealogy of Nicholas Biddle. If he did not derive a great name from his ancestors, he *made* the name of Biddle dear to Americans. He was the sixth son of William Biddle of New Jersey, and who removed to Philadelphia to prosecute commercial business.

He discovered his propensity for a nautical life in the early period of his existence. However much his parents might have wished to retain him in their domestic circle, until more mature age, and greater literary and scientific acquirements rendered him better qualified for a bold adventurer into a dangerous and pityless world, they found it wholly impossible to restrain his juvenile ardour, or prevent him from accomplishing his darling object.

At the age of thirteen, he made a voyage to Quebec, in Canada. It was a pleasant and prosperous voyage ; and he became fascinated with the charms of the ocean, and the exhilarating scenes of a sailor's life.

Having explored a portion of the American coast, he became anxious to penetrate farther into an element with which he had become enamoured.

This adventurous youth little anticipated the disastrous scenes he was about to encounter. Indeed, if it were only

partially revealed to men, what their future destiny should
be, it would produce inconsiderate rashness in some, and
in others,—

" The native hue of resolution, would
Be sicklied o'er by the pale cast of thought."

The second voyage the ardent Biddle made, was from
his native city to the Island of Jamaica, from thence to the
Bay of Honduras. After having accomplished the object
of the voyage to this bay, the master of the vessel sailed
for Antigua, at near the close of the year 1765.

Upon the night of the 2nd of January '66 in a violent
gale of wind, the vessel was wrecked upon a fatal and im-
passable shoal. The crew remained upon the deck,
through the night of the 3d, and until late in the morning of
the 4th. Finding it impossible to sustain themselves upon
the wreck, they resorted to the forlorn hope of wrecked
mariners—the *boat*. After enduring the imminent hazard
of an agitated ocean, in a feeble boat, crowded with a crew,
whom it was scarcely able to keep above water, they landed upon a desolate and unpeopled island, ten miles from
the shoal where they were wrecked. After remaining a
number of days upon the island—famishing with hunger,
and making what repairs the scanty means in their power
afforded, a part of the crew ventured off to the wreck, and
procured a small supply of ruined provisions; which, like
the *fœtus* of a camel, or a putrified wen, to Robbins, was
to them a delicious repast !

Soon after, one of the most appalling and distressing
scenes, which the destitute, forlorn and miserable sons of
Adam have to pass through in this " vale of tears," was to
be acted by this hard-fated crew.

They could not sustain themselves upon the island ; and

the damaged boat could not carry them all from it. Four were to be left, and to suffer what Providence should decree, or had decreed. Who should remain upon this region of barrenness, and who should enter the boat, (both desperate chances,) was to be determined by the usual, uncertain, and capricious mode—by lot. This mode, according to sacred history, decided the fate of a prophet; and it has often determined the dark and gloomy prospect of life when " shadows clouds and darkness rest upon it."

Young Biddle at this time was a boy of fourteen years of age. He was in that period of life, when most boys continue to hang upon the arms of their mothers, for effeminate indulgences, and who look to their fathers for protection. When the lots were cast, it fell upon Biddle to remain upon the island ; to perish or escape as the dark future should determine. With his three companions in calamity, he endured all the privations and anguish which man can endure, and yet survive. Inheriting from his ancestors a constitution which possessed the real *stamina* of the European emigrants to America, and an original strength of mind which was not to be daunted by adversity nor effeminated by prosperity, he passed through scenes of sufferings, and privations, which might well have appalled the heart of matured manhood. I do not mean those sufferings inflicted by a barbarous and relentless foe, who pursues an enemy " with a step steady as time, and with an appetite keen as death," nor those dangers which surround an ardent and adventurous youth, who would glory to die on the field of battle, or on the deck of a vessel, in fighting the battles of his country ; but those sufferings and dangers are meant which are occasioned by a diminution of the wonted supplies which nature demands, and the gloomy

and distressing consideration that a total destitution of them
is near at hand.

For sixty days, young Biddle, and his three associates,
(who were advanced far into manhood,) endured those distresses and privations, which, to those who have always
lived in the midst of temporal enjoyments, would seem to
be absolutely beyond the endurance of human nature. It
is in such situations, that the native energy and fortitude of
men develope themselves. To retain firmness of soul, in
a state of hopeless destitution and solitude, where there is
" no eye to pity nor arm to save," but those of Omnipotence—to wear away life with fortitude upon a desolate
island like Selkirk, or to wander, in slavery, over an outspread desert like Robbins, where no sympathizing mortal
can witness or alleviate suffering, surely evinces the original greatness of the sufferer's soul. Such was the soul of
Biddle in the days of his youth. But he was created for
a different destiny than to perish by famine, or the hand of
slaves.

At the expiration of two months, he was taken from the
island, and returned to his native city, in an American vessel, and immediately again resorted to his adopted element,
the ocean.

As it regards Americans, the remark may safely be made,
that disasters, storms, shipwrecks, and " hair breadth
'scapes," instead of driving them to the dull and perpetually recurring scenes of domestic life, rather stimulates
them to press forward to new encounters, to enable them
to enjoy the exultation of success.—Life may be called a
lottery—the prize-holder still hopes to gain, and the loser
to retrieve his losses.

Young Biddle continued in the merchant service, and

made frequent voyages from the American, to the Eastern
continents. But there was something too tame in this business to fill a soul, created for " noble daring." He had,
to be sure, made himself an able seaman, but that is an acquisition within the reach of ordinary capacity.

In the year 1770, the unsatiated ambition of Britain, induced that unsatisfied power, to cast a wishful eye at the
Falkland Islands, in the possession of Spain. A war was
expected between England and that power ; and Biddle
wished to be engaged in some pursuit, which should evince
his ardent love of the country which gave him birth, and
the King of England, who swayed his sceptre over it.

Altho' born an American, with that high sense of independence which characterized Americans, as well before as
after their allegiance to Britain was dissolved, Biddle wished
to serve his country as a warrior. The dispute concerning
the Falkland Islands, eventuated in no other warfare than
that which was carried on between the Opposition, and the
Ministerial party in England. At the head of the first,
stood the unknown, and the unrivalled JUNIUS. The ministry stood aghast and terror-struck, at the peals of eloquence and satire, which were poured forth from the pen
of this unsurpassed champion of constitutional freedom.
The descendants of the house of Stuart trembled ; and the
house of Brunswick was tortured into agony. Grafton,
Bedford, and Mansfield trembled—and the throne itself
seemed to totter under the tremendous shocks of eloquence
which rolled forth from this resistless political essayist.
Once more the imperious JOHNSON advanced with the artillery of his pen, and commenced a war of words in sup
port of majesty. His " Taxation no Tyranny" was considered as a bull of excommunication against high-minded

Americans, who could not be brought to bow to parliamentary usurpation. He now came forward and attacked all that portion of Englishmen, who manfully struggled for the wreck of freedom, which had survived the numerous breaches made upon the constitution. While the literary world admire Johnson as an Essayist, Moralist, and Lexicographer, the patriot abhors him as the pensioned advocate of despotic power.

Biddle much more ardently wished to be amidst the roar of broadsides, and the thunder of batteries, than the " paper bullets of the brain," which issue from the artillery of the press. But a reconciliation between Spain and England deprived him of serving his then " king and country" as a warrior. But his propensity for a naval life predominated over every other consideration ; and the appointment of Midshipman in one of H. B. Majesty's ships, commanded by Capt. Stirling, was the consummation of his wishes.

It was in this station that he commenced the study of naval tactics. He began to acquire a theoretical knowledge of that almost mysterious system which imparts such a mysterious power to floating bulwarks. Although Britain, for many centuries past, has been almost constantly engaged in war, yet at the time Midshipman Biddle entered the navy, that nation happened to be at peace. The ardent Midshipman, not sufficiently aware of the importance of acquiring the theory of naval tactics by long and patient service, impatiently and impetuously determined to enter into some more active and adventurous employ. He had that natural inquietude,—that impatience for enterprize which rendered inaction to him the greatest misery.

An opportunity presented, when the Admiralty of Britain determined to despatch two of their best fitted vessels of their class the *Race-Horse* and *Carcase*, for a voyage of Discovery toward the North Pole ; and a most distinguished British officer, Lord *Mulgrave*, was designated as commander of the expedition.

There was something too splendid in this object to be overlooked by the aspiring Biddle. He solicited a discharge from the station he held in the British navy for the purpose of entering into this expedition. He had become a favorite of Capt. Stirling—had been promoted to a lieutenancy, and he strongly remonstrated against his leaving the service of the king in his navy. But, it was wholly impossible to restrain a spirit like Biddle's from sacrificing the rank he had obtained in the navy, and the certain prospect he had for promotion, from gratifying his ardent wishes, for advancing forward into scenes of enterprize and danger.

When Biddle found that Capt. Stirling would not consent to the gratification of his wishes, he resolved to become the master of his own conduct and run the risque of its consequences. He flung off his naval uniform—divested himself of every insignia of office, and assumed the garb of a common seaman. When the Race-Horse and Carcase were nearly ready for departure, Biddle seized a boat, rowed off to the Carcase—jumped on board of her, and entered as a seamen before the mast. He was recognized by a seaman who had served under him, and whose manly cheeks were immediately moistened by the copious tribute of tears which grief forced from his eyes. He thought his beloved Lieutenant had been degraded ; but when he learned from Biddle the facts just related, his exultation surpassed his

dejection.   This affectionate tar continued the unaltera-
ble friend of Biddle, during the whole of the perilous voyage to the Pole.   This simple fact shows that Biddle, in
very early life, possessed the rare talent of securing respect by his dignity, and attachment by his benevolence.

That prodigy of a man—that paragon of naval greatness,
and human weakness—that matchless commander upon
the ocean, and easy victim of seductive charms upon land—
HORATIO NELSON—was on board this vessel.   Two more
congenial spirits, so far as it regarded manly energy and
naval ardor—could not be associated than BIDDLE and
NELSON : and had the fortune of war have placed the
AMERICAN in the same situation it subsequently did the
English hero, it is not presuming too much to suppose that
he would have acquired laurels of equal splendour.

Their commander soon appointed them cockswains.—
This designation evinces the estimation in which these ardent and aspiring young heroes were holden by the noble
commander of this interesting and hazardous expedition.
The duty of cockswain requires the most dauntless, skilful
and intrepid spirits to execute it ; and these adventurous,
and fearless candidates for fame, soon discovered their native energy, and displayed their nautical skill.   This voyage was made in 1773.

Although the polar regions were not then altogether unexplored, yet perhaps no preceding navigators ever accomplished more than the officers and crews of the Race-
Horse and Carcase. It presented to the view of the younger as well as to the more advanced sons of the ocean the
stupendous works of nature in lofty mountains and floating
islands of ice.   To encounter an enemy upon the ocean,
in the usual mode of fighting upon that element, where the

8

prospects of victory, and the numerous chances for escape, remove all ideas of despair, is next to amusement when compared with encountering an iron-bound shore, or floating regions of ice which defy the utmost exertion of human power to resist.   But even in such situations, the fury and the terror of the elements seem to yield their destructive power to the skill and prowess of man.

The vessel in which Biddle sailed reached nearly as far as the 82° of north latitude, and subsequent navigators have never penetrated farther than to the 84°.*

A minute detail of the events of this voyage would be inconsistent with the objects of this sketch, which is intended to present a miniature picture of the gallant Biddle. For a number of days, the vessel and crew to which he was attached, was in the most imminent danger of destruction.   Indeed, for five days, her destruction seemed inevitable, as the Carcase was completely surrounded and hemmed in by mountains of ice.   No imaginable situation could be calculated to produce in the mind more horror and despair.   But Biddle, a second time, escaped a disastrous death, to meet with one, if possible still more tragical.   He returned to England and exhibited his own journal of the incidents of the voyage, which was lost when he was lost to his country, and the world.

At the time Biddle returned to England, the long protracted dispute between the American colonists and the crown of Britain was drawing to that issue, when encroach-

* The voracious devourers of wonderful news have lately been amused with the story that Capt. —— had actually " doubled the North Pole ;" and that if the *ukase* of Alexander did not detain him, he would sail home peaceably through the *Pacific Ocean.* Perhaps some subsequent navigator may enter " Symmes' Hole" and *sail through the earth.*

ments and remonstrance, impositions and concessions, petitions and rejections, were all to give place to the decisions of the sword.

Every suggestion and inducement, excepting those of patriotism and devotion to country, would have led Biddle to devote his services to the king and country in whose service he commenced his naval life, and with whose almost boundless power he had become familiarly acquainted. In that power he recognized the imperious Queen of the Ocean. Her floating batteries were riding triumphantly in every sea and ocean. With the "mind's eye" he viewed the ports and shores of his native country, feeble, defenceless, and unprotected, save by the imperfect fortifications, and the bayonets of his countrymen. But this patriotic son of a rising Republic would not suffer himself to "*debate which of the two to choose, slavery or death.*"

He returned again to the bosom of his native, and then endangered country, in the year 1775. The Thirteen Colonies then had not a single frigate, sloop of war, brig or gun boat belonging to the government. But a daring and ardent spirit like Biddle was not born to despair of the commonwealth. Merchants and ship-owners, deprived of their wonted commercial pursuits, converted many of their heavier vessels into privateers, and the hardy sons of the deep impetuously rushed forward to lend their aid in repelling the cruel and implacable enemy who were devastating the country; and though with apparently feeble means, to chastise the insolent foe upon the element of which she claimed herself to be mistress.

The immense disparity of Naval power between the Republic and Britain, in the second sanguinary war which commenced in 1812, was pointed out by the writer in attempting to present the American reader with the Life and Character of the unrivalled DECATUR ; but in the first war, which commenced in 1775, there was nothing with which to compare the overwhelming naval power of Britain, in the Thirteen Colonies, for as to naval power, THEY HAD NONE. But the Old Congress—the Colonial Assemblies, patriotic combinations, and even single individuals, suffered not the paralyzing effects of fear or despondency to check the ardor of patriotism ; but promptly seconded the noble wishes of their noble countrymen upon the ocean as well as upon land. They, did not suffer themselves even to hesitate or doubt, knowing that—

" Our doubts are traitors, that make us lose the good
" We oft might win, by fearing to attempt."

The language of each Statesmen, Soldier and Seamen of that gloomy and portentous period was—

" I dare do *all* that may become a *man ;*
Who dares do *more* is *none.*"

It was indeed a period when the *ordinary* calculations of prudence, and the dictates of moderation, were in some measure to be disregarded from the *extraordinary* and almost unparalleled circumstances in which Americans were placed by the imperious crown of Britain in 1775.

In NICHOLAS BIDDLE was recognized an exalted American, in the ardour of youth, and with a heart glowing with patriotism, fitted for the time and the occasion. A large galley was fitted suddenly up for the defence of the river Delaware, upon which his native city was situated, and called the Camden. The command of it was offered to Capt. Biddle, which, for the want of a more active and adventurous service, he accepted.

Although but twenty-five years of age, his previous ser-

vice in the British navy, and his voyage to the polar regions, had rendered him as familiar with naval tactics and
nautical skill as any American, at any age, at that period.
Although to navigate the Delaware with an armed galley,
might now (1823) be considered an humble station, yet
Capt. Biddle then deemed it his duty to act in any station,
sobeit he could render any service to his then almost unprotected country.   He was willing to move in a minor,
although well calculated for an exalted station.   He could
not become *small* by being in a *little* place.

He continued in this service until an expedition was fitted out for the island of New-Providence, one of the West
India islands.   This expedition might even now be considered as a daring one, were America at war with Britain ;
then it might be considered as a desperate one.

Capt. Biddle, whose qualifications had become known to
the government for such an undertaking, was appointed to
the command of the armed brig Andrew Doria.   She rated at fourteen guns, and her crew consisted of an hundred
and thirty men.   He was indefatigable in preparing his
crew for the service, as at that period, naval service was
almost wholly unknown to American seamen, who had
spent their lives in the merchant service.

While at, or near the shore, a very stout and able bodied
seaman, by the name of Green, shrinking from the hazard
of the expedition, and dreading to desert alone, induced
another of the crew to desert with him.   They were de-
tected and lodged in prison, but little distance from the
Capes of Delaware, where Capt. Biddle was lying with his
brig.   He sent one of his Lieutenants on shore to regain
the deserters.   The Lieutenant returned, and assured the
Captain, that the deserters, with a number of other despe-

radoes had fortified themselves in the prison, and bidden defiance to the civil and military power to take them. They were supported in prison by the loyalists and tories, and encouraged in their desperation.

This pusillanimous conduct in the organized powers, and desperate determination in two dastardly deserters from the flag of their country, afforded the young and fearless Biddle an opportunity to develope his character. He selected a favourite Midshipman only to attend him on shore. Full armed, he approached the prison door, and with a manly and commanding voice demanded entrance. It was refused. The door being strongly secured within, he ordered it to be forced; although Green and his associates had repeatedly declared that instant death should be the fate of any one who had the presumption to pass the threshold. Biddle entered with a loaded pistol in each hand, and, bringing his heart and soul into his face, sternly advanced towards Green, who was well armed, exclaiming with a stentorian voice, " Take good aim, Green, or you are surely a dead man." The agitated and trembling deserter dropped his weapon, and he, with his deluded comrade, returned to their duty on board of the Andrew Doria. Death on the yard arm, like that of the British deserters taken from the Chesapeake frigate, in more modern days, would unquestionably have been their fate, had they belonged to a British, instead of an American vessel. But the Captain, who awed these men into submission by his fearless firmness, secured their attachment to him and to their country by the suavity and humanity of his conduct. Capt. Biddle's early example of uniting the dignity of the warrior, with the humanity of the man, has been happily followed in our day.

Commodore Hopkins was the commander in chief of this expedition.   The expected rencontre with the British forces upon the island of New Providence was anticipated as a most desperate one.   Capt. Biddle, well acquainted with the firmness and courage of Britons, with whom his country was now at war, prepared his crew as well as he possibly could for the approaching scene.   Cool, collected, and fearless, he left no duty undischarged to prepare for the approaching attack.   He was well aware that he had entered into a service encircled with dangers; but, in the language of one of the finest painters of the human passions, he was—

> " Serene, and master of himself,—prepared
> For what might come—and left the rest to heaven."

Uncertain whether he should ever again revisit his native shores or city, he thus addressed his brother :—" *I know not what my fate may be ; be it, however, what it may, you may be assured I will never cause a blush in the cheeks of my friends or countrymen.*"   His brother, whom he thus pathetically addressed, was a distinguished scholar; and it would remind the classical reader of what Pope wrote to Lord Harley " My mother, such as she is, never caused me a blush, and her son, such as he is, never caused her a tear."

Capt. Biddle's crew were chiefly Pennsylvanians; and had survived that once alarming and mortal disease, the small pox.   The crews of the other vessels of Com. Hopkins' squadron were mostly New Englanders, who had never taken that loathsome and appalling disorder.   They became infected with it after they had put to sea; and it raged with almost resistless violence.   It became the melancholy business of the well to watch over the births of the

134337

sick—to cast the lifeless bodies of the dead into a watery
grave, and then become victims themselves to the raging
pestilence.

> " 'Twas all the business then to tend the sick,
> And in their turn to die."

Capt. Biddle with that feeling humanity which is always
a concomitant with real greatness, exerted every mean in
his power to assuage the distresses of his languishing countrymen. His crew, being uninfected, he despatched his
boats from time to time to the other vessels, and brought
on board the Andrew Doria, such officers and seamen as
were in the most dangerous condition. Amongst them he
recognized an elegant young midshipman, who was in the
last stages of this dreadful distemper. He laid him in his
own birth—watched over him with the most tender solicitude—slept himself upon the lockers, until death relieved
the accomplished and distressed young Midshipman from
his agony.

But with his slender force, reduced essentially by disease
and death, Com. Hopkins bore down with his little squadron for N. Providence. Meeting with little opposition, he
acquired possession of the island, levied a contribution upon the inhabitants, and brought off a great amount of naval
stores. This affair will not be particularly mentioned in
this place. It more properly belongs to the biography of
Com. Hopkins.

Capt. Biddle's crew became sickly with the disorders
peculiar to the West Indies ; and, when ordered to return
to America, he had scarcely able seamen sufficient to navigate his vessel.

He arrived at New London, (Conn.) where a salubrious
climate and the urbanity of the citizens, restored them to

health, and rendered them fit for any duty they should be ordered to perform.

The officers and crew of the Andrew Doria under the discipline of Capt. Biddle, had become somewhat familiarized with the principles of naval tactics, entirely devoted to their commander, and ardent in the cause of their country.

He refitted his brig at New London ; and soon after received the orders of the " Marine Committee" of *Congress,* (for there was *then* no *Navy Department,*) to proceed to sea, and cruise against British merchantmen upon the coast of *Newfoundland.*

He eluded the numerous British cruisers upon the American coast ; and, before he reached his destination, captured two of the enemy's transports, containing half a regiment of Highland troops, to reinforce the British troops, under the perfidious Gage.*

This was a most seasonable capture, as it enabled the government to make exchanges for American prisoners, and to ensure better treatment to them before exchanged.

---

* It will be recollected that Gov. Gage pledged himself to the people of Boston, to "let the people go" if they would surrender up their arms. It is thus happily touched off by the Hon. JOHN TRUMBULL, in his inimitable Hudibrastic poem " M'Fingal."

> " So Gage of late agreed you know,
> To let the Boston people go ;
> Yet when he saw, 'gainst troops that brav'd him,
> *They* were the only guards that sav'd him ;
> Kept off that Satan of a PUTNAM,
> From breaking in to maul and mutt'n him,
> He'd too much wit such leagues t'observe,
> And shut them in again to starve."

                                        Canto I.

9

It served another purpose—to enable the intrepid Biddle to compel a British admiral to regard the right of war. One of his Lieutenants, Josiah, an excellent officer, had been captured in a prize vessel, despatched by Capt. Biddle, by a British frigate. Capt. Biddle wrote an indignant letter to admiral Howe at New York, remonstrating against the treatment Lieut. Josiah received. " If, sir, you see fit to mal-treat a noble and patriotic young officer, whom the fate of war has placed in your possession, rest assured the law of retaliation will be resorted to by me." Amongst *his* prisoners, he had the son of an English nobleman ; and considering one of *his* Lieutenants as equal in rank to *any* nobleman, he determined that *he* should feel the weight of necessary severity, instead of inflicting it upon a *common* British subject. This determination was worthy of this truly noble American officer.

Not satisfied with this, as the only means in his own hands to insure the good treatment of his Lieutenant, he addressed Congress upon the subject.

At this period it excites not only astonishment, but indignation, that the officers of a nation which then claimed the first rank amongst the nations of the earth, for civilization and christianity,—that her Commons, which were graced by a Burke, a Fox, and a Barre, and her Peerage, which contained two arch-bishops and twenty-four bishops, decorated with the sanctity of the lawn, and lords temporal robed in the ermine of justice, should have been guilty of barbarity toward prisoners of war, taken in defending the dearest rights of their country. The enormity of it was increased from the consideration, that Britain considered herself all-powerful, and America as all-impotent ; for it is one of the attributes of real greatness, to be humane. They ought to have remembered the sentiment of the prince of *their* poets.

> " O ! 'tis excellent to have a giant's strength,
> But tyrannous to use it like a giant."

By examining the Journal of the " Old Congress" it will be found that that majestic body of statesmen would readily lend all their aid and call forth, if necessary, all their power, to avenge the injuries which a single individual sustained.   This every government is bound to do ; for if rulers will be tame and unmoved spectators of cruelty inflicted upon *one* of its citizens, the *whole* become endangered.   The same nation who were then violating the rights of civilized warfare, upon the person of Lieut. Josiah, owe their boasted *habeas corpus* act to the injuries which an obscure individual suffered.   The treatment an American, by the name of *Meade* recently sustained from the government of Spain, and the decided and spirited conduct of the American minister, in regard to that subject, convinced the Spanish monarchy that every citizen of our Republic, is ready to give efficacy to the declaration of a Roman—" *Nemo me, impune lascessit*" (no one shall injure me with impunity.)

In the Journal of Congress, August 7th 1776, is the following entry.—" That the general remonstrance to Lord Howe, on the cruel treatment Lieut. Josiah has met with, of which the Congress have received undoubted information, and a letter from Capt. Nicholas Biddle, to the Marine Committee, was laid before Congress and read— Whereupon, Resolved that Gen. Washington be directed to propose an exchange of Lieut. Josiah, for a Lieutenant of the navy of Great Britain."   Although this resolution was passed the next month after the declaration of Ameri-

can Independence—and although the Confederation was
considered by its vaunting enemy, little stronger than a
"reed shaken by the wind," yet such a proposition, from
such a body, and to be offered by such a man as GEORGE
WASHINGTON, awed the enemy into compliance, and the
gallant Lieut. Josiah was restored again to his station in the
little marine force of his country.

Doctor Ramsay, in his excellent and authentic " *History
of the American Revolution*" thus remarks. " The American
sailors, when captured by the British, suffered more than
even the soldiers which fell into their hands. The former
were confined on board prison ships. They were crowded
together in such numbers, and their accommodations were
so wretched, that diseases broke out, and swept them off in
a manner that was sufficient to excite compassion in breasts
of the least sensibility."—" Eleven thousand persons perished on board the *Jersey*, one of these prison-ships."—
" On many of these, the rites of sepulture were never but
imperfectly performed."—This is the language of history.
Let me add, that within a few years past the whitened
bones of these gallant ocean-warriors laid scattered along
upon the shores of Long Island,—monuments of their devotion to country, and of the Gothic barbarism of Britain
in the first war. Praise to a preserving God, and thanks
to our energetic countrymen, in the *Second War*, Britons
dared not *thus* treat American soldiers or seamen.

Amongst a great variety of interesting incidents in the
War of the Revolution, many of which are but little known,
and generally forgotten, the following is apposite to the
present subject. It ought not to be forgotten, that in the
early part of that sanguinary contest, American prisoners
were denied the rights of prisoners of war. Witness the

treatment of the gallant youths, Robert and Andrew Jackson ; and more especially of Col. Allen, wafted in irons, across the Atlantic, to be exhibited in London, as a *Rebel Colonel*. Witness also, the incarceration of the great Henry Laurens, in the Tower of London. Let the following *morceau* be read, and let the memory of the Old Congress be venerated.

" A memorial having been presented to Congress, from Lieut. Christopher Hale, of the British Navy, praying to be exchanged, and to have leave to go to New York upon his parole, for a few days, to procure a person in his room, that Assembly resolved, " That Mr. Hale be informed, that the Prayer of his Memorial cannot be granted until Capt. Cunningham is released, as it has been determined that he must abide the fate of that Officer."

Capt. Biddle, in his little brig, now went on " conquering and to conquer." A very great number of British storeships, transports, and merchantmen, with munitions of war and property to an immense amount, were captured by him, and sent into American ports.

At that period, when the country was impoverished and constantly impoverishing, from being deprived of the thriving and prosperous pursuits of husbandry, commerce, fishing, and whaling, such acquisitions were of more consequence than can well be conceived in the *forty-seventh year* of *American Independence*.

He kept constantly at sea himself ; and, from time to time, despatched his officers and seamen into different ports with his prizes and prisoners. Many of the prisoners he took, entered cheerfully into his service, and, in this way, he kept his crew good. When he found it necessary to land in a port, his vessel was so crowded with prisoners, that, for some days before landing, he remained constantly upon deck. After he arrived, and inspected his muster-roll, he found he had but *five* of the original crew he had, when he sailed from New London !!

While Capt. Biddle, with his slender means was thus making an impression upon the enemy, and animating his countrymen upon land by his brilliant success upon the ocean, the " Marine Committee" were preparing for him a more important command. A frigate of 32 guns was rapidly built, and called, The Randolph, and Capt. Biddle was appointed to the command of it at the commencement of the year 1777.

His ardent and restless spirit would scarcely give ' sleep to his eyes or slumber to his eyelids,' until he had fitted the frigate for sea. Although probably much inferior to the fine frigates of her class which now belong to our noble navy, yet she was probably the finest ship then belonging to America.

Capt. Biddle, at this period of his life, might have retired to enjoy the independence he had acquired by his valour. But that independence which the fortunate children of wealth display in splendid equipage, and by soaring abroad like the gaudy butterfly, which spreads the variegated wing to the rays of a summer's sun, was littleness itself in such a soul as guided and governed the actions of Nicholas Biddle. He was an advocate for that independence which proceeds from self-government, and was anxious to exert his faculties, and if necessary to lose his life, in establishing the independence of his native country.

At that dangerous and doubtful period, it was difficult to obtain American seamen to enter on board the few ships which belonged to the Republic. But the British seamen which Capt. Biddle had captured, equally regardless of the monarchy under which they were born, and into the service of which they were daily liable to be impressed, as they were for the Republic which was striving for independence, enlisted under Capt. Biddle. He was aware that they were good seamen, but he had good reason to doubt their fidelity. They were mostly composed of beings who were hired to die, or compelled to spill their blood in supporting and defending the pageantry of royalty. They considered themselves as mere " food for powder," and cared little in what cause they died. But the determined Captain was resolved to put to sea, and once more to face and defy the enemies of his country.

He sailed from Philadelphia in the month of February. 1777. He had been at sea but a few days before he discovered the mutinous and perfidious machinations of his crew. The English seamen entered into a combination to rise upon the Captain, his officers, and the American seamen—take the frigate into their own command, and present the ship and crew to the British admiral, or become pirates. They possessed the *physical* power to carry this determination into effect. It required all the energy and intrepidity of Capt. Biddle and his officers to defeat this nefarious design. Indeed, it is upon occasions like this, that the native greatness of man is displayed. To bear a ship into action, with an equal antagonist, with a crew like that of the junior Decatur, whose hearts beat in unison with that of their commander, is pastime and pleasure, when compared with the danger that arises from disaffection and treachery. Said a noble Spartan—" May the gods preserve me from *friends*—my *enemies* I am always prepared to encounter." The disaffected part of the

crew, as a signal for rising, were to give three cheers---
rush into the cabin—put the officers in irons, and assume
the command of the frigate.

The noble, the fearless, and determined Biddle, re-acted
the scene he had passed through at the prison, when he re-
took his deserters. His presence of mind—his thundering
denunciations—his consummate and wonderful power of
commanding, struck instantaneous terror into the hearts
of the numerous host that opposed him. He was, indeed,
a host of himself. The awe-struck mutineers submissively
returned to their duty ; and would afterwards as soon set
Omnipotence itself at defiance, as to wink an eye-lid in
hostility to their commander.

No sooner had he restored order in his floating garrison,
than he had to endure the distressing scene of beholding
all his masts go by the board, from their original defects.
He put into Charleston, S. C. to refit. Every hour's detention seemed like a whole *calender* to this unsurpassed
ocean warrior. The means of refitting a dismasted frigate
in 1777, were next to nothing to what they are in 1823, at
our well furnished naval depots. Capt. Biddle's whole
soul was entwined around the cause of his country ; and
he ardently panted to be constantly facing her enemy.
He was not to be restrained by the cold and icy suggestions
of prudence, from venturing all his temporal possessions,
and his life too, in the holy cause of his country, which he
loved better than he did himself. He was lavish to excess,
in spending his blood and treasure for it.

His short stay at Charleston, excited toward him the admiration of its patriotic citizens. The enemy had learned
that an American Frigate had been to sea, and they were
determined to add it to the Royal Navy of Britain. Capt.

Biddle sailed from Charleston with the patriotic wishes
and fervent prayers of every true American for his success.
The third day's sail brought him into contact with four
valuable British ships. The commander of one of them,
the True Briton, had expressed his urgent wishes to fall in
with the Randolph. As soon as he recognized the ship,
he hove to, and at long shot commenced the action. The
fire was incessant, although ill directed from the True
Briton.

Capt. Biddle set the example, which has so successsful-
ly been followed by the modern officers of our navy, of
bearing down upon the enemy, reserving fire—coming into
close action—and settling the contest at once. The astonished and vaunting Briton, at the moment the Randolph
was about to pour in her first broadside, struck his flag,
and surrendered his ship to Capt. Biddle.

He instantly officered and manned his prize ; and, with
the Randolph, went in pursuit of the other vessels, every
one of which he captured. The citizens of Charleston had
hardly expected that Capt. Biddle had left the American
coast, before he gladdened their eyes and rejoiced their
hearts with the sight of his frigate and four prizes of very
great value.

At that time, such an achievement, and such an acquisition, produced perhaps more real joy than the more recent achievements of our matchless navy. It was but sev-
en days from the time Capt. Biddle sailed from Charleston
before he entered the same port with his frigate and prizes.
His presence diffused animation through all ranks ; and the
possessors of wealth readily advanced it to augment his
force. Every exertion was made to prepare a squadron
for Commodore Biddle. " The north gave up, and the
10

south kept not back," as it regarded North and South Carolina. The very souls of the people were devoted to the cause of their country ; and the wonted enjoyments of private luxuries, and the more splendid display of glaring and magnificent equipage, were forgotten in the cause of the Republic which must have sunken into the degradation of slavery, had it not risen into the majesty of independence by the unparalleled exertion of the undaunted spirits of '76.

Com. Biddle's reputation stood so high at this period, that the ardent youth of South Carolina were solicitous to adventure their lives under his command. In a very short time, the Commodore raised his broad pendant upon the Frigate Randolph,* and had in his squadron the ship General Moultrie,† the brigs Fair American and Polly,—and

* This frigate was named Randolph, in honour of Peyton Randolph, first President of the Old Congress under the confederation.

† This ship was named General Moultrie, in honour of William Moultrie, Maj. Gen. in the Revolutionary army—the defender of Sullivan's island, and the victor at Beaufort. Lord Montague, ex-governour of S. Carolina, offered a princely bribe to Gen. Moultrie, as Gov. Gage did to Gen. Putnam, to join the British forces. Although the literary acquirements of the latter general, would not enable him to repel the audacious insult so *elegantly* as the former, his patriotic heart, repelled it as *indignantly.* As Gen. Moultrie's letter is in my possession, I am persuaded the reader will be gratified in perusing the noble sentiments of a warm friend of the exalted Biddle.

Haddrell's Point, March 13, 1781.

My Lord—

" I received yours this morning. I thank you for the wish to promote my advantage, but I am much surprised at your proposition. I flattered myself I stood in a more favourable light with you. I shall write with the same freedom with which we used to converse, and doubt not you will receive it with the same candour. I have often heard you express your sentiments respecting this unfortunate war ;

sloop **Notre Dame.** The Randolph had lost one of her masts by a stroke of lightning. It was immediately restored,

when you thought the Americans injured ; but am now astonished to find you take an active part against them ; though not fighting particularly on the continent ; yet the seducing their soldiers away to enlist in the British service, is nearly similar.

" My lord, you are pleased to compliment me with having fought bravely in my country's cause, for many years, and, in your opinion, fulfilled the duty every individual owes it ; but I differ widely from you in thinking that I have discharged my duty to my country, while it is deluged with blood and overrun by British troops, who exercise the most savage cruelties. When I entered into this contest, I did it with the most mature deliberation, with a determined resolution to risk my life and fortune in the cause. The hardships I have gone through I look upon with the greatest pleasure and honor to myself. I shall continue to go on as I have begun, that my example may encourage the youths of America, to stand forth in defence of their rights and liberties. You call upon me now, and tell me I have a fair opening of quitting that service with honor and reputation to myself, by going with you to Jamaica. Good God ! is it possible that such an idea could arise in the breast of a man of honor ? I am sorry you should imagine I have so little regard to my own reputation, as to listen to such dishonorable proposals. Would you wish to have that man honored with your friendship, play the traitor ? Surely not.

" You say, by quitting this country for a time I might avoid disagreeable conversations, and might return at my own leisure, and take possession of my estates for myself and family ; but you have forgot to tell me how I could get rid of the feelings of an injured, honest heart, and where to hide myself from myself. Could I be guilty of so much baseness, I should hate myself and shun mankind. This would be a fatal exchange for the present situation, with an easy and approving conscience, of having done my duty, and conducted myself as a man of honor.

" My lord, I am sorry to observe, that I feel your friendship much abated, or you would not endeavour to prevail upon me to act so base a part. You earnestly wish you could bring it about, as you think it will be the means of bringing about that reconciliation we all wish for. I wish for a reconciliation as much as any man, but only upon hon-

and the frigate was fitted for sea, with a lightning rod on her main-mast.

orable terms. The repossessing of my estates ; the offer of the command of your regiment, and the honor you propose of serving under me, are paltry considerations to the loss of my reputation. No, not the fee-simple of that valuable island of Jamaica, should induce me to part with my integrity.

" My lord, as you have made one proposal, give me leave to make another, which will be more honorable to us both. As you have an interest with your commanders, I would have you propose the withdrawing the British troops from the continent of America, allowing independence, and propose a peace. This being done I will use my interest with my commanders to accept the terms, and allow Great Britain a free trade with America.

" My lord, I could make one more proposal ; but my situation as a prisoner, circumscribes me within certain bounds. I must, therefore, conclude with allowing you the free liberty to make what use of this you may think proper. Think better of me.

" I am my lord, your lordship's most humble servant.

Wm. Moultrie."

" To lord Charles Montague.

Can the present generation of Americans, at this remove of time, contemplate upon the firmness of Moultrie, when a prisoner of war, and of Biddle, his youthful friend, without the highest exultation, mingled with the deepest veneration?

Joseph Reed, was secretary and aid de camp to Gen. Washington, in the revolution, and afterwards governour of Pennsylvania. The Royal Governour Johnston, assured the inflexible patriot " That ten thousand pounds sterling, and the best office in the gift of the crown in America should be at his disposal, if he could effect a reunion of the two countries." He replied, " *That he was not worth purchasing ; but such as he was, the king of Great Britain was not rich enough to do it.*"

A London paper, (1780) says,—" The following were the terms that were offered to Gen. Washington, viz.—To be given rank in the British service ; a landed estate in England purchased for him, of 7000l. a year, and great promotions for 12 such persons as he should name."

At this period the Continental infantry in the vicinity of Charleston, were under the command of a man, whose name is now associated with the proudest recollection of our countrymen,—a man, whose talents, science and patriotism has added vast weight to the character of American greatness ;—whose acquirements as a diplomatist and statesman, have excited the undissembled admiration of the courts of St. Cloud and St. James—CHARLES COTESWORTH PINCKNEY. The approbation of such a man was a volume of eulogy in favour of Com. Biddle. The country at that time had nothing like a well organized marine corps ; and Gen. Pinckney offered a detachment from a regiment to serve in the squadron, provided the men would consent to change their service from soldiers to marines. Notwithstanding the perfect devotion of the regiment to their accomplished commander, a competition arose amongst the captains and subalterns in the different companies, who should have the honour of entering into the more dangerous service of Com. Biddle.

These noble and gallant spirits little anticipated the awful fate that was shortly to await them, and their adored commander. As the writer approaches toward the relation of the direful catastrophe, he sensibly feels his incompetency to delineate it.

The coast of S. Carolina was infested with British cruisers, from *Seventy-fours* down to *Schooners ;* yet Com. Biddle rendezvoused with his little squadron in what was then called " *Rebellion Roads,*" toward the last of February.

The British commanders, in order to decoy him into greater danger, left the coast and bore away for the West Indies. Capt. Biddle resolved to carry the arms of America, where the enemies of America were to be found ; and to conduct his squadron to those regions where he could inflict the severest injury upon the enemy, and render his country the most essential service.

Let not the reader conclude that this admired and lamented commander, had that daring rashness which would carry his ships and crews into danger, that could not be escaped. Although but twenty-seven years of age—although the gristle of youth had but just ripened into the bone of manhood, he had devoted himself with such assiduity to his profession, and had seen so much service, that he had acquired the coolness and prudence of an experienced admiral.

Upon the 5th March, a number of the officers of the squadron, dined on board the Randolph. The Commodore observed to them, " We have been some days cruising here, and having spoken a number of vessels, some of them have undoubtedly given information of us. But in this ship, I think myself a match for any thing floating, that carries her guns upon one deck." He captured one valuable ship and cargo, and sent her to America.

From the time he took command of the *Andrew Doria*, to this period of his life, this dauntless and vigilant navigator and tactician, had probably given more annoyance to British commerce, and aid to his country than any other of the intrepid American Heroes upon the ocean. During a considerable portion of the time, his native city and the adjoining country, was in the hands of an enemy whose " tender mercies are cruelties." To adopt the language of the patriotick Humphreys, " Add to the black catalogue of provocations,—their insatiable rapacity in plundering— their libidinous brutality in violating the chastity of the female sex—their *more* than Gothic rage in defacing private writings, public records, libraries of learning—dwellings of individuals—edifices of education, and temples of the Deity —together with their insufferable ferocity, unprecedented indeed among civilized nations, in murdering on the field of battle, the wounded while begging for mercy"—and " carrying their malice beyond death itself, by denying the decent rights of sepulture to the dead." Such is the just and pathetic description of a young and gallant officer, who was then encountering the enemies of the rising Republic, upon land, as Biddle was upon the ocean. But mark the difference of the conduct of this noble American, when he had captured a king's ship, or a merchantman. His humane conduct made prisoners forget that they were in the possession of an enemy ; and although their property had fallen a sacrifice to the depredations of war, the magnanimous Commodore shielded them from individual distress ; and restored to them every thing needed, for personal necessity and convenience.

Although American Naval Officers have always been distinguished for a dignified deportment and feeling humanity, to a vanquished enemy, yet the example set by Biddle in the First, may well be supposed to have had much influence upon officers in the Second war with Britain.

But as if " death loves a shining mark" and designates his sudden victims amongst the most brilliant ornaments of dying man, this favourite of his then warring and distressed country—the delight of his friends, and the admiration of his enemies was, by the most appalling, sudden, and terrific shock of warfare, to be torn from time into eternity.

The 7th of March 1778, was the day upon which this admired Officer, and one of the most gallant Crews of that age, were to be lost to their friends and country.

At 3 P. M. a sail, at the windward, was descried from the Randolph. A signal being made from the frigate, the squadron hauled upon a wind, to speak the strange sail. As the sail neared the Randolph and came directly before the wind, she had the appearance of a heavy sloop,* with only a square-sail set. It was not until 4 P. M. that she was discovered to be a ship. At about 7 P. M. the Randolph had the windward, the General Moultrie being to the leeward, when the ship fired ahead of the General Moultrie and hailed her. Her answer was, " The Polly from New-York," (then in possession of the British forces.) The ship suddenly hauled her wind and hailed the Randolph. The sail was H. B. Majesty's ship of the line Yarmouth, Capt. Vincent, of sixty-four guns.

According to the opinion of the most scientific and experienced naval officers, the Yarmouth was a fair and equal match for *three* ships of the rate of the Randolph.† As she ranged along side Com. Biddle's ship, an English lieutenant exultingly exclaimed, " *The Randolph! the Randolph!*"—and instantly poured into her a full broadside. The fire was returned from the Randolph, and the little Moultrie, with the utmost rapidity ; and, from the disparity of force, with astonishing effect. The night was excessively dark ; the Yarmouth shot ahead of the Randolph, and brought her between that ship and the Moultrie. One broadside from the last mentioned ship, in the hottest of the

* To a landsman, like the writer, this would appear improbable ; but I have been assured by accomplished seamen, that this deception is by no means unusual.

† The reader is referred to the report of Com. CHARLES STEWART of the American navy, made to the department of the navy in 1812, in support of this position ; which was confirmed by Captains HULL and MORRIS. Mr. Secretary Hamilton expressly alludes to the battle of the Randolph and the Yarmouth.

action, through mistake went directly into the Randolph, the moment Com. Biddle was wounded dangerously in the thigh ; and one of the survivors of the crew conjectured the wound was received from that fire.

And here, another example was set by the dauntless Biddle, which, to the admiration of Americans, and astonishment of the world, seems to have been universally followed by the modern heroes of our navy—never to leave the deck in consequence of a wound, however severe. After the Commodore fell, and they were about to carry him below, he exclaimed with a voice which was almost like a voice from the tomb—" Bring me a chair ; carry me forward ; and there the surgeon will dress my wound."— While this painful operation was performing, he animating the crew, the Randolph firing three broadsides to the Yarmouth's one ; while the thunder of an hundred cannon reverberated over the ocean ; while the vivid flashes of three armed vessels increased the horrors of the surrounding darkness, the Randolph was blown into atoms, and the mangled fragments of the whole crew, (excepting four) consisting of about three hundred and twenty gallant and patriotic Americans, fell sudden victims to their devotion for the cause of their country.

Doct. Ramsay in his admirable history of the American Revolution, very briefly alludes to this disastrous event, and says : " Four men only were saved, upon a piece of her wreck. These had subsisted for four days on nothing but rain water, which they sucked from a piece of blanket." It is with real pleasure I record, as *one* instance of *British* humanity, that upon the 5th day of their sufferings, Capt. Vincent of the Yarmouth, suspended a chase to rescue

11

these despairing Americans from certain death, and restored them to their country.

Although the naval heroes of the revolution are but seldom mentioned in the histories of that sanguinary contest,
yet Doct. Ramsay has left upon *his* record the following
testimony of the merits of this justly admired hero : " Capt.
Biddle, who perished on board the Randolph, was universally lamented. He was in the prime of life ; and had excited high expectations of future usefulness to his country
as a bold and skilful naval officer."

The consternation produced by this disaster can neither
be imagined nor described by one who was not a witness
to it. The Yarmouth and Randolph were in such close action, that the Fair American concluded it to be the former
that blew up, and her Captain, (Morgan) hailed her to inquire after Com. Biddle, knowing him to have been wounded. Alas! he, and also his valiant crew, were insensible to
the solicitude of the remaining part of the squadron, which
but a few minutes before, he so gallantly commanded. The
Yarmouth was in a condition so shattered that Capt. Vincent could not capture either of the little vessels which
were near her, and they all effected their escape.

The explosion of an armed vessel, with a large magazine of powder, is universally allowed to be one of the most
awfully solemn and tremendously horrid scenes that can be
presented to the eye of man. The mind of the reader of
these imperfect sketches is almost irrisistibly hurried forward
from the gloomy catastrophe of the 7th of March 1778, to
the no less horrid one of Sept. 4th 1804, when the gallant
Somers, Wadsworth and Israel became victims in chastising a barbarous foe, as the gallant Biddle and his associates did in defending his country against a Christian ene-

my. From the very nature of such catastrophes, it is impossible to develope the causes of them. Whether they are occasioned by the inattention of the crew, or the accidents occasioned in a close and furious engagement, can scarcely ever be determined.

Thus lived, and thus died NICHOLAS BIDDLE, one of the early champions of American Independence. His premature death deprived him of the honours and rewards of a grateful, protected, and Independent Republic, and the enjoyment of the opulence which he had acquired by his valour. But even these enjoyments are trifling and evanescent, when compared to that glory which descends to late posterity. It was for this glory that the immortalized Biddle toiled, fought, bled, and died for his beloved country. Let the ardent and rising youth of the Republic ponder upon the example of this young and exalted hero ; and when their country shall again be called to defend the independence acquired by the heroes of the Revolution, and secured by the war of 1812, may they emulate his virtues and patriotism ; and like him, and Biddle the younger, acquire fame which will descend to the remotest posterity.

CHARACTER OF NICHOLAS BIDDLE.

NICHOLAS BIDDLE was born at a period of the world pregnant with the most important events, and was peculiarly adapted for a distinguished actor in them. Ever since the discovery of the Magnetic Needle enabled man to traverse oceans from the equator to the arctic and antarctic circles, the watery element has been the fruitful nursery of unsurpassed heroes. But thirteen years had bloomed the cheek of Biddle, when he found his " home upon the deep;" but early scenes of danger, sufferings, and miraculous preservations, soon converted the sailor boy, to the manly seaman. Sufferings endured and dangers escaped, so far from dissuading, rather stimulated him to one deed of noble daring after another.

In early life, he became a skilful navigator, and well versed in commercial pursuits. But its dull routine was irksome to his ardent and aspiring mind. His manly qualifications procured for him a midshipman's warrant in the Royal Navy of Britain; and he was in full prospect of rapid advancement. He was thus early initiated into the science of naval tactics, and made that science familiar by practical knowledge. It happened to be a period of peace with almost perpetually warring Britain, and Biddle had no opportunity then, to face an enemy.

In HORATIO NELSON, BIDDLE found a spirit congenial with his own; and both became cockswains in Mulgrave's renowned voyage of discovery towards the north pole.— Stupendous mountains of ice, wafted upon billows mountain high, presented the ocean to the view of the lieutenant, acting as cockswain, in all its majestic awful, and destructive grandeur. While Nelson was encountering the snow-white bear, Biddle, encompassed with frowning cliffs of ice, was awaiting the awful crush which was threatening momently to send the ship and crew to the bottom. But he returned to England with Nelson and both became favorites with the proud admiralty of Britain, the modern Carthage.

Notwithstanding he had become familiar with the immeasurable power of the British marine—notwithstanding he was making rapid strides on the lofty waves of promotion with his ship-mate Nelson—notwithstanding the shining orders of knighthood, and the "blushing honours" of nobility were within the reach of this ardent aspirant for honourable fame—he frowned indignantly upon a powerful monarchy which was about to let fall the uplifted arm of vengeance upon the land of his birth. At a time when the menaces of the House of Brunswick *awed*, and the promised honours and gold of Britain *bought*, hordes of American loyalists and tories—Biddle was above corruption— above price. The bank of England, nor that over which his respected connexion presides, never had gold enough in their vaults to buy him.

He re-crossed the Atlantic whose waves were soon to roll him forth as a warring champion against the "king and country" in whose service he commenced his short and brilliant career of naval glory. With a diminutive force, suddenly fitted out by the almost destitute, infant states, he dashed forth like a rude and fearless intruder upon the imperious "Ocean Queen," and her commerce instantly felt and feared his presence.

The profound judgment and deep penetration of the Old Congres, placed the dauntless BIDDLE in command of a squadron. His broad pendant upon the Randolph waved defiance to any equal hostile force upon the ocean. Such was the celerity with which he moved and the number of prizes that he captured, that his ship was singled out as a victim to British prowess. The fate of naval warfare forced him into an awfully unequal contest. The powerful foe, of treble force, descried the devoted ship, while yet the light of heaven directed his unerring course ; and when sable night enveloped the troubled deep in horrid gloom and rendered "darkness visible," the vaunting enemy, sure of victory, vomited forth the thick messengers of death upon

the Randolph. BIDDLE, cool, collected, animated and
fearless, with blood gushing from wounds, animating his
comrades, and defying the enemy whom he could not escape, breasted the tremendous shock. Amidst the roar of
an hundred cannon, and a shower of reddened balls, the in-
discribable catastrophe of an exploding war-ship, hurled
him and his unrivalled associates from temporal warfare to
eternal peace, in a brilliant flame of blazing glory. Thus
did the heroic, the patriotic, the exalted BIDDLE, in the
bloom of life, in heaven-approving warfare, give his mangled corse to the deep—his immortal spirit to the God of
battles, and his imperishable fame to the Republic.

BIOGRAPHICAL SKETCH

OF

JOHN PAUL JONES,

COMMODORE AND POST-CAPTAIN

IN THE

CONTINENTAL NAVY,

IN THE WAR OF THE REVOLUTION.

His Life and Character as drawn by a British Biographer.....Early incidents of his life....Enters a slave ship....Slave Trade....Goes to service at the Earl of Selkirk's, and is discharged....Becomes a "Smug," gets married, has the *hypo*, and leaves his wife....Becomes the "Prince of smugglers"....Goes to France, gets married again, plays the gentleman landlord, "runs out," and again "sets up business" as a grand smuggler, and afterwards as a merchant. ....Gains wealth, goes to London, dashes and gambles, and "comes upon the world"....Smuggles again....Makes a voyage to America, and assumes a new and decided character....He is employed by Congress upon a secret expedition to England....Accomplishes his object, and returns to America....He is appointed to the command of a Continental ship, and successfully assails British merchantmen ....He joins Com. Hopkins' squadron as commander of the Alfred, distinguishes himself in the capture of the British island of New-Providence....Upon his return takes command of the Providence. of 12 guns, in which he convoys vessels and transports.....He receives the first Captain's commission after the 4th of July, 1776.... Capt. Jones sails again in the Providence, is encountered by the frigate Solebay of 30 guns; takes valuable prizes; sails for Nova Scotia; is attacked by the Milford of 32 guns; escapes; effects a landing; destroys fisheries; takes 17 prizes, and returns....He is appointed to a squadron....Com. Jones sails in the Alfred ; takes the rich transport Mellish, three prizes, and a Liverpool privateer of 16 guns....Is again attacked by the Milford; escapes with his prizes to Boston....Receives a vote of thanks from Congress....He takes command of the Ranger, of 18 guns ; sails for France ; takes numerous prizes ; announces the defeat of Burgoyne....Repairs to Paris, returns to the Ranger, and receives the first salute to the American Flag....Enters Brest, is saluted by Count D'Orvilliers... He lands at Whitehaven, carries the fort, spikes 40 cannon, and returns on board....He visits his father....Captures the Drake of 20 guns ; enters Brest, and visits the court of Louis XVI...Com. Jones sails in a squadron of five vessels, on board the Good Man

THE naval hero now to be introduced to the reader, is
a sort of phenomenon in human nature. He was an ano
maly in the human character. Born within the dominions
of Britain, at a period when his native kingdom was striding on from conquest to conquest—from usurpation to
usurpation, he caught the adventurous spirit of his countrymen, and seemed in his own character, to have revived
the ancient spirit of chivalry. His life has been sketched
by one of his own countrymen, with that malignant asper-
ity which characterizes the writers of that country, when
treating of the daring spirits who espoused the cause of
America in the unparalleled war of the revolution. In
order to cast a shade over his wonderful achievements in
that contest between the rectitude of weakness and the
usurpation of power, they have endeavoured to blast his
fame, by attributing to him the most infamous and detestable vices.

While it is readily admitted that it is the business and
duty of the biographer to give a faithful portrait of the
character delineated, yet, it must also be admitted, that
the eccentricities, the irregularities, and the aberrations of
untutored judgment and misguided passions, in the early
period of life, ought not to be glaringly painted for the
purpose of tarnishing the fame of mature manhood. It is
unhesitatingly asserted that almost without exception, the
private lives of the most distinguished ornaments of human
nature are not without *some* blemishes. But when a man
has become a benefactor to his country in the state, the

church, the army, the navy, or in the walks of literature, why should the just admiration of the world be diminished by publishing his little, private foibles? One of the biographers of Nelson carries his enraptured readers along through the life of that wonderful man from the days of boyhood, when he encountered a bear in the polar regions, until, in the full fruition of glory, he fell at Trafalgar. Another biographer of the same naval hero, makes the reader almost despise him, because he makes him a victim to the fascinating charms of Lady Hamilton. But, without saying more by way of introduction to the Life of JOHN PAUL JONES, and as perhaps too much has been already said, I will proceed in a brief sketch of his eventful life.

He was born at Dumfries, in Scotland, in the month of June, 1748, two years before his associate in war, Nicholas Biddle. His parents were in what is called, the humblest grade of life, but which, in reality, is the most exalted—tillers of the earth. They were amongst the peasantry of Scotland, so renowned for their sobriety, industry, intelligence, and devotion. Like Robert Burns, Jones, from the circumstances in which he was born, seemed to be destined for the useful, although dull and unvarying scenes of a peasant's life. But young Jones possessed that restlessness of spirit—that inquietude—that insatiable desire to accomplish something beyond the highest achievements of the comrades with whom he was associated, that he could not be limited to their dull pursuits. He would neither be chained down to the business of a hewer of wood, a carrier of water, a heaver of coal, a thresher of oats and barley, or a dresser of flax.

It was the misfortune of young Jones, that the first ad-

12

venture he made beyond the humble pursuits of domestic life. was the most detestable of all pursuits— *the slave trade.* That wicked, that infamous, that infernal and diabolical traffick, above all others, is most directly calculated to divest the human breast of every exalted sentiment, and of every moral and religious principle. The slave dealer unites in his own character, the murderer, the robber, the ravisher, and the thief. He directly or indirectly violates the precepts of the whole decalogue. The Law that came by Moses, and the Grace that came by the Redeemer, are equally broken and defied by the slave dealer. But the anathemas of angels and of men against these " devils incarnate," must be omitted, to remark, that Jones acquired a cruelty and ferocity of temper in the first and only voyage he made to Guinea. The natural humanity and magnanimity of his heart was tarnished by this horrid traffick, but it was subsequently ameliorated by association with humane and dignified Americans.

After his return to Scotland the Earl of Selkirk, an excellent Scots nobleman, received Jones under his protection ; but he proved to his patron, as Savage did to Lord Tyrconnel, too turbulent, too boisterous, too regardless of " the method of regular life," to be endured in a mansion where every thing was to " be done decently and in order."

He was turned loose and destitute into the world, which is but little disposed to espouse the cause of such a being. From the whole tenor of Jones' life, it may be inferred that he could not endure restraint, or submit to authority. He aspired to be his own commander and to command others. He seemed to prefer to fall by his own directions, than to stand by the guidance of others, and—

"Strong as necessity, to fight his way,
Struggle with fate, and brighten into day."

An opportunity presented itself, in joining a gang of smugglers. A better " Smug," than Jones, could not be found. He was made for that business, and the hazardous business seemed to be calculated for him. But he had no idea of acting in a subordinate station ; and the hardy smug-glers would not consent to be commanded by a young des-perado. Jones left them in disgust, and once more " came upon the world ;" and after leading a vagabond sort of life for a time, he entered on board a Sunderland brig, which was a regular trader. He devoted himself with the utmost assiduity to his business, and shortly made himself an ac-complished navigator and seaman. By this pursuit he be-came perfectly well acquainted with the coast which was afterwards to become the theatre of his unequalled exploits, and imperishable glory.

From this brig he was impressed on board a man of war. " The floating dungeons" of the British navy almost invari-ably secure impressed seamen for life, unless the admiralty discharge them. But as soon as Jones had acquired a pretty competent knowledge of naval tactics, he took his own time and manner to be discharged, i. e. by *desertion.* Fear of the yard arm, was probably the occasion of Jones' desperate fighting in his subsequent life.

At this period, Jones "took to himself a wife," and a fortune of twelve hundred dollars. At this age and in this country, this sum would excite a smile when speaking of " fortune." But at that age, in Scotland, it amounted to an independence.

To such a character as Jones, the honey-moon is gene-rally of short duration, and such a sum might readily be

squandered. Notwithstanding the glowing representations
of hymeneal joys, and domestic felicity, they were entirely
too insipid for the romantic and adventurous Jones. He
felt that inquietude which the uninteresting and dull routine
of regulated life produces in the mind of an ardent spirit.
He experienced that feeling which the French call *ennui*—
which equally defies *translation* and *description*. Americans call it *hypo*, and whoever is afflicted with this non-
descript in the long catalogue of the " miseries of human
life," may well justify Jones in striving to tear himself away
from this paralyzing *incubus*.

His former companions, with his aid, purchased a stout
vessel, and Jones became her commander. He now filled
a station which filled his desires. The marauders upon
the coast of Scotland and Ireland, at this period, were numerous. Captain Jones was not deterred, from any conscientious scruples from pursuing a business which others
pursued. He was a child of fortune ; and, in the language
of his eccentric countryman, he was determined to follow
his advice in his epistle to a young friend.

" To catch dame fortune's golden smile,
" Assiduous wait upon her."—
" And gather gear by ev'ry wile,—
*   *   *   *   *

Like a comet, his eccentric course defied calculation.
He suddenly acquired a considerable amount of wealth,
and not wishing to return to the " dull pursuits of civil life"
amongst the virtuous peasantry of Scotland, he landed in
France, at the port of Boulogne.

This was a new scene for a Scottish peasant. The fascinating blandishments of that captivating country, allured
Jones into the good graces of a widow who kept what is

called a *Restorateur* or hotel. But she could not give her
hand to an adventurer, or fortune-hunter, until she was convinced that she should receive something besides the hand
of a rough and boisterous Scotsman. But Jones, to convince her of the sincerity of his profession, placed in her
hands two hundred guineas, and once more resorted to his
favorite element—the ocean.

Possessing requisite funds, he became a first rate smuggler, and established himself at Dover, the nearest port to
the coast of France, where some of his treasure, and all of
his heart, were deposited. He resumed the business of a
smuggler; and his success exceeded his most sanguine expectations.

But Capt. Jones was not satisfied with the mere accumulation of wealth. He was disgusted with a pursuit which
did not embrace something bold and daring. Having cruis-
ed against defenceless merchantmen, he resolved to commence an attack upon an English cruiser designed to chastise the Barbarians up the Mediterranean.

However much the cool calculator of chances may con-
demn the temerity of Jones, it was an attempt that perfectly comported with his character. With his feeble force he
captured a well-fitted, armed vessel, and made her his own.
In this vessel, he dashed into the midst of armed ships and
peaceful coasters : and, although opposed by an overwhelming superiority of force, either by nautical skill, or
deep laid stratagem, he effected his escape.

Having acquired enough to return to Boulogne "in style"
his thoughts were turned to his amorous French widow
who still remained there. He transferred his vessel to
his ascociates—disembarked ; and, with a very considerable fortune, proceeded to Boulonge. The widow, with

the artful finesse, of affected rapture, no longer hesitated
to take Jones to her bosom, since it made such an augmentation to her wealth.

Captain Jones now appeared in a capacity, the worst of
all fitted to his genius and disposition—that of a *landlord*.
It was like Hercules at the distaff—it was like an eagle upon a shrub. He, who could not endure the control of any
one, was now, in a measure, under the control of every
one. He was a slave to slaves ; and subjected to the calls,
the whims and caprices of every one who visited his hotel.
But he figured away in most splendid style—gave sumptuous entertainments to his customers, and appeared more
like one of the French noblesse, than a retailer of champaigne, soups, and pastry. This was a grand scene for a
Scots peasant who seemed to have been born to subsist
upon oaten cakes, barley broth, and "gude parritch."
But these halcyon days, like an autumnal squall, only portended the storms of winter. Jones became outrageous—
drove away his customers, and prepared again to drive into more boisterous scenes.

It would not comport with the limits prescribed for this
sketch, to give a minute detail of the numerous and diversified incidents of the life of this extraordinary man—extraordinary he surely was, for he completely transcended
the ordinary traits of the human character. He left his
hotel in the care of his wife—embarked for the Isle of Man,
which had just come into the possession of Great Britain,
and commenced business as a sort of prince of smugglers.
He amassed riches ; and, as money is the sinew of enterprise, he repaired to Dunkirk, and prosecuted business
with success—not the business of a regular merchant, for
there was nothing at this time of regularity in his character.

Having once deserted from a king's ship ; having been engaged in an illicit trade, and fearing to be betrayed by some of his numerous comrades, he hesitated whether to visit his native country or not. But with his usual rashness, he dashed into London, that world in miniature, that resort of every thing that elevates, and every thing that degrades the human character.

The Captain here began to display the "high character." He rolled in splendour, and figured at the gambling table. Here, to use a familiar expression, *he found his match*, and was soon outmatched. He was reduced almost to indigence ; and finding he could not regain his wealth by *honest gambling* upon land, he resorted to the business of an *honest smuggler* at sea. Here he was perfectly at home ; and having a crew as daring as himself, he soon acquired a large amount of property.

Towards the latter end of the year 1773, Capt. Jones turned his attention towards America, and was determined to make a voyage to this country. He sailed from Havre. in France, in the spring of 1774.

Upon his arrival in America, he found the Colonies in a state of turbulence exactly suited to his wishes. Despising the idea of joining the strongest party, and having the utmost detestation for tyrannical usurpation, he resolved to espouse the cause of America, which he made his adopted country.

With his high sense of independence—his hostility against English power, from having been impressed—his perfect acquaintance with the coast of England, Scotland and Ireland ; his skill as a navigator and naval tactician, added to his undaunted courage, rendered the acquisition of such a man, at such a time, of the highest importance. It was a time of daring expedients, and required daring spirits to act.

Capt. Jones took the earliest opportunity to impart the most important information to the high minded and indignant whigs of that day. He was received and treated with every mark of distinction by these unrivalled patriots and statesmen.

This was a new sphere for the ambitious Jones to move in. His associates, in his own country, had been men of desperate fortunes, and contaminated hearts ; and he must have been most favourably impressed with the American character, when contrasted with that of his own countrymen. From an irregular and dissolute life, he became the steady, cool, and determined hero, in the great cause of freedom against oppression.

The confidence reposed in him by the master spirits who were to direct the storm that was lowering over the Thirteen Colonies must have been highly gratifying to a man who was born, and might have died, an humble peasant.

Being deemed of high importance that every information possible should be obtained concerning England, and especially of her naval depots and commercial ports, Capt. Jones was selected for the purpose of repairing to Great-Britain for this purpose. This evinced the sagacity of the early patriots of the revolution. Such information was deeply interesting, as it regarded the contest which was just commencing, and Jones, the best calculated of any man to obtain it. His Scotch accent was calculated to elude suspicion ; and his previous pursuits to lead him to proper subjects of inquiry. He explored London ; mingled in society ; learned the sentiments of all classes con-

cerning the Americans, and their "*rebellion.*" He repaired to the docks and roads where armed vessels and merchantmen were moored—learned their destination, and objects—purchased maps, charts, and soundings of the coasts,
and obtained information which became afterwards of vast
importance.

Capt. Jones returned to America in 1775—communicated with the leaders of the patriotic and ardent heroes
amongst our ancestors who dared to resist, and even defy
the gigantic power of Britain, when that imperious power
presumed to wrest from their American Colonies their municipal and chartered privileges, and to deprive them of the
rights of self-government.

He was appointed to the command of an American armed vessel; and British merchantmen found the same adventurous hero upon the ocean, preying upon their commerce, who was recently viewing their ports and preparing
for more important enterprizes.

His success, in this first of his efforts in the cause of
America, excited great applause, and raised the hopes of
intrepid American seamen, who like Com. Biddle, wished
to face the enemy upon their adopted element.

A small ship called the Alfred, was fitted for sea, belonging to a small squadron under Com. Hopkins, who, it is
believed, was the first commander of a squadron under the
American government. Jones was a Lieutenant of this
ship; and on board of her, with his own hands, hoisted the
first "star spangled banner" which ever waved from the
mast of an American public ship. It was in this squadron
that Lieut. Jones became acquainted with the gallant and
accomplished Capt. Nicholas Biddle, who soon discovered
his fitness for a commander, and distinguished him with his

13

particular attention. Com. Hopkins also bestowed upon him the highest approbation. The expedition of this squadron to the British island of New-Providence was exceedingly successful. They took at this island a large quantity of the munitions of war ; took some valuable prizes on the homeward bound passage, and entered the port of New-London to refit.

The squadron was here broken up, and the different vessels were despatched to different stations, and upon various services. Capt. Biddle continued in the command of the Andrew Doria, and Capt. Jones was ordered to the small sloop Providence, of twelve small guns and the small crew of seventy men.

His skill and intrepidity were so well known, that the government ordered him to the hazardous and important duty of convoying transports with troops from the Eastern states, to the city of New-York. This was in the early part of the year 1776.

Lord Howe's naval forces lined the coast from Halifax to Chesapeake bay, and rendered the utmost vigilance indispensable. In convoying the transports, he had a running engagement with H. B. M. frigate Cerberus; but he escaped with his vessel and convoy and arrived at the port of destination in safety.

He was then ordered to convoy a ship containing naval stores, of great value. He again encountered the Cerberus, and some other of the enemy's vessels,—again effected a complete escape, and arrived in the Chesapeake twenty-seven days after the DECLARATION OF AMERICAN INDEPENDENCE.

The importance of his services were duly appreciated by the Old Congress, and the President of that august body.

with his own hand, presented JOHN PAUL JONES, with the
first commission of CAPTAIN, issued after the states were
declared " FREE, SOVEREIGN, AND INDEPENDENT." It
bore date 8th August, 1776.

At this early period, there was scarcely any thing on
board the few armed ships which had sprung up, as if by
magic, which is like that *discipline*, which now, (1823) is
established in the navy of the Republic, and which was begun in the naval warfare with France, in the administration
of ADAMS—advanced in the war with Tripoli, in the administration of JEFFERSON ; and which was almost perfected
in the second war with Britain, in the administration of
MADISON.

The stern and resistless voice of command could hardly,
with safety, be given, lest the restless spirits of that turbu-
¹ent, and doubtful period, should mutinously disobey it.
Captain Jones with a crew of high-minded AMERICANS, but
yet little accustomed to rigid discipline, and strict obedience, was differently situated from Captain Jones, with a
crew of Scotch, Irish, Welsh, and English, smugglers.

His perfect acquaintance with the human character, in
all its ramifications, made him fully aware of this ; and
convinced him that he must govern more by the influence
of persuasion, than by the exercise of authority. He was
but twenty-eight years of age—had been in America but
two years, and was by birth a Scotsman—circumstances
not very favourable for conciliating a race of men who
had thrown the gauntlet of defiance at kings, dukes, lords,
generals, and admirals. But the subject of this sketch,
seemed to be endued with faculties calculated for almost
every possible emergency.

Soon after Capt. Jones was honoured by a commission
from Congress, he repaired to sea in his old shi , the little
Providence. His orders were indefinite, and he was left
to govern himself by the dictates of his own judgment.
He run down the Bermudas, and fell in with a large convoy, under the protection of the frigate Solebay, of 30 guns.
His object was to escape ; but his officers and seamen
were bent upon capturing some part of the convoy. He
was attacked by the Solebay—for nearly six hours maintained a distant contest with this vast superiority of force,
and by a masterly manœuvre effected an escape. His
crew were now convinced that they needed his judgment
in going into action, as his skill had saved them by disen-
gaging the ship from such an unequal contest.

He now bore away for Nova Scotia, and soon captured
several merchantmen. He was now placed in a situation
where he could not avoid a contest with a ship of war, still
superior to the Solebay. It was the celebrated Frigate
Milford, of 32 guns. Capt. Jones manœuvred the Providence so as to keep at a considerable distance from the enemy, as he must have done, to withstand a cannonade from
10 A. M. until 6 P. M. with such a force as the Milford.
He then, by a favouring breeze, made his escape into a
small harbour, into which the Milford could not pursue
him.

He here made the enemy feel the distress and the losses
from which his crew and ship had just escaped. He destroyed the vessels in the harbour, and the fisheries ; but
he did not destroy a single habitation of the people.

He continued some time in this region, taking valuable
prizes,—sinking or burning vessels, and destroying fishe-
eries. After a cruise of seven weeks, in which time he

nad been attacked by, and escaped from two heavy frigates, he returned to Rhode Island, having sent in, or bringing with him sixteen valuable prizes ! !

This gallant and successful cruise of course, augmented the reputation of Capt. Jones ; inflicted a severe wound upon the enemy, and aided the resources of the country, to which he had become devoted.

Thirteen ships, called frigates,* had previously been ordered to be built ; but upon the return of the Providence from her third cruise, were not ready for sea.   An expedition had been planned however, for Capt. Jones, well calculated for his active and daring spirit.

Amongst American prisoners taken by the British, there were about three hundred and fifty incarcerated in the coal mine, on Isle Royale.   To restore these unfortunate Americans, and to destroy the very valuable whale and cod fishery at that place, was the two-fold object of this expedition.   The vessels designed for this important service, were the Alfred, Hampden, and Providence.   Commodore Jones now hoisted his pendant on board the same ship which first displayed the American banner.

As the season was advancing, and as the expedition was destined for a northern and boisterous region, Jones felt extremely solicitous to weigh anchor and get under way. The Hampden, not being fitted for sea, was left in port.

Upon Nov. 2d, 1776, Com. Jones set sail in the Alfred, the Providence in company.   He soon had the satisfaction of falling in with and capturing the British armed ship, the Mcllish.   She was a fine ship of her class, having a vast amount of stores for the army of Gen. Burgoyne.

At this period, the American land forces were in a state

* See Introduction.

of destitution, which, if described, would excite the incredulity of the younger class of readers. One of the best appointed British armies, under Burgoyne, that ever landed in America, was forcing its way through the northern states to form a junction with sir Henry Clinton's army at New York. Gen. Washington was retiring with the disheartened wreck of a little army through New Jersey; and the Thirteen Colonies recently declared independent seemed to look like so many trembling victims, about to be immolated upon the sanguinary altar of monarchial vengeance.

Com. Jones sent in his prize, containing 10,000 complete suits of winter uniform, and other materials of war. As by weakening the enemy, by destroying their materials of war, the strength of the successful party is augmented, so by preserving them, it gains a double advantage. The loss to the army of Burgoyne can hardly be calculated—the gain to that of Washington, cannot be estimated. The campaign of '76 closed by the victory of Trenton, where Washington triumphed—that of '77, when Burgoyne fell at Saratoga.*

* A recent perusal of Burgoyne's "State of the expedition into Canada, during the campaign of 1776 and 1777," induces me to extract the following as a signal instance of female fortitude and affection in Mrs. Ackland; and as exhibiting a fine trait in the Revolutionary Hero, HORATIO GATES, as daring and successful in the army, as JONES was in the navy.

"At the time the action began, she found herself near a small uninhabited hut, where she alighted. When it was found the action was becoming general and bloody, the surgeons of the hospital took possession of the same place, as the most convenient for the first care of the wounded. Thus was this lady in hearing of one continued fire of cannon and musketry for some hours together, with the presumption, from the post of her husband at the head of the grenadiers, that he

In the Mellish, Com. Jones also made two British naval officers prisoners, one of whom was afterwards exchanged for Lieut. Josiah, a favourite officer of the gallant Biddle.

was in the most exposed part of the action. She had three female companions, the Baroness of Reidesel, and the wives of two British officers, Major Harnage and Lieutenant Reynell; but, in the event, their presence served but little for comfort. Major Harnage was soon brought to the surgeons very badly wounded; and a little while after came intelligence that Lieutenant Reynell was shot dead. Imagination will want no helps to figure the state of the whole group.

" From the date of that action to the 7th of October, Lady Harriet with her usual serenity, stood prepared for new trials. And it was her lot that their severity increased with their numbers. She was again exposed to the hearing of the whole action, and at last received the shock of her individual misfortune, mixed with the intelligence of the general calamity; the troops were defeated, and Major Ackland, desperately wounded, was a prisoner.

" The day of the 8th was passed by Lady Harriet and her companions in common anxiety; not a tent or a shed being standing, except what belonged to the hospital, their refuge was among the wounded and the dying.

" I soon received a message from Lady Harriet, submitting to my decision a proposal (and expressing an earnest solicitude to execute it, if not interfering with my designs) of passing to the camp of the enemy, and requesting Gen. Gates' permission to attend her husband.

" Though I was ready to believe (for I had experienced) that patience and fortitude, in a supreme degree, were to be found, as well as every virtue, under the most tender forms, I was astonished at this proposal. After so long an agitation of spirits, exhausted not only for want of rest, but absolutely for want of food, drenched in rains for twelve hours together, that a woman should be capable of such an undertaking as delivering herself to the enemy, probably in the night, and uncertain of what hands she might fall into, appeared an effort above human nature. The assistance I was enabled to give was small indeed; I had not even a cup of wine to offer her; but I was told, she had found, from some kind and fortunate hand, a little rum and dirty water. All I could furnish to her was an open boat, and a

The Providence, in a manner wholly inexplicable, left the ship Alfred ; and Com. Jones, encumbered with prisoners—encountered by storms—and surrounded by enemies, prosecuted his cruise alone. He effected a landing, demolished every building and establishment connected with the whale and cod fisheries, and also a rich transport. Bearing away for Isle Royale, as if "*fortune always favours the brave*," he captured three valuable transports, while the frigate Flora, which was convoying them, was hard by, concealed in a fog. Soon after, he captured a large Liverpool privateer, mounting sixteen heavy guns. Thus surrounded with prizes, and having more prisoners than crew, he steered for an American port. Off Massachusetts Bay he was a second time encountered by the frigate Milford. But the little Alfred still proved to be " Alfred the great." He instructed his prize-masters to

few lines, written upon dirty and wet paper, to Gen. Gates, recommending her to his protection.

" Mr. Brudenell, the chaplain to the artillery, readily undertook to accompany her, and with one female servant, and the major's valet de chambre, (who had a ball which he had received in the late action, then in his shoulder,) she rowed down the river to meet the enemy. But her distresses were not yet to end. The night was advanced before the boat reached the enemy's outposts, and the sentinel would not let it pass, nor even come to shore. In vain Mr. Brudenell offered the flag of truce, and represented the state of the extraordinary passenger. The guard, apprehensive of treachery, and punctilious to their orders, threatened to fire into the boat, if they stirred before daylight. Her anxiety and sufferings were thus protracted through seven or eight dark and cold hours ; and her reflections upon that first reception could not give her very encouraging ideas of the treatment she was afterwards to expect. But it is due to justice, at the close of this adventure, to say, that she was received and accommodated by General Gates, with all the humanity and respect, that her rank, her merits, and her fortunes deserved."

make all possible sail for the nearest port; and as darkness approached, placed the Alfred between them and the frigate—raised his lights, and suddenly changed his course. The Milford continued in chase, and the next day, at 3 P. M. engaged the Alfred.

This gallant warrior could not endure the thought of lowering that flag which he first raised. The contest was fearfully unequal; but the Commodore, by dauntless courage, and nautical skill saved his ship and prizes, and triumphantly entered Boston harbour, Dec. 1, 1776.

Regardless of wealth, as he was ambitious of fame, he paid the crews of the Alfred and Providence their wages and prize money out of his own purse, and transmitted the remainder of it to Congress, to aid in the glorious cause in which he was now so enthusiastically engaged.

A vote of thanks from such a body of men as the Old Congress, by the recommendation of such a man as George Washington, must have elated such a champion as John Paul Jones to the highest elevation of joy. Such thanks he received, and became more and more devoted to the cause of American Independence.

To speak of the American Navy at the beginning of the last quarter of the eighteenth,—at near the close of the first quarter of the nineteenth century, would almost excite a smile. Indeed American armed ships were then but "cockboats" to the navy of the Republic in 1823. This was not the only difficulty. Although there were many gallant and accomplished commanders, there was no "Commander in chief of the Navy;" like him whose matchless wisdom guided the armies of the struggling States. Further; there was but little of naval discipline, system, or subordination—and there was no concert.

14

Commodore Jones, after his arrival in Boston, proposed to Congress an important expedition to the Gulf of Mexico and the West Indies. It met the entire approbation of that body; but was relinquished from either the cowardice, malice or jealousy of a senior naval officer who will not be named. But this ardent hero could not endure a state of inaction or suspense. He knew what he had accomplished, and was prepared to attempt any enterprise within the accomplishment of human exertion.

Early in the year 1777, he took command of the sloop of war Ranger, of 18 guns, destined for France. This cruise, as it would carry him to near the scenes of his early life, in a new, and in an important capacity, he entered into it with avidity.

Upon the coast of France, and the opposite coast of Britain, he was unceasingly vigilant, and uncommonly successful in taking prizes and sending them into French ports.

In December, 1777, he had the honour and the satisfaction of entering the port of Nantz, and communicating the first intelligence of the splendid victory of the American forces under Gen. Gates, over those of Britain, under Gen. Burgoyne.

The bearer of official intelligence of a great victory, is regarded with a respect almost equal to the one who achieves it. By communicating this exhiliarating intelligence, Commodore Jones attracted the attention of the courtiers of the splendid court of Louis XVI. By this victory, France was induced to aid the British colonies in America, in breaking the ligament that previously bound them to *their* natural enemy—Great Britain. France acknowledged the independence of " The United States of

America," which was deemed a declaration of war against Britain.

Commodore Jones was now determined to sustain the character in ,Europe, which he had acquired in America. He repaired to Paris early in 1778, to concert measures with the American minister at the Court of St. Cloud. He returned to the Ranger, and convoyed a great number of American vessels from Nantz to Quiberon Bay, where a French fleet with stores for America, and destined for that country was lying. That gallant and noble friend of America, and of the rights of man, Marquis Fayette was on board this fleet.

As the Ranger was entering the bay, Com. Jones sent in a Lieutenant to know if his salute would be answered? By a signal he was assured it would. He immediately saluted the French Admiral, and he immediately saluted Com. Jones—the first salute the American Flag ever received from a foreign power.

When the treaty of alliance between America and France was announced to him, he entered the port of Brest in the most gallant style, and saluted the Admiral, Count D'Ovilliers, who returned the salute and received Com. Jones on board the Bretagne, his flag ship.

It would seem that this would have been the consummation of this aspiring man's wishes ; but when a Scotsman begins to acquire wealth, he is like the daughter of the horse-leach, crying " give give."--When he begins to acquire power, he is unsatisfied, until it becomes as near absolute as possible.

Commodore Jones now resolved to accomplish something beyond convoying merchantmen and capturing prizes. He steered for Carrickfurgus, Ireland, from whence the an-

cestors of Andrew Jackson emigrated to America, about
ten years previous. He omitted to take prizes because it
would diminish his crew ; being determined to achieve some
heroic deed. He intended to attack the Drake, a heavy
armed 20 gun ship. Boisterous weather prevented him at
this time from a *tete a tete* with that ship, and led him into
another, the most daring deed in the annals of desperation.

He selected thirty volunteers, with whom he was determined to make a landing in Whitehaven, a large shipping
port on the Firth of Solway.

He left the Ranger, and entered a boat at ebb-tide, in the
night season, when the vessels could not escape—landed
near the fort, and was the first who mounted the walls. He
carried the fort—spiked forty pieces of cannon—set fire to
the shipping, and, by daylight, entered again on board the
Ranger. The alarm spread rapidly through the country
and the shores were lined with soldiers, who could only
look with fear and chagrin at the American Flag proudly
waving upon the little Ranger.

Commodore Jones, landed at his birth-place, and visited
his father, who still remained the humble industrious, and
pious peasant. Probably he would not have exchanged the
happiness he derived from that Scotch devotion so admirably described by Burns in his "Cottager's Saturday-night"
for the wealth and fame of his son.

The reader will recollect that the Earl of Selkirk dis-
carded Jones in early life. The Commodore now determined to take his Lordship prisoner, and entertain him on
board the Ranger. In this he was disappointed, as the
Earl was in Parliament in London. His officers and men,
contrary to his wishes, rifled the castle of a large amount of
plate, which Jones afterwards purchased and returned to

his Lordship, and received from him a letter of thanks, couched in the most grateful and flattering terms.

This was perfectly in character with this gallant and peculiar man. He would have given more to have had the Earl a prisoner on board the Ramger, than to have had the fee-simple of all his Lordships domains in Scotland.

The commander of the British ship Drake, now in turn went in pursuit of the Ranger. In the latter end of April, 1778, about six weeks after the loss of Com. Biddle in the Randolph, the two ships hove in sight of each other. Com. Jones disguised his ship as much as possible—masked his guns—concealed his men, and had the appearance of a merchantman. A boat's crew from the Drake approached to reconnoitre the Ranger, and were suddenly made prisoners. The Drake immediately bore into action. The Ranger laid to, until the enemy came within pistol shot. She then poured in her fire with such admirable gunnery and rapidity, that in one hour, the hull and rigging of the Drake were severely injured—her Captain and 1st Lieutenant slain, and over forty men killed and wounded. She struck her flag to the Ranger, and was carried triumphantly into Brest on the 7th May, 1778.

Com. Jones had beside taken a number of prizes, and had with him more than 200 prisoners, for which the imperious court of St. James was necessitated to deliver the same number of American Rebels.

Count D'Orvilliers sent an express to Dr. Franklin, American minister, informing him of this brilliant affair, and his majesty Louis XVI. gave an order for Com. Jones to repair to Versailles.

France and England were now seriously at war, and very important designs were communicated to him. It is unnecessary to detail the various plans conceived, and then relinquished. He was illy calculated to digest a system of extensive operations. The negotiations of the courts at Versailles and Amsterdam were not so well calculated for the genius of John Paul Jones, as negotiation at the cannon's mouth. That was a language he better understood than he did that of the diplomatist. Although in the midst of the blandishments and charms of France, he became impatient at the delays which from time to time occurred. He was determined to take his little Ranger, and range where he chose.

At length an ill-appointed and ill-fitted squadron was prepared for him. The American frigate Alliance was in France. An old ship, which he named *Le Bon Homme Richard*, (the Good Man Richard) was fitted up with old cannon, unfit for a ship of war. She was called a 40 gun ship; but was no ways equal to the late American frigate Essex, of 32 guns. The Pallas was a large merchantmen, and was furnished with about 30 little eight pounders. The Vengeance with 12 three pounders, and Cerf with 18 nine pounders.

The crews were of the worst possible description. Undisciplined, inexperienced, mutinous, and turbulent; of almost all nations and tongues, they cared little about glory, and were almost wholly bent upon plunder. Prize money instead of glory was their object.

With this incongruous mass of materials, called a squadron, Com. Jones sailed from Groays, in France, upon the 14th August, 1779, the Richard, flag ship.

The object was to cruise for the Baltic fleet, which was known to be on the homeward bound passage.

The squadron was dispersed either by the weather or the

insubordination of the crews. Com. Jones captured a
number of prizes and privateers with the Richard, and sent
them to the most convenient ports in France.

At length, upon the 23d September, the Baltic fleet, under convoy of the Seraphis, one of the heaviest and best appointed frigates in the British navy, of 44 guns; and the
new Countess of Scarborough of 22 guns; two ships, considering their batteries and munition, equal to Com. Jones'
whole squadron, appeared off the coast.

They had approached within two leagues of the coast of
England, and in sight of Scarborough Castle. The Alliance was at a distance, lying to; and the Pallas hauled her
wind; so that the Good Man Richard was to encounter the
Seraphis and Countess, single handed. Her crew was diminished, and there was but one lieutenant on board.

Before mentioning any particulars of the engagement, I
have the satisfaction of presenting the reader with Com.
Jones official account of the desperate battle which followed. In point of brevity and perspicuity, it will suffer
but little from a comparison with the justly admired, naval
letters in the second war with Britain—

* Copy of a letter from John Paul Jones, late commander
of the ship of war Good Man Richard, dated on board
the ship of war Seraphis, off the Texel, Oct. 31, 1779.

" I have only time, my dear friends, to inform you, that
I have this day anchored here, having taken this ship in the
night of the 23d ult. on the coast of England, after a battle
of three hours and a half; two hours and a half of that time
the Good Man Richard and this ship being fast along side of
one another, both ships being in flames, and the Good Man
Richard making water faster than all the pumps could deliver it. This ship mounts 44 guns, and has two entire

batteries, one of them eighteen pounders, so that my situation was severe enough, to have to deal with such an enemy, in such a dreadful situation.   Judge then, what it must
have been when the Alliance came up, towards the close of
the action ; and, instead of assisting me, directed her whole
fire against the Good Man Richard, not once or twice, but
repeatedly, after being spoke to, and shewing a private signal of recognizance.   The Alliance killed eleven men and
mortally wounded an officer on the Good Man Richard's
forecastle, at one volley.   I have lost, in killed and wounded, the best part of my men.   The Good Man Richard
went to the bottom on the morning of the 25th ult. in spite
of every effort to bring her into port.   No action before
was ever, in all respects, so bloody, so severe, and so lasting.   I beg of you to communicate this, with my best respects, to the gentlemen of your port.

" The fire was not quite extinguished on board of the
Good Man Richard, till eight hours after the enemy had
struck : and at last it had reached within a few feet of the
magazine.   We lost all the stores and all our private effects ; but no lives were lost from the conflagration.   The
Pallas took, at the same time, an armed ship of twenty 6
pounders.
                         JOHN PAUL JONES.

N. B. The prizes taken and ransomed by the Good Man
Richard during her cruize of about three months, amount
to at least about a million of livres."

As this action excited astonishment and wonder in Europe as well as in America, I offer the letter of Capt. Pearson, of the Seraphis, as a specimen of British veracity half a
century ago.   The antiquity and scarcity of such revolutionary papers, give them a great value at this time—

" Pallas, French frigate, in Congress service, }
Texel, October 6, 1779. }

Sir,

You will be pleased to inform the lords commissioners of
the Admiralty, that on the 23d ult. being close in with the
Scarborough, about 11 o'clock, a boat came on board with
a letter from the Bailiffs of that corporation, giving information of a flying squadron of the enemy's ships being on
the coast, and a part of the said squadron having been seen
from thence the day before, standing to the southward. As
soon as I received this intelligence, I made the signal for
the convoy to bear down under my lee, and repeated with
two guns; notwithstanding which, the van of the convoy
kept their wind, with all sail stretching out to the southward from under Flamborough head, till between twelve
and one, when the headmost of them got in sight of the
enemy's ships which were then in chase of them; they
then tacked and made the best of their way under the shore
for Scarborough, &c. letting fly their top-gallant sheets and
firing guns; upon which I made all the sail I could to the
windward, to get between the enemy's ships and the convoy, which I soon effected. At one o'clock we got sight of
the enemy's ships from mast head, and about four we made
them plain from the deck to be three large ships and a brig,
upon which I made the Countess of Scarborough's signal to
join me, she being in shore with the convoy, at the same
time I made the signal for the convoy to make the best of
their way, and repeated the signal with two guns; I then
brought to, let the Countess of Scarborough come up, and
cleared ship for action. At half past five the Countess of
Scarborough joined me, the enemy's ships then bearing
down upon us, with a light breeze at S. S. W. at six tacked,

15

and laid our head in shore, in order to keep the ground the
better between the enemy's ships and the convoy : soon after which we perceived the ships bearing down upon us to
be a two decked ship and two frigates ; but from keeping off
and on upon us, on bearing down, we could not discern
what colours they were under. At about 20 minutes past
seven, the largest ship of the three brought to, on our larboard bow, within musket shot : I hailed him, and asked
him what ship it was ; they answered in English the Princess
Royal ; I then asked who they belonged to, they answered
evasively ; on which I told them, if they did not answer directly, I would fire into them ; they answered with a shot,
which was instantly returned with a broadside ; he backed
his topsails, and dropped upon our quarter within pistol
shot, then filled again, put his helm a-weather, and run us
on board upon our weather quarter, and attempted to board
us, but being repulsed, he sheered off, upon which I backed our topsails, in order to get square with him again,
which, as soon as he observed, he then filled, put his helm
a weather, and laid us athwart hawse; his mizen shrouds
took our jib boom, which hung him for some time, till it at
last gave way, and we dropt alongside of each other head
and stern, when the fluke of our spare anchor hooking quarter, we became so close fore and aft, that the muzzles of
our guns touched each others sides. In this position we
engaged from half past eight till half past ten ; during which
time, from the great quantity and variety of combustible
matters which they threw in upon our decks, chains, and
in short into every part of the ship, we were on fire not less
than ten or twelve times in different parts of the ship, and
it was with the greatest difficulty and exertion imaginable
at times that we were able to get it extinguished. At the

same time the largest of the two frigates kept sailing round us the whole action, raking us fore and aft, by which means she killed or wounded almost every man on the quarter and main decks.

About half past nine, either from a hand grenade being thrown in at one of the lower deck ports, or from some other accident, a cartridge of powder was set on fire, the flames of which running from cartridge to cartridge all the way aft, blew up the whole of the people and officers that were abaft the mainmast, from which unfortunate circumstance all these guns were rendered useless for the remainder of the action, and I fear the greatest part of the people will lose their lives.   At ten o'clock they called for quarters from the ship alongside, and said they had struck: hearing this, I called upon the captain to know if they had struck, or if he asked for quarters ; but no answer being made, after repeating my words two or three times, I called for the boarders, and ordered them to board, which they did ; but the moment they were on board her, they discovered a superior number laying under cover with pikes in their hands ready to receive them, on which our people retreated instantly into our own ship, and returned to their guns again till past ten, when the frigate coming across our stern, and pouring her broadside into us again, without our being able to bring a gun to bear on her, I found it in vain, and in short impracticable, from the situation we were in, to stand out any longer with the least prospect of success ; I therefore struck, (our main-mast at the same time went by the board.)   The first Lieutenant and myself were immediately escorted into the ship along side, when we found her to be an American ship of war, called the Bon Homme Richard, of 40 guns, and 375 men, commanded by Capt.

Paul Jones; the other frigate which engaged us proved to be the Alliance, of 40 guns, and 300 men ; and the third frigate, which engaged and took the Countess of Scarborough, after two hours action, to be the Pallas, a French frigate of 32 guns and 275 men; the Vengeance, an armed brig of 12 guns and 70 men, all in Congress service, and under the command of Paul Jones. They fitted out and sailed from Port l'Orient the latter end of July, and came north about ; they had on board 300 English prisoners which they have taken in different vessels in their way round, since they left France, and have ransomed some others. On my going on board the Bonne Homme Richard, I found her in the greatest distress; her quarter and counter on the lower deck entirely drove in, and the whole of her lower deck guns dismounted ; she was also on fire in two places, and six or seven feet water in her hold, which kept increasing upon them all night and the next day, till they were obliged to quit her, and she sunk with a great number of her wounded people on board her. She had 306 men killed and wounded in the action ; our loss in the Seraphis was also very great. My officers and people in general behaved well, and I should be very remiss in my attention to their merit were I to omit recommending the remains of them to their lordships' favour. I must at the same time beg leave to inform their lordships that Capt. Piercy, in the Countess of Scarborough, was not in the least remiss in his duty, he having given me every assistance in his power, and as much as could be expected from such a ship, in engaging the attention of the Pallas, a frigate of 32 guns, during the whole action.

I am extremely sorry for the misfortune that has happened, that of losing his Majesty's ship I had the honor to com-

COM. JOHN PAUL JONES.

mand ; but at the same time, I flatter myself with the
hopes, that their lordships will be convinced that she has
not been given away ; but on the contrary, that every exertion has been used to defend her ; and that two essential
pieces of service to our country have arisen from it ; the
one in wholly oversetting the cruise and intentions of this
flying squadron ; the other in rescuing the whole of a valuable convoy from falling into the hands of the enemy,
which must have been the case had I acted otherwise than
I did. We have been driven about in the North Sea ever
since the action, endeavouring to make to any port we possibly could, but have not been able to get into any place
till to-day we arrived in the Texel.

Herewith I inclose you the most exact list of the killed
and wounded I have been able to procure, from my people
being dispersed amongst the different ships, and having
been refused permission to muster them. There are, I
find, many more, both killed and wounded, than appears in
the inclosed list, but their names as yet I find impossible to
ascertain ; as soon as I possibly can, I shall give your
Lordships a full account of the whole.

I am, Sir, your most obedient and most humble servant,

R. PEARSON.

P. S. I am refused permission to wait on Sir Joseph
Yorke, and even to go on shore.

Abstract of the list of killed and wounded.

Killed, 49.   Wounded, 68.

Among the killed are boatswain, pilot, 1 master's mate,
2 midshipmen, the coxswain, 1 quarter-master, 27 seamen,
and 15 marines.   Among the wounded are the second
lieutenant, Michael Stanhope, and Lieut. Whitman, second
lieutenant of marines, 2 surgeon's mates, 6 petty officers, 46
seamen, and 12 marines."

From other publications of that period, and from the writings of Com. Jones, the following facts may safely be relied upon as authentic.

The action commenced at 7 P. M. within pistol shot. The Richard sustained it for an hour and was on the point of sinking. Any body but John Paul Jones, and David Porter would have struck ; but, in a state of desperation, he grappled the Seraphis ; and, with his own hands, fastened the Richard to that ship. In a short time, every one of her guns, except four, upon the forecastle, were burst, or rendered useless. Com. Jones repaired there himself ; and although dark, he could discover the *yellow* mainmast, of the Seraphis, at which he fired with great effect. The swivels, grenades, and musketry in the tops of the Richard were annoying the crew of the Seraphis in a terrible manner. The fire from her almost ceased, when a panic struck the surviving crew of the Richard, from losing the use of one of the pumps by a shot. A report run through the ship that Com. Jones and the only Lieutenant were slain. The gunner ascended the quarter deck to strike the flag ; and there found the undismayed Commodore, working his three remaining guns.

The admiration of the Captain of the Seraphis was excited to the highest pitch, at the dauntless courage of Jones, and he exclaimed to him, " I give you an opportunity to strike ; if you do not, I will sink you at the next broadside." The indignant Jones replied, in a rage,—" Sink me if you can—if I must go to the devil, I had rather strike to him than to you." The Alliance came up ; and from the excessive darkness of the night, and the unusual closeness of the action, injured the Richard more than she did the Seraphis. (See preceding letter.) The battle continued to rage in a manner not equalled in ancient or modern naval warfare, unless it were in the action of the Essex with the Phœbe and Cherub in 1813. Towards the close of it, a seaman in the tops of the Richard, seized a bucket of hand grenades ; and, with a lighted match, passed along the main yard, until he was directly over the deck of the Seraphis. He then let them off one at a time, to the terror and consternation of the crew. Com. Jones, with his three little guns had shot away the mainmast of the Seraphis. The commander then called for quarters, and struck his flag.

The gallant and proud commander of the Seraphis, with his officers, now approached Com. Jones, who was in the habiliment of a common seaman ; and presented him with his sword.

This was at 11 P. M. Ten of Jones' seamen escaped in a shallop, and were afterwards examined by English magistrates. The Richard, after every exertion to save her and carry her into port, as an object of curiosity, went to the bottom two days after the battle, carrying to the bottom all the property of Jones, excepting what he was to derive from the prizes, which he had sent into French ports ; from these, however he obtained nothing until after the peace between America and England.

The admiralty of Britain sent out more than forty vessels of different classes, to capture Com. Jones.

The following extract from an English paper, points out the following as a part of them. " Portsmouth, Monday afternoon, Sept. 13, 1779. Sir John Lockhart Ross having struck his flag from on board the Royal George, and hoisted it on board the Romney, has this instant got under way, with the Berwick of 74 guns, the Hon. Keith Stewart ; the Biensfaisant. of 64, Capt. M'Bride ; the Jupiter of 50,

Captain Reynolds ; and the following frigates, viz. Diana, Phœnix, Southampton, Ambuscade, Crescent, Milford, Brilliant, and Porcupine ; the Bonetta, Cormorant, and Helena sloops ; the Griffin, and Nimble cutters ; and Firebrand and Incendiary fireships."

It is a circumstance, not unworthy of notice, that the " Milford" which twice before, in 1776, had encountered Jones upon the American coast, was one of this fleet.

An European statesman, under date of Nov. 19, 1779, says " The Dutch seem at present entirely to disregard Great Britain ; notwithstanding Sir Joseph Yorke's memorials, they allow Captain Paul Jones to refit his little squadron, and give him every assistance possible ; nay, he is even allowed possession of a small fort in the Texel, in which he has put his sick and wounded seamen,—his own marines constantly mount guard, and Continental colours are hoisted. The English do him the honour to attend with eight ships at the south and four at the north entrance of the Texel to watch his motions." It may be added—the Dutch peremptorily refused to deliver up the Seraphis, and Countess of Scarborough, when demanded.

He shifted his flag to the Alliance, American frigate ; and, in view of the British Squadron in the Downs, effected his passage to Corunna, in France, where he arrived in the height of glory, and in the depth of bankruptcy, in January 1780. He soon after repaired to Paris—was received by Doct. FRANKLIN with distinction—at public places with applause, and finally had an audience with LOUIS XVI ! !

It excites a smile at this period that the appearance of Jones upon the coast of England, in 1779 with an ill-fitted little squadron should have excited such consternation, when, in 1805, they treated with sovereign contempt the vast preparation of Bonaparte to effect a landing. But while they feared him as a gallant ocean-warrior, they were compelled to admire him for his magnanimity. He never made war upon defenceless villages, or drove the harmless cottagers houseless and destitute into a cruel world. To repel the infamous aspersions of his infamous British biographer, who calls him the " American Corsair," I will here present the reader with a few extracts from more dignified British writers who dared to speak the truth of Americans and of Jones, in the face of a corrupt and imperious court. The commendation, coming from an enemy, is doubly valuable. The following is from a London Gazette of Sept. 1779.

" By an examination of the four men belonging to one of Paul Jones' squadron, before the mayor and magistrates of Hull, it appears that Jones' orders were *not to burn any houses or towns*. What an example of honour and greatness does America thus shew to us! while our troops are running about from town to town on their coasts, and burning every thing with a wanton, wicked and deliberate barbarity. Dr. *Franklin* gives no orders to retaliate. *He is above it.* And there was a time when an English Minister would have disdained to make war in so villainous a mode. It is a disgrace to the nation. But notwithstanding the moderation hitherto shewn by the Americans upon our coast, it is to be feared that moderation will cease in a little time.

" Paul Jones could have burned Leith the other day with the greatest ease, and another little town near it ; but his orders were peremptory not to burn any town. Bute and Knox must whitewash Lord George Germain, and say,

16

that the burning the towns lately in America, was not done
by his orders. Falsehood agrees with all their characters.

  " Many of the particulars of the burning the two towns
in Connecticut, viz. Fairfield and Norwalk, have been received, but they are too shocking to relate. The brutality
and cruelty of the soldiers in several instances, are too
dreadful, as well as unfit to be printed. These horrible
scenes are an indelible scandal to our arms. And the
ministers and officers, who can order and execute such
proceedings, must be detested by all mankind."

  Another London Gazette of the same month thus pours
forth the language of indignation :

  " What will be the consequence of burning Fairfield and
Norwalk ? Paul Jones has done no mischief yet : But had
he known of the burning of these towns, is it not probable
he would have burned Leith and Hull ? They were as
completely at his mercy. When this burning business
comes to be retaliated upon our own coasts, we shall then
see our ministers' scribblers expatiating upon the cruelty
of it, of its being contrary to the rules of war, &c. and those
public prints, which are paid and bribed by the public
money, for deserting and betraying the public interest,
who print every lie for ministers, but refuse every truth
against them, will be the foremost to publish those complaints, which they now approve in others. The nation
cannot be misled much longer ; the tricks of the court in
buying up the newspapers, and sending about their runners,
are become so obvious, people cannot now be duped by
them as they have been."

  The French minister of Marine, now furnished Com.
Jones with the Ariel of 20 guns, a king's ship, in which he
sailed for America, in October, 1780. On his passage he

engaged and captured the British ship Triumph, of 20 guns. He arrived in America early in the year 1781.

He repaired to Philadelphia, where the highest honours awaited him. In April, 1781, Congress passed a vote of thanks "For the zeal, the prudence, and the intrepidity, with which he sustained the honour of the American flag ; for his bold and successful enterprise, with a view to redeem from captivity the citizens of America, who had fallen into the hands of the English ; and for the eminent services by which he had added lustre to his own character and his associates."

That august body, also presented him with a Gold Medal, as a token of the high estimation in which he was held by the Congress of the American Republic.

At this time, the long and arduous contest between America and Britain was drawing to a close by the resistless and powerful attitude in which the American Republic appeared. Britain, instead of devastating what she still called her American Colonies by armies, fleets, conflagration, massacres, and destruction, was now willing to acknowledge their Independence,* and enter into negotiations for peace. But until a definitive treaty of Peace was concluded, the active spirit of Jones could not rest.

A ship of the line, the AMERICA, of 74 guns, had been built, designed for Com. Jones ; but she was presented to Louis XVI. to supply the place of the Magnifique, French 74, lost on the American coast.

* In a London paper, the beginning of 1780, is this paragraph. " A cessation of arms has again been proposed on the part of France and the rebel Colonies, through the mediation of the King of Sardinia, which the British cabinet have refused to listen to, unless the dependence of America on the parent state, be made the ground work of such cessation."

He now entered the Triumphant, flag ship, of the Marquis D'Vandreuil,—was received with the utmost distinction, and assigned to one of the highest births on board. The object of the Marquis's expedition was prevented by a general peace, by which the Independence of the American States was fully acknowledged. Jones returned to America to enjoy the political Independence of the Republic ; but as to that independence which arises from wealth, he could not enjoy it, for he was in possession of none. His wealth was on the other side of the Atlantic. In 1783, he went to France—obtained for himself his officers and seamen the full amount of prize-money due them, and returned to the bosom of his adopted country, to enjoy the blessings of that freedom which he had so gallantly and unceasingly aided in obtaining.

He selected the then new state of Kentucky, as his place of residence. In the midst of a high-minded and noble race of Americans, he enjoyed the inestimable blessings of a free government ; and lived long enough to behold the Republic rise from a state of political infancy, to the majestic state of national greatness.

He closed his active, eventful, and diversified life in 1801, at the age of fifty-three years ; leaving an example to the youth of his native and his adopted country, of the astonishing effects resulting from " decision of character." The foibles of his early life serve as beacons to avoid the rocks and quicksands of rash precipitation. His whole life, most clearly evinces, that the most humble birth, and disheartening circumstances, furnish no insuperable obstacle against an ardent and determined spirit, and a decided character.

ADDENDA TO THE PRECEDING SKETCH.

Persuaded that the reader will be gratified with European details, both English and French, concerning the daring expedition of Com. Jones, I present them exactly as published in *their* papers in 1779. It will serve the double purpose of confirming the preceding sketch, and also to show, that the hireling editors of his Majesty in London, under Lord Germaine, could traduce and slander American champions, as well as the "royal printer" Rivington in the city of New York under Sir William Howe.

Extract of a letter from Scarbro, Sept. 21, 1779.

" Yesterday a ship (1 two decker) a frigate, a sloop and a cutter, appeared about a mile off the Pier, supposed to be French ; they fired at several ships, took two, and obliged two others to run into the harbour, damaging their rigging and sails, by keeping a continual fire after them ; they then steered their course to the northward."

Sept. 27. A letter from Sunderland, dated the 20th of September says, " that an express arrived there the 18th from Aymouth, with information, that Paul Jones was off there, with five sail of ships of war, and 2000 troops on board ; that on the 19th they appeared off Sunderland, and came up within two miles, which put the inhabitants into great confusion, as they expected them to land every hour, or destroy the ships in the harbour. The inhabitants and soldiers got immediately under arms, and continued so at the writing of the letter, as they were still in sight."

Extract of a letter from Stockton, Sept. 21.

" Copy of an express which arrived here this day from Sunderland, dated September 21.

" The under mentioned ships having appeared off this

place under the command of Paul Jones, we have sent the
bearers to inform all light colliers they may meet with, to
take harbour as soon as possible, and there to remain till
they receive advices of their being off the coast; the bearers are to proceed to Bridlington with all speed. Two
ships appearing to be 50 guns each; one frigate about 40
guns; one brig, like a collier; two sloops; one snow, and
one brig both armed.   E. Linshell,   J. Young,
                         J. Marshall,   J. Smith."

On Saturday noon, two gentlemen of the corporation of
Hull, arrived express at the Admiralty with the alarming
account, that the celebrated *American corsair*, Paul Jones,
had entered the river Humber on Thursday last, and chased
a vessel to within a mile of the Pier, where he sunk, burned and destroyed 16 sail of valuable vessels, which threw
the whole town and neighbourhood into the utmost consternation; as a very few men in armed boats, might have
laid the town in ashes. He had taken nine or ten colliers
and other vessels a day or two before he appeared at Hull;
one of which, being left to the charge of only four men,
her former crew rose upon them, and carried the vessel into a port near Hull; and which men state the strength of
his squadron to be as follows:

A Boston built frigate with 40 guns upon one deck,
(Jones' ship.)

A French ship (an old Indiaman,) of 44 guns.

Two American frigates of 32 guns each, new.

One 20 gun ditto.

Two brigantines of 18 guns, and two small tenders.

Some of this squadron conducted the prizes they had made
to the coast of France, and returned to Hull the Friday
noon, attended by other Dunkirk privateers.

On Saturday night another express arrived at the Admiralty from Hull, (which set out at three in the morning) with the further disagreeable intelligence, that Paul Jones' squadron, after having done more mischief in the shipping on Friday, had fell in with the Baltic fleet, (for which purpose he principally ventured to cruise in the North Channel) and had taken their convoy, the Seraphis man of war, of 44 guns, Capt. Pearson, and the armed ship hired to government by a gentleman of Hull called the Countess of Scarborough, Capt. Percy, of 24 guns. This action was seen by thousands of spectators, and the last express was despatched in consequence of it, and seeing the other ships of Jones' squadron making havock among the fleet ; most of which, however, had taken shelter near Flamborough and the Head.

From the four captured Americans it was discovered that this fleet sailed with stores for three months, from Brest the beginning of August ; and that two other small squadrons were to sail soon after them for the coasts of Ireland and Wales. They were all in the service of the Congress, and few or no French seamen on board.

Their plan generally was to alarm the coasts of Wales, Ireland, the western parts of Scotland, and the North Channel, while the combined fleets kept Sir Charles Hardy at bay to the westward. Jones took several prizes on the coast of Ireland, particularly two armed transports with stores for New York, in the North Seas, and near the Firth of Forth, and had it in his power to burn Leith ; but his orders are only to destroy shipping. His squadron is now but weakly manned, owing to the great number of prizes he has taken, and it will likely fall an easy conquest to the 16 sail of men of war who have orders to go after him.

The Seraphis, man of war, lost her main-mast, bowsprit, and mizen top mast, before she struck ; and the Countess of Scarborough made an exceeding good defence against one of the 32 gun frigates. The enemy's 44 gun ship was not in the action, and the Seraphis struck to Jones' ship and the other 32 gun frigate.

Expresses also arrived on Saturday from Sunderland, stating that Paul Jones had taken 16 sail of colliers.

In consequence of the capture of so many colliers, and the interception of the trade ; the price of coals will be enormous.

Instead of having the dominion of the sea, it is now evident that we are not able to defend our own coast from depredations.

Extract of a letter from Newcastle, Sept. 25.

" The little squadron commanded by Paul Jones, after leaving the Firth of Forth, directed its course along the coast southward, and excited no small fears in the inhabitants along shore as they passed. About five on Sunday afternoon, they appeared off Tynmouth, and after parading a while in the offing, proceeded onwards to Sunderland, and so much alarmed the inhabitants of that place, that many of them immediately had their valuable effects buried in the earth, or conveyed up the country. The militia there beat to arms, and, with many of the town's people, lined the shore until the next morning : but no descent was attempted, the enemy continued their course to the southward.

" The Emerald frigate of 32 guns, appeared off Sunderland on Monday morning, when four foy-boat men were sent off to her, to give information of the above squadron ; the sea running exceeding high at the time made the spectators on shore fear much for their safety ; but happily they effected their errand, and were kindly received on board.

" Monday the Content sailed from Shields, and joined the Emerald frigate to go in quest of the above squadron.

" The following particulars are from the information of the master of the Speedwell sloop, of Hull, which was taken and ransomed by the said squadron, and who made oath to the fact thereof before the Mayor of this town on Wednesday.

" Sunday last, about four leagues off Tynmouth bar, the Speedwell sloop of Hull, and the Union brig of Chatham. were taken by the Pallas, an American friate or barque, of 34 nine pounders, in company with a two decked ship of 44 eighteen pounders, (name not known) commanded by Paul Jones, and a snow of 14 nine pounders, called the Vengeance, (master's name not known.) After taking them, Jones and the master of the Pallas disagreed concerning the capture. Jones proposed to turn the brig into a fire ship, and to send her into Shields harbour, to which the commander of the Pallas would not consent ; the master of the Pallas proposed to ransom the sloop, as she had a woman with child on board, to which Jones would not consent. However, the next day, about 12 leagues off the land, between the Scarborough and Filay Bay, the brig was plundered and sunk, and the sloop ransomed for 300l. the mate taken hostage. Jones had one or two, and the Pallas three or four English masters, and a number of other prisoners on board, belonging to ships that had been taken and destroyed. The master of the sloop said he was informed that Jones had 200 marines on board. Jones declared that his orders were to ransom none, but to burn, sink, or destroy all. The master of the Pallas, in the ransom bill

17

styles himself thus : " Denis Nicolas Cotineau, of Keloguen, Captain of a man of war in the service of the United States of America, and Commander of the American frigate the Pallas." They hoisted English colours, but the captain of the sloop saw that they had also American and Swedish colours."

Friday morning the principal inhabitants of Yarmouth met, and agreed to petition the lords of the Admiralty for a number of ships to be sent down for the better protection of that town and trade.

The Fly sloop of war, that beat off the two privateers, who engaged him in hopes of capturing the packets, allured by the expectation of a large ransom for the noble passengers, is got safe into the Elbe. The Fly carried only 14 guns, and was scanty of powder. The privateers were stoutly manned, and one of them carried 20 guns, and the other 18.

Extract of a letter from Hull, Sept. 25.

" On examination of one of the ship's crew retaken from Paul Jones, we learn, that he had pilots on board for every part of this coast, from Edinburgh to Harwich, and that he had taken 15 sail of vessels ; some he had ransomed and others sent to France—that he had 500 men on board his own ship, when he left Brest ; and that the complements of the whole fleet were above 2000 ; that they had provisions for three months, and an amazing quantity of military stores, as shot and gun powder ; that the seamen were exercised daily with small arms, in case of their going on shore, as a debarkation was intended, when a convenient place and opportunity offered ; that the major part of the crews were English and Irish, many of them taken out of the prisons at Brest and St. Maloes, where any prisoner was offered his liberty to serve on board his fleet—There were very few Americans, but more French, and some neutrals, as Dutch and Germans. They gave them but small bounties at first for the men to enter, as the promises that were made them that they would all return with fortunes, had a great effect ; but men growing scarce, they were obliged to pay very handsomely for them, and some of the ships were obliged to come away without the complement intended, as they all brought more away than they had need to work the ship and fight the guns, in order to be the better enabled to man the prizes they should take, and not reduce their proper complement, in case of meeting with a powerful enemy."

The master of a sloop from Harwich, who arrived yesterday in the Pool, saw, on Saturday last, no less than 11 sail of men of war going in search of Paul Jones, and among them was the Edgar of 74 guns.

LONDON, October 1.

Extract of a letter from Scarborough, dated the 26th of September, 1779.

" Last Wednesday the red flag was hoisted at the castle, as a signal that the enemy was in sight. It proved to be Paul Jones and his squadron. He kept our coasts several days, and spread so universal a terror, that the inhabitants quitted the city. He cannonaded the town most severely. The following circumstances are mentioned in a deposition of a sailor, who escaped from the squadron : The squadron consisted of 8 vessels ; they sailed from L'Orient to the western coast of Ireland, from thence to the north shore of Scotland, where they took a most valuable prize, bound to Quebec with military stores, and a Liverpool letter of marque, and sunk several colliers near Whitby. Having cruized six days between Berwick and Humber, they met the Baltic fleet, escorted by a 40 and a 20 gun ship, They first attacked Jones' ships ; the contest continued four hours, when Jones' fire was interrupted, but the British man of war was finally obliged to strike, on the coming up of the American frigate Alliance, one of Jones' squadron. Jones' crew were then obliged to call for the boats of the Alliance, to save them, as their ship was sinking. This sailor and six others took that opportunity to escape. They add the following particulars :   Towards the end of the combat, the British captain called to Paul Jones to strike or he wonld sink his ship the next broadside. The intrepid American answered, " sink me if you can, if I must go to the devil, I had rather strike to him than to you." Jones fought in sailor's frock and trowsers, with a large girdle round his waist, in which hung twelve pistols, and a large cutlass in his hand. The sailors say they saw him blow out the brains of seventeen of his men, for abandoning their posts. During the action an attempt was made by a few British desperadoes he had picked up in France, to relieve the prisoners he had below decks, with a view to surrender the ship—the Seraphis (the vessel he now fought with and took) was new, and built on a new construction, sailed wonderfully fast, and was copper bottomed. Twenty-five vessels in different divisions have been sent in pursuit of Jones, but it is thought he is gone towards Norway.

Fxtract of a letter from L'Orient, dated Oct. 22, 1779, to a gentleman in this city.

" The gallant behaviour of Capt. Paul Jones, at present engages the whole attention here. In my last I informed you, that he had the command of a small squadron then on a cruise. He sailed round Ireland and Scotland, spreading

terror and devastation in every part.   He took, burnt, and
sunk a great number of vessels, among them a ship bound
to Quebec, extremely rich.

" On the 23d of Sept. in the evening, having under his
command the Poor Richard, of 40 guns, the Alliance of 36,
and the Pallas of 28 guns ; he fell in with the Baltic fleet,
consisting of about 40 sail, under convoy of the Seraphis,
of 44 guns, and the Countess of Scarborough of 20 guns ;
the Pallas, after an engagement of about an hour, took the
latter, and Jones in the Poor Richard attacked the former :
they fought three hours and a half, with inconceivable rage :
two hours of which time they were fast to each other, and
almost all the time one or the other was on fire.

" The Poor Richard was obliged to keep all her pumps
going during the greater part of the engagement ; it being
night, and the two vessels enveloped in smoke, the Capt.
of the Pallas could not distinguish which was friend or enemy, so could give Jones no assistance.   The Alliance lay
out of gun shot for the greatest part of the engagement, and
when she came up to his assistance, through mistake, instead of firing on the enemy, gave the Poor Richard two
broadsides, which killed 11 men, besides doing other considerable damage.*   Notwithstanding all this, Jones continued the engagement until he obliged her to strike.

The Seraphis is a fine new ship, sheathed with copper,
on an entire new construction, and thought to be the fast-
est sailing vessel in Europe ; she has two entire batteries,
the lower of which is 18 pounders ; so that she may be said
to be almost double the force of the Poor Richard.   This

* This corresponds with Com. Jones official letter, and directly
contradicts the British account.

last ship, notwithstanding every assistance from the others, sunk the second morning after the engagement."

Extract of another letter from the same place.

" Capt. Jones came to town from the Texel, and he is gone to the Hague ; his presence will, I am persuaded, embarrass this Republic, and may probably produce warm altercations in the senate.

I cannot give you a very particular account of the engagement, only that the conflict between the two ships exceeds description ; upwards of 230 men killed and wounded in both, and so shattered, that it was a matter of doubt which of the vessels would sink first. The captain of the Seraphis, behaved with great bravery.

" The Poor Richard with all the assistance afforded from the other ships after the action, could not be kept above water, and Jones had the mortification to see her go down, not being able to save any material part of her stores. He (it may be said) has made a good exchange, but he wished to have got the poor Richard into port, shattered as she was, as a picture of curiosity and distress."

By the following note, it seems the conjecture relative to the Hague was correct.

Yesterday in the afternoon despatches were sent from the Secretary of State's Office to Sir Joseph Yorke at the Hague ; and, it is reported, that they contain a request to the States General to stop Paul Jones the pirate, and his ships, and to deliver him up that he may be brought to England, and punished according to law.

In consequence of these despatches, the following " demand" was made by Sir Joseph.

" High and Mighty Lords,

" The undersigned Ambassador Extraordinary and Ple-

nipotentiary of the King of Great Britain, has the honor
to communicate to your High Mightinesses, that two of his
Majesty's ships, (the Seraphis and Countess of Scarborough) arrived some days ago in the Texel, having been
attacked and taken by force, by a certain Paul Jones, a
subject of the King, who according to treaties and the laws
of war can only be considered as a rebel and a pirate.
The undersigned is therefore in duty bound to recur to
your High Mightinesses, and demand their immediate orders that those ships with their officers and crews may be
stopped, and he especially recommends to your humanity,
to permit the wounded to be brought on shore, that proper
attention may be paid to them at the expense of the King
his master.

YORKE."

What ineffable contempt must Americans have felt
towards the ministry of Great Britain at that period when
their prostituted presses were whining forth their piteous
wailings and lamentations, for the loss of a few armed
ships which would weaken their marine—a few merchantmen, which would diminish their treasury ; and a few
"Colliers," which would make " the price of coals enormous ?"   What puerile gasconade was it to pronounce the
fearless, the intrepid, and magnanimous Jones, the American Corsair, Rebel and Pirate, when he, scrupulously
kept within the recognized boundaries of civilized warfare, and never applied the torch, to even a sheep-cote.
Nevertheless, he had every personal reason to feel a spirit
of revenge against Englishmen.   He had been impressed
aboard their ships,---abused---compelled to fight his friends
---had been swindled by sharpers, and driven from the
kingdom.   But the American Commodore, forgot the in-

juries of John Paul Jones. He fought in the cause of freedom, of religion, and humanity, against despotism, superstition, and barbarity ; and he fought in a manner worthy
the cause he espoused.

Let the tables be reversed, and for a moment examine
what kind of warfare was carried on in America at the very
time. Com. Jones was conquering ships of war, capturing
privateers, taking forts, spiking cannon, and making prizes
of merchantmen on the coast of Britain. Let the following proclamation of an incendiary knight of Britain be
read with the highest indignation by Americans, and with
the deepest shame by Englishmen.

" By Commodore Sir George Collier, Commander in Chief
  of his Majesty's ships and vessels in North America,
  and Major General William Tryon, commanding his
  Majesty's Land Forces on a separate expedition.

  Address to the Inhabitants of Connecticut.

  " The ungenerous and wanton insurrection against the
sovereignty of Great Britain into which this colony has
been deluded by the artifices of designing men, for private
purposes, might well justify you in every fear, which conscious guilt could form respecting the intentions of the present armament.

  Your towns, your property, yourselves, lie within the
grasp of that power, whose forbearance you have ungen-
erously construed into fear ; but whose lenity has persisted
in its mild and noble efforts, even tho' branded with the
most unworthy imputation.

  The existence of a single habitation on your defenceless
coast, ought to be a constant reproof to your ingratitude.
Can the strength of your whole province cope with the
force which might at any time be poured through every

district in your country? You are conscious it cannot. Why then will you persist in a ruinous and ill judged resistance? We hoped that you would recover from the frenzy which has distracted this unhappy country; and we believe the day to be now come, when the greater part of this continent begin to blush at their delusion. You who lie so much in our *power*, afford the most striking monument of *mercy*, and therefore ought to set the first example of returning allegiance.

Reflect on what gratitude requires of you; if that is insufficient to move you, attend to your own interest: we offer you a refuge against the distress, which you universally acknowledge broods with increasing and intolerable weight over all your country.

Leaving you to consult with each other upon this invitation, we do now declare, that whosoever shall be found and remain in peace at his usual place of residence, shall be shielded from any insult either in person or property, excepting such as bear offices either civil or military, under your present usurped governments; of whom it will be further required, that they shall give proofs of their penitence and submission, and they shall then partake of the like immunity.

Those whose folly and obstinacy may slight this favourable warning, must take notice, that they are not to expect a continuance of that lenity which their inveteracy would now render blameable.

Given on board his Majesty's ship Camilla, in the Sound, July 4, 1779.

GEORGE COLLIER,
WM. TRYON."*

* The following Hudibrastic version of this proclamation appeared originally in the Connecticut Courant, published by Hudson and Good-

18

The addition of William Tryon's name, ex-governor of
New York, shews that the army and navy of Great Britain

win, July 27, 1779, the leading Gazette in New England, in the revolutionary war. The production carries strong internal evidence
that it emanated from the same " Connecticut Butler" who produced
that inimitable burlesque poem—" M'Fingal."

" By Collier George, Sir commodore,
Of all the ships that line this shore ;
Of vessels too, and all the squadron.
In North America, the Lord on :
And Major General Tryon Billy,
Of separate party sent to kill ye :
The Royal, mighty, arch director,
And of the Tories kind protector.
To all Connecticut folks greeting,
Let this address save you a beating.
    When people blinded by delusion,
Have set the world in dire confusion :
When factious freemen dare cabal
Against the Royal MUST and SHALL ;
The conscious rogues may well feel chilly
At the approach of George and Billy.
You see until the time that now is,
We have forborne t'exert our prowess ;
Thankless rebels ! with wanton sneer,
You've construed mildness into fear ;
When long ago you might have lost
Each house and barn upon your coast.
Each moment now a force at hand,
Might spread wild horror through the land.
Nor all your vile militia rabble,
Could cope with Britons in the squabble.
Why then resist almighty force,
And every day grow worse and worse?
We waited long that we might then see
If you'd recover from your frenzy ;
And we believe the day now present,

produced twin Goths in Collier and Tryon in the first, and
Cockburn and Ross in the second war with Britain.

Let the American reader peruse this short extract from

When all from Congress down to peasant,
Who've not obtain'd the king's protection,
Begin to blush at their defection.
All those in reach of cannon shot,
We can destroy as well as not.
Since you're expos'd to British power,
And death's before you every hour,
And not recover'd from your blindness,
You're striking proofs of British kindness.
The wings of mercy you've not flew to,
And must find shelter with old Pluto,
A dismal cloud with vengeance dire,
Hangs o'er your heads and now grows nigher,
'Twill fall intolerably severe,
On all you rebels far and near.
On this invite and threatning thunder,
We leave you to consult and ponder.
We therefore solemnly declare,
Which is as much as 'tis to swear,
That he in usual place who stays,
Shall not be injur'd several ways ;
We'll only rob him, and his person,
Let soldiers have to make a farce on.
But officers in state and army,
You've something more that ought t'alarm ye ;
'Tis fell submission, penitence,
Entitles you to like defence.
But they who still may choose to slight us,
And rashly dare to arm and fight us,
Who disregard this friendly warning,
Must feel the effects to morrow morning.
    In seventeen hundred seventy-nine,
July the fourth, at sun's decline ;
Given on board King's ship Camilla,
Sir Collier George and Tryon Billy.

the speech of the patriotic Lord Camden in the House of
Lords, in 1778, and the Protest drawn by his unequalled
pen.   How striking must have been the contrast between
Lord Camden and Lord Mansfield, when one arose as an
advocate for humanity—the other for barbarism.

" What did the *desolation* of war mean, but destruction
of the houses, and massacreing the people in an enemy's
country ? The declaration in his opinion, held forth a war
of revenge, such as Moloch, in the Pandemonium of Hell
advised."

His lordship added, " That the Proclamation ought to be
damned ; for it would fix an inveterate hatred in the
Americans against the very name of Englishmen, which
would be left as a legacy from father to son to the latest
posterity.   If there was any doubt of the intention of it,
let a comparative retrospect prove it : What had been done
by that fellow, Colonel Butler.   Had he not surprised a
little peaceable settlement, and put the poor people, men,
women, and children to the sword ? He hoped he did not
now bear the King's commission."

The following are the inscriptions on the flags captured
at the taking of York, conveyed by major Armistead to
Washington :

" The standard of the notorious plundering, burning,
murdering, scalping corps of rangers, commanded by col.
Butler, in the service of England, in the revolutionary war,
whose savage barbarities will long be remembered by the
inhabitants of Mohawk and Susquehanna river; taken at
Fort George, Upper Canada, May 27, 1813."   [This flag
was held in great veneration by the savages.]

The declaration alluded to by Lord Camden, is presented
to the reader for the double purpose of shewing the Gothic

rage of the British ministry, and the exalted magnanimity of thirty-one Peers of the realm, who protested against it in language, humane as it is Christian—just as it is forcible. As they " chose to draw themselves out, and distinguish themselves to posterity," as enemies to " ferocity and barbarism in war," let the present generation of Americans venerate their memories as friends to the infant colonies.

The declaration says, " If there *be any persons*, who, *divested of mistaken* resentments and *uninfluenced by selfish interests* really think *it is for the benefit* of the Colonies to separate themselves from Great Britain, and that so separated they will find a constitution more mild, more free, and better calculated for their prosperity, than that which they heretofore enjoyed, and which we are empowered and disposed to renew and improve ; with such persons we will not dispute a position, which seems to be sufficiently contradicted by the experience they have had. But we think it right to leave them fully aware of the *change* which the maintaining such a position must make in the *whole* nature and future conduct of this war, more especially when to this position is added *the pretended alliance with the court of France.* The policy, as well as the benevolence of Great Britain, have thus far checked the *extremes* of war, when they tended to distress a people still considered as our fellow subjects, and *to desolate a country* shortly to become again a source of mutual advantage ; but when that country possesses the unnatural design, not only of estranging herself from us, but of mortgaging herself, and her resources, to our enemies, the whole contest is changed, and the question is, how far Great Britain may, by every means in her power, destroy or render *useless* a connection contrived for her ruin, and for the aggrandizement of

France. Under such circumstances, *the laws of self-pre-servation* must direct the conduct of Great Britain ; and if the British Colonies are to become an accession to France, will direct her to render *that accession of as little avail as possible to her enemies ! !*"

Dissentient,

1st. Because the public law of nations, in affirmance of the dictates of nature, and the precepts of revealed religion, forbids us to resort to the extremes of war upon our own opinion of their expediency, or in any case to carry on war for the purpose of desolation. We know that the rights of war are odious, and instead of being extended upon loose constructions and speculations of danger, ought to be bound up and limited by all the restraints of the most rigorous construction. We are shocked to see the first law of nature, self-preservation, perverted and abused into a principle destructive of all other laws ; and a rule laid down, by which our own safety is rendered incompatible with the prosperity of mankind. The objects of war which cannot be compassed by fair and honorable hostility, ought not to be compassed at all; an end that has no means but such as are unlawful, is an unlawful end. The Manifesto expressly founds the change it announces from a qualified and mitigated war, to a war of extremity and desolation, on the certainty that the provinces must be independent, and must become an accession to the strength of the enemy. In the midst of the calamities by which our loss of empire has been preceded and accompanied; in the midst of our apprehensions for the farther calamities which impend over us, it is a matter of fresh grief and accumulated shame to see, from a commission under the Great Seal of this kingdom, *a declaration for desolating a*

*vast continent, solely because we had not the wisdom to retain,
or the power to subdue it.*

2dly. Because the avowal of a deliberate purpose of
violating the law of nations, must give an alarm to every
state in Europe. All commonwealths have a concern in
that law, and are its natural avengers. At this time, surrounded by enemies, and destitute of all allies, it is not necessary to sharpen and embitter the hostility of declared
foes, or provoke the enmity of neutral states. We trust
that by the natural strength of this kingdom, we are secured from a foreign conquest, but no nation is secured from
the invasion and incursions of enemies. And it seems to
us the height of frenzy, as well as wickedness, to expose
this country to cruel depredations, and other outrages too
shocking to mention (but which are all contained in the
idea of the extremes of war and desolation) by establishing
a false, shameful, and pernicious maxim, that where we
have no interest to preserve, we are called upon by necessity to destroy. This kingdom has long enjoyed a profound internal peace, and has flourished above all others
in the arts and enjoyments of that happy state. It has
been the admiration of the world for its cultivation and its
plenty; for the comforts of the poor, the splendour of the
rich, and the content and prosperity of all. This situation
of safety may be attributed to the greatness of our power.
It is more becoming, and more true, that we ought to at-
tribute that safety, and the power which procured it, to
the ancient justice, honour, humanity, and generosity of
this kingdom, which brought down the blessing of Providence on a people who made their prosperity a benefit to
the world, and interested all nations in their fortune, whose
example of mildness and benignity, at once humanized

others, and rendered itself inviolable. In departing from
those solid principles, and vainly trusting to the frailty of
human force, and to the efficacy of arms, rendered impotent
by their perversion, we lay down principles, and furnish
examples of the most atrocious barbarity. We are to
dread that all our power, peace and opulence, should vanish like a dream, and that the cruelties which we think safe
to exercise because their immediate object is remote, may
be brought to the coasts, perhaps to the bosom of this kingdom.

3dly. Because, if the explanation given in debate, be
expressive of the true sense of the article in the manifesto,
such explanation ought to be made, and by as high authority as that under which the exceptionable article was originally published.   The natural and obvious sense indicates, that the extremes of war had *hitherto* been checked,
that his Majesty's Generals had *hitherto* forborne (upon
principles of benignity and policy) to desolate the country ;
but that the whole nature, and future conduct of the war
must be changed in order to render the American accesion
of as little avail to France as possible.   This in our apprehension, conveys a menace of carrying the war to extremes and to desolation, or it means nothing.   And as
some speeches in the House (however palliated) and as
some acts of singular cruelty, and perfidy, conformable to
the apparent ideas in the manifesto, have lately been exercised, it becomes the more necessary, for the honour and
safety of this nation, that this explanation should be made.
As it is refused, we have only to clear ourselves to our con-
sciences, to our country, to our neighbours, and to every
individual who may suffer in consequence of this atrocious
menace, of all part in the guilt, or in the evils that may be-

come its punishment. And we choose to draw ourselves out, and to distinguish ourselves to posterity, as not being the first to renew, to approve, or to tolerate the return of that ferocity and barbarism in war, which a beneficent religion, enlightened manners, and true military honour, had for a long time banished from the christian world.

Camden,	Abergavenny,	Beausieu,
Abingdon,	Coventry,	Harcourt,
Fitzwilliam,	De Ferrars,	Effingham,
Fortescue,	Ferrars,	Wycombe,
Grafton,	Stanhope,	Scarborough,
Craven,	Rockingham,	Cholmondeley,
J. S. Asaph,	Tankerville,	Devonshire,
Richmond,	Ponsonby,	Foley,
Bolton,	Derby,	Spencer.
Radnor,	Manchester,	
Egremont,	Portland,	

LONDON, December 12.

The list of noble Peers, who protested against "the extremes of war and desolating America," on Monday last, is one of the most respectable that has appeared for some years, as, independent of their great characters in private and public life, there are ten of them whose fortunes altogether make up above two hundred thousand pounds per year; yet these are the men whose sentiments must avail nothing at so critical and important a crisis as the present; whilst a mad and impracticable war is carrying on for the purposes of a false pride, the aggrandizement of vicious, ignorant statesmen, and the rapacity of hungry contractors."

It was certainly a studied, as it was a low insult. to date this conflagration edict upon the anniversary of American

19

independence : and, like the ancient Nero, who fiddled while Rome was burning, these modern Vandals were " grinning horribly ghastly smiles," while, in three days only, after its date, the beautiful towns of Fairfield and Norwalk,* were in smoking ruins.

No wonder that the prophetic Lord Camden foresaw that such barbarism " would fix an inveterate hatred in Americans against the very name of Englishmen, which would be left as a legacy from father to son to the latest posterity."

Although the powerful empire of Britain may boast, that in the eighteenth century she carried her conquests thro' the four quarters of the globe, let her not again, in the nineteenth, attempt to subdue that portion of America, which lies between the Atlantic and the Western ocean— the 45th degree of north latitude, and the Gulf of Mexico.

At the sessions of the common pleas at Whitestown, N. Y. in September 1820, Kirkland Griffin, Esq. a veteran of the revolution, appeared in person to witness an assemblage of heroes of the revolution, who appeared before the court, to procure the proper vouchers to enable them to obtain the pension munificently granted to them, through the exertions of JAMES MONROE, who was himself a severely wounded lieutenant at the " Victory of Trenton," in 1776, and now (1823) President of the United States. The venerable Griffin, did not come to ask for himself, but to congratulate those who asked conscientiously, and who received gratefully. The scene revived his ardour, and he proceeded as follows :

" Who could forbear to go into service, when fathers,

---

* The British general Garth, one of Collier's torch bearers, was taken by the Experiment, and 80,000 guineas with him.

mothers, sisters, and friends, all implored it, and all would give every thing and do every thing in their power to prepare the young men. Those were the days of devotion to our country. I went on board a privateer. We were soon captured. We could not help it. We had but 10 guns, and they came upon us with 64--we could not resist, and surrendered. It was early in the war, and we were not considered or treated as prisoners of war, but as rebels.

We heard nothing from our country but from our keepers, who gave us the most dismal and gloomy accounts ; until after a long confinement a clergyman happened to say to us that there was good news from America for us. After he was gone we had a long consultation about what it could mean, and finally concluded that it must be, that Burgoyne,* of whose invasion and progress we had heard the most exulting statement from our keepers, had surrendered. We immediately mustered a crown and bribed a poor woman to bring us a paper that had in it the account of Burgoyne's capitulation, and a candle : for we had not seen the light either of a fire or a candle for many months. Having procured them, we mounted one of the best readers on a beam, for we occupied a second story, and had no floor over head, and all gave attention. He read the account in a loud voice, and it was with difficulty that order was preserved until he had finished, and the moment he had, there was a tremendous shouting. The guards were roused, we heard them and retired. They examined and left us. We went at it again ; they returned—we retired as they approached. They took off a few and departed ; we re-assembled and determined that we would rejoice. How to do it we knew not ; for we had nothing to drink, and precious little to eat ; but rejoice we must and would.

* Com. Jones announced this victory to the French Admiral.

Finally, we concluded we would dance.—We had a few fiddles, and we set two or three to playing, and then all throughout the whole extent of our long prison went at it, and in spite of the keepers and guards we had a real Connecticut dance." After an imprisonment of more than two years, our Paul Jones* was liberated, and again went into the service under the brave commander of that name, and was with him during his most successful cruises, and particularly in the terrible engagement between the Good Man Richard and Seraphis, when the engagement was decided by boarding. The Americans lost 150 out of 350 men, and the British suffered a still greater loss. The American Frigate was old, and not built for war, and it was believed, during the battle, that she would sink : ' Never mind it,' said Paul, ' we shall have a better one to go home in,' and so it proved. All, said our Paul, that I ever received for my services, except a little prize money, was 180 dollars in continental money, and that I have now."

Since the preceding sketch was written, the writer has enjoyed the high gratification and the amusement and intelligence of an acquaintance with Mr. William Henderson, a remote connexion of Capt. Matthew Henderson, immortalized by the elegy and epitaph of the charming bard of "Old Scotia," Robert Burns. This inimitable bard, who, like Pope, " lisped in numbers," was often hospitably entertained at the house of Mr. Henderson's father, situated upon the estate of the Earl of Mansfield. At this hospitable mansion, Burns wrote many of his unsurpassed effusions ; and Mr. Henderson's brother, who, with him, left "Old Scotia," for " New (Nova) Scotia," during the last war, has in his possession a large poem in the hand writing of Burns, never yet published.

* In his vicinity Mr. Griffin was so called.

Mr. Henderson had explored almost the whole of Scotland, England and Wales, before his desire for novelty and enterprise led him to the province of Nova Scotia; and, late in 1821, to New England.

He has been acquainted, from early life, with that part of Scotland, so long menaced by one of his own countrymen, and the adopted champion of American freedom, John Paul Jones. He assured me, that amongst the elder portion of the people still surviving, the achievements of Jones are still a subject of animated, yet fearful conversation. As the Scots peasantry are remarkable for superstitious belief in ghosts, witches, warlocks, &c. they probably still fear Jones, " though he be dead," as much as Sir John Falstaff did " that gunpowder Percy." It is with the highest satisfaction I present the following anecdote, so perfectly characteristic of the ancient Presbyterian clergy of the kirk of Scotland, in the language of Mr. Henderson.

" About the time that Jones visited Whitehaven, he went round to the Firth of Forth, and made his appearance off the harbour of Kirkaldy, a noted small town on the borders of Fifeshire (called by the Scotch the ' *Lang toun o' Kirkaldy*,' owing to its length.) No other enemy however formidable, could have created in the minds of the inhabitants, such consternation and alarm as that which then approached. Paul Jones was the dread of all, old and young, (and pamphlets of his depredations were as common in every house as almanacs.) He was looked upon as a sea-monster, that swallowed up all that came in his power. The people all flocked to the shore to watch his movements, expecting the worst consequences. There was an old Presbyterian minister in the place, a very pious and good old man, but of a most singular and eccentric turn, especially in addressing the Deity, to whom he would speak with as much familiarity as he would to an old farmer, and seemingly without respect, as will appear from the following ; he was soon seen making his way through the people with an old black oak arm chair, which he lugged down to low water mark, (the tide flowing) and sat down in it. Almost out of breath, and rather in a passion, he then began to address the Deity in the following singular way.

" Now *deed* Lord, *dinna* ye think its a shame for *ye* to send this vile *Pireet* to *rub* our *folk o' Kirkaldy ;* for ye *ken* they're *a' puir* enough already, and *hae naething* to *spaire.* They are *a' gaily guid,* and it *wad* be a *peety* to serve them in *sic in a wa.* The *wa* the *wun blaws,* he'll be here in a *jiffie,* and *wha kens* what he may do. He's *nane* too *guid* for *ony* thing. *Meickle's* the mischief he has *dune* already. *Ony pecket gear* they *hae* gathered *thegither* he will *gang wi' the heal o't ;* may burn their *hooses, tak* their *vary claes,* and *tirl* them to the *sark;* and *waes me ! wha kens* but the *bluidy* villain might *tak* their lives. The *puir* weemen *ere maist freightened* out *o'* their *wuts,* and the *bairns skirling* after them. *I canna' tho'lt ! I canna' tho'lt !* I *hae* been *lang* a *faithfu'* servant to *ye, Lard;* but *gin ye dinna* turn the *wun* about, and *blaw* the scoundrel out *o'* our gate, I'll *na stur a fit,* but will *juist* sit here, until the tide comes and *drouns* me ; *Sae take yere wull o't.*"

Whether the wind suddenly turned or not, Jones altered his course, and moved off. The good old man took up his chair and went home ; expressing his thanks to the Lord for the favour, in a more humble manner than he requested it.

To Mr. P. WALDO, from his ob't servant,

WM. HENDERSON."

P. S. I will send you the original poem, by ROBERT BURNS.

I at first thought of furnishing a glossary explanative of the Scotticisms in this singular specimen of Scots devotion, which Mr. Henderson repeatedly heard recited by his father, and many aged people of Kirkaldy ; but there is so much "sprinkling of Scots," as Burns says, it is all offered in modern English under the correction of Mr. Henderson.

"Now, indeed, Lord, do not thou think it is a shame for thee to send this vile Pirate to rob the people of Kirkaldy ? for thou knowest they are all poor enough already, and have nothing to spare. They are all, in great measure, good ; and it would be a pity to serve them in such a way. The course the wind blows he will be here in a jiffin ; and who knows what he may do ? He is none too good for any thing. Much is the mischief he has done already. Any little wealth they have gathered together, he will go off with the whole of it. He may burn their houses—take their very clothes, and strip them to the very shirt ; and woe be to me ! who knows but the bloody villain might take their lives. The poor women are almost frightened out of their wits ; and the little children are screaming after them. I cannot endure it ! I cannot endure it ! I have long been a faithful servant to thee, Lord ; but if thou dost not change the wind about, and blow the scoundrel out of our way, I will never stir a foot ; but will sit here until the tide flows and drowns me.—So let thy will be done."

CHARACTER OF JOHN PAUL JONES.

JOHN PAUL JONES was a phenomenon in human nature, and an anomaly in the human character. However sacred and endearing is the principle to Americans, that " all men are born equal, and born free ;" a Scots peasant has but a

faint conception of native equality or native freedom—yet,
although *Paul of Dumfries* was born of humble peasants,
he might, with " Paul of Tarsus" have said, " *I was born
free.*" The devotion of the Scots peasantry is proverbial
for its fervor; but the fervor of Jones seemed to have but
little reference to Heaven! He divested himself of devotion and humanity also, and attached himself to an infernal,
blood-stained, slave dealer. He left the diabolical traffic
in human flesh, and became commander in chief in smug-
gling goods. He left the business of defrauding the revenue, for the daring employ of capturing the war ships of
his king.

He found himself an outlaw from the land of his birth,
and sought a new home in France. As he had been a
prince of smugglers on a little island,* he became a princely
tavern-keeper on the continent : Disgusted with retailing
wine and soup at Boulogne to replenish his purse, he dashed into London to fill it by gambling. Calculating himself
a match for any thing, he there suddenly found himself
outmatched. He once more appeared like a piece of
abandoned goods, ready to be taken up by the first fortunate finder. This thoughtless and inconsiderate being, at
length began to consider and think. Driven from two kingdoms in the Old World, he sought an asylum in a rising
Republic in the new.

A passage across the Atlantic dissipated all the incongruous eccentricities of his character. From soaring like a
comet, where the varying gusts of flames and winds hurled
him, he began, and continued to move like a planet in a
regular orbit. Furnished with secret instructions from
WASHINGTON and the Old Congress, he repaired, *incognito*,
to the proud capital of Britain. With a minute knowledge

* Isle of Man.

of the preparations of the Admiralty of the first naval power on the ocean, he returned to the struggling colonies, and suddenly ascended the "mountain wave" with the first "star-spangled banner" that ever waved upon a war ship of Independent America, bearing the first Post-Captain's commission, under the signature of WASHINGTON, that issued after the "Declaration of American Independence," and sailed in a ship, bearing the name of the first legitimate Saxon Prince who first gave regulated existence to English Liberty; which, after being banished from degenerate Britain, was rearing her mild and majestic front amidst a new race of Freemen, sprung from an old stock of subjugated and unresisting vassals.

The new-born Jones, a champion of the new-born Republic, wafted forth, violating the mechanical rules of studied naval warfare, and defying an enemy, who defied heaven and earth, nor shrunk at the power of "profoundest hell." He rushed on from victory to victory, from "conquering and to conquer," till the Genius of Conquest claimed him as a favourite son. From the time of his defection from his tyrant king, and the beginning of his achievements in the cause of his "rebel colonies," he was sought after as a "piece of lost silver," and pursued, by the arm of vengeance, as a daring traitor. Jones eluded their search and their wrath; and, with a squadron of ill appointed ships, excited alarm for the homeward bound fleets of British merchantmen—captured their convoy, and compelled St. George's Cross to fall before the Republican Banner of America.

He menaced the cities of Old Scotia—visited the place of his birth as a conquering Commodore—took the plate of a Scots Peer for his own cabin, and drew from him a letter

20

of thanks for his magnanimity in restoring it. Upon one month he spread consternation and dismay upon the coast of Britain—upon the next, he received the congratulations of a Prince of Bourbon, and their High Mightinesses of Holland. He announced the victory over Burgoyne, and received the first salute ever given by a foreign power to the American flag. He re-crossed the Atlantic, like a prodigy, conquering as he passed, and received the highest meed of praise ever bestowed upon a hero—a Vote of Thanks from the Old Congress by the recommendation of WASHINGTON. At the height of glory, and the depths of bankruptcy, he once more rolled across the ocean—placed in his coffers the reward of his valor—again made his last voyage to the admired Republic—his adopted country. In the bosom of that favoured land, he lived an object of wondering contemplation, and died with the glory of one of the first heroes of the eighteenth century. His birth, his life, and his death, evinces that the most disheartening circumstances furnish no insurmountable barriers against an ardent and determined spirit ; and that, by exertion, with the smiles of heaven, man can arise from obscurity to distinction, from penury to competence, and from degradation to glory.

MONUMENT,

erected in the Navy Yard at Washington by the Officers
of the Mediterranean Squadron, commanded by Com. Preble,
in honour of those who fell in the Bay of Tripoli. It was bar-
barously dilapidated by the British in 1814.——

BIOGRAPHICAL SKETCH

OF

EDWARD PREBLE,

LIEUTENANT IN THE

CONTINENTAL NAVY

IN THE WAR OF THE REVOLUTION;

AND

COMMANDER IN CHIEF OF THE

AMERICAN SQUADRON IN THE MEDITERRANEAN,

IN 1803 AND 1804.

His birth, early propensities, pursuits, obtains a midshipman's warrant
—enters the Protector 26 gun ship—engages the Admiral Duff, 36
guns, takes her, and she explodes—Epidemic on board the Protector—Preble is promoted to 1st Lieutenant—Enters the Winthrop
in that capacity—Capt. Little designates him for a daring enterprise in Penobscot bay, which he executes, brings out his prize,
and enters with her into Boston harbour—Peace is concluded—
Lieut. Preble commences the merchant service, accumulates property, and marries an excellent wife.—Incidents of domestic life
omitted—He is appointed a lieutenant in the modern navy in 1798
—Capt. Preble is appointed to command the Essex—Repairs to the
East Indies—Returns to America—He is appointed commander of
the Mediterranean squadron—Mahometan depredations upon Christian merchants—Com. Preble's squadron, names and force of vessels, and commanders—Modesty and reserve of naval officers—
Com. Preble's measures with the emperor of Morocco—Lays his
squadron before Tangier—Is invited to land—Declines to lay off
his arms when on shore—His unshaken firmness and decision—Before he returns to the squadron, effects an accommodation—Proceeds to his ultimate destination—Loss of frigate Philadelphia, and
bondage of the crew—Lieut. Decatur captures a Tripolitan corsair—Difficulty and importance of Com. Preble's situation, and his
fitness for it—His general rendezvous, Syracuse—Jussuff, Bashaw
of Tripoli—Com. Preble designates Lieut. Decatur to command an
expedition against the Philadelphia frigate—Danger of it—Masterly execution of it—Com. Preble obtains two bombards and six gun-
boats from Naples—Gen. Eaton's attempt to aid Com. Preble—
Carramalli ex-bashaw—First general attack upon Tripoli, Aug. 3,
1804—Desperate engagement of the gun-boats—Death of Lieut.
James Decatur—Effects of the engagement—Second attack Aug.
7th—Proposition from Com. Preble to the Bashaw—Third attack,
Aug. 27—Fourth attack, Sep. 3d—Upon the 4th Sept. Lieut. Som-

ers, &c. enters the harbour with a fire-ship, which explodes—Re-
mark—Com. Barron arrived Sept. 9th, and Com. Preble returns to
America—Employed in Navy Department—Died at Portland,
Maine—His character.

THE man whose life and character I now attempt to present to the reader, moved in a subordinate station in the first
war between America and Britain—for he was then but a
youth. He was born in Portland, the capital of the then
District, and now State of Maine, in the year 1761. His
native country, then under the dominion of Britain, was
struggling, hand in hand, with what was then called, " the
mother country," against Frenchmen and Indians. Born
in a frigid, and what was then deemed a sterile region, as
he advanced along into that stage of life when the " ruling
passion" evinces itself by overt acts, he manifested his predilection for a nautical life.

His surviving companions in boyhood, relate many incidents of his early life, which clearly show the original firmness and greatness of his mind. Although habit, education, pursuits, associates, and innumerable other circumstances, give a tone and direction to the human mind, yet
there is a certain native trait of character which distinguishes one boy, as well as one man, from another. It
seems to be born at their birth, to grow with their growth,
and strengthen with their strength. Neither the mother in
the nursery,—the father in the active scenes of life—the
preceptor in the school, nor the president in the university, can divert the mind of some youth from their predom-
inant aim and object. Although it is said " the stream is
made by nature, but the channel is cut by custom ;" yet
EDWARD PREBLE would float in the stream which nature
made for him ; and it was as vain to attempt to change his
course, as it would be to strive to divorce the sun from the
ecliptic, or the earth from the zodiac.

The parents of young Preble, being amongst the most respectable class of citizens, designed their son for one of the learned professions. He was placed in one of the best seminaries, and under the tuition of one of the most accomplished preceptors of that period, to pass through studies preparatory for a university. He made rapid progress in his studies ; but while his eyes were upon his books, his thoughts were upon the ocean.

The remonstrances of his parents could not long dissuade, nor their threatenings deter him. They were compelled to part with a favourite son, or dampen his ardour by thwarting his inclination , and the adventurous youth wafted from his native shore, to his adopted element, as a cabin-boy. Disgusted with the humble duties of the cabin, he was almost constantly on deck, or hanging in the rigging, " in calm and in storm." He was too inquiet for a cabin-boy, and fitted by nature for some duty more manly and daring.

He continued at sea in the merchant service until the year 1779. He was then of the stature of manhood, and had a heart beating ardently for heroic enterprise. Having influential friends, they obtained for him from government a midshipman's warrant.

Although this was but a humble rank, it is the " first degree" that is now obtained in the British navy. Even then it became necessary for lord Nelson, and the duke of Clarence, (son of Geo. III.) to pass through the duties of this station as a passport to one of higher grade.

Young Preble in this capacity, entered on board the Protector, then commanded by Capt. J. F. Williams. Preble soon discovered his qualifications for the station he filled. Although like a true seaman, he was to all,

" Manly and honest, good-natured and free."

he maintained and exercised the authority vested in him with a firm, steady, and undeviating hand. Although but eighteen years of age, he had entirely divested himself of the frivolous puerilities of boyhood.

The year 1779, was a year, memorable in the desperate struggle which eventuated in the independence of the American Republic.

The armed ships belonging to the Thirteen Colonies were like little barques, thrust into the midst of powerful fleets; and they were compelled to swim or sink by the most unparalleled exertions of human courage. Swimming or sinking, their crews, inspired by the patriotic sentiments which the genius of liberty infused into their hearts, were cool, dauntless and undismayed in the hour of disaster—humane and dignified in the midst of victory.

The first cruise the Protector made was upon the coast of Newfoundland. It was the theatre upon which the first Jones* and the first Biddle† began to act their splendid parts in the tragedy of the Revolution. The Protector afforded every possible protection to American commerce, and gave every possible annoyance to that of Britain. She mounted 26 guns, and her crew were principally " Yankee seamen," prepared for the most desperate enterprise.

An opportunity was afforded them to display their courage when the Protector fell in with the British ship Admiral Duff, of 36 guns. Capt. Williams might well have wished to avoid an engagement with a ship so much superior to his own. But he chose not to strike the American Flag, which so lately began to wave over the Atlantic in a hostile capacity. He laid his ship along-side the Admiral

---

* Com. John Paul Jones.   †Com. Nicholas Biddle.

Duff, and entered into action as close as possible, unless it were by boarding.

This was the first serious engagement young midshipman Preble ever entered into. The men under his immediate command, were inspired to the highest pitch of enthusiasm by his fearless example. The ships laid so near together, that as the survivors relate, the men actually cast balls at each other from the decks with their hands.

After a short, but most furious contest, the Admiral Duff struck to the Protector. Midshipman Preble with his superior officers, was on the point of taking possession of her, when she was blown to pieces by the explosion of the magazine.

Whether it was occasioned by the chagrin of the British commander at being compelled to strike to a Yankee ship, of inferior force, or by accident, never was, and never can be determined. Instead of taking possession of the ship, the officers and crew of the Protector, were now engaged in picking up the surviving crew of the enemy, from the fragments of the destroyed ship. Five minutes before, Preble would have encountered a whole gang of them, single handed—but now, when he saw them at the mercy of the waves, he strove to save human beings who could no longer resist him as enemies.

The consequence of taking on board the Protector the surviving crew of the Admiral Duff, was the spreading of a malignant disorder, on board the ship, and losing two thirds of the crew.

The humanity and benevolence of American Naval Heroes, were displayed at this early period of the naval glory of the American Republic. It was not in the instances of a few individuals only that these exalted sentiments were displayed—it was a sentiment common to the American character.

The moderation of our ancestors during the sanguinary struggle of the revolution, must excite the admiration of their descendants, and the applause of the world. No race of people upon earth, however, ever had more cause to resort to violent measures. Americans were denounced as rebels, and threatened as traitors. Wanton destruction and Vandal devastations, marked the presence and the passage of the enemy. The capital of Preble's native District was burned, Charlestown, (Mass.) was in ashes, New London, Fairfield,* and Norwalk, (Con.) were reduced by conflagration. The beautiful island of Rhode-Island was turned into a waste. But why extend the long catalogue of barbarous deeds ? It might indeed be extended ; and as the character of Britons approximated to that of Vandals, that of Americans would remind the historian of Romans in the best days of Rome.

Capt. Williams returned into port to refit the Protector, and recruit his crew, so alarmingly reduced by a dreadful malady. This was soon effected, and the Protector once more wafted into the midst of the enemy. It was her last cruise under American colours. She was obliged to strike to a heavy British Frigate, and Sloop of War in company ; as it would have been the height of desperation to have contended with a force so vastly superior.

The severe treatment the crew of the Protector received, was unquestionably occasioned by their unrivalled gal-

* Vide Gen. Humphreys " Elegy on the burning of Fairfield." Also preceding Sketch of Com. Jones. The debates in Parliament, in the most vindictive language condemned the conduct of British officers in America.

lantry in compelling the frigate, Admiral Duff, to strike ;
but which really ought to have excited the admiration of
the British Captains.   Instead of paroling the officers and
exchanging the seamen for British prisoners, the gallant
Capt. Williams, Lieut. George Little, and many other unrivalled patriots in the cause of freedom, were transported
to England, and lodged in Plymouth prison.   Midshipman
Preble, however, by the intervention of influential friends,
obtained his release in America.

Mr. Preble, for his gallant, and his highly meritorious
services on board the Protector, received the commission
of first Lieutenant.   He was but twenty years of age, at
the time he was placed in this highly responsible station.
The British might be led to suppose that the favours bestowed upon the Lieutenant by his exchange, would have
conciliated his feelings towards the crown of England.   But
while he was gratified at being in the bosom of his country
—receiving the approbation of the Old Congress, and being promoted to a station in which he might again serve
his country ; he could not forget the gallant Williams and
Little, incarcerated in a British dungeon, three thousand
miles distant.   He was not long separated from the determined Little.   He scaled the wall of his Plymouth prison
—made his escape to France, and returned to Boston.   He
was immediately promoted to the rank of Captain.

A fine sloop of war, called the Winthrop was prepared
for sea ; and Capt. Little, and Lieut. Preble entered on
board ; and very soon had a crew well calculated for such
officers.   They immediately put to sea, and these young
officers soon gave evidence of those exalted qualities which
afterward raised them both to the acme of glory.

At this time, Penobscot Bay, and the adjoining country,

21

was in possession of the British forces. How much benefit the possession of it was to Britain or detriment to America, cannot well be calculated, considering the state of that portion of the country at that period. At any rate, in the war of 1812, the British forces were permitted by the constituted authorities of Massachusetts, to remain for a long time in peaceable and undisturbed possession of a large portion of the State of Maine; and Castine, became a commercial, rather than a naval depot.

The British had erected considerable batteries upon the shore, and had a considerable marine force in the harbour. Capt. Little and Lieut. Preble conceived the daring design of capturing a heavy armed ship and her tender, as they lay at their moorings. The design was to be executed in the night season, and Lieut. Preble was honoured with the immediate command of the expedition. Forty dauntless New-Englanders were selected to accompany the gallant Lieutenant. To avoid confusion arising in a night battle, from mistaking friends for foes, the Americans were all clad in white frocks. The enterprize was a most desperate one. When every thing was ready, and a night favourable to the expedition came round, Capt. Little bore into the harbour, and alongside the British ship. The unsuspecting enemy supposed the Winthrop to be *their* tender. The sea was running high; and the sentry of the British ship exclaimed—" You will run us aboard!" The cool and collected Preble, in a tone of decision, answered—" Aye, aye, we are coming aboard." His forty " white frocks" were all ready to follow him; but from the head-way the Winthrop had made, and the state of the waves, but fourteen could follow him to the deck of the British ship.

The solicitude of Capt. Little was excited to the high

est pitch at the situation of Lieut. Preble, and his fourteen fearless comrades. When doubtful of the result of the arduous contest between fourteen of his crew, and over 200 British seamen, he hailed Lieut. Preble, and demanded of him. " Do you not want more men ?" Lieut. Preble, with the thundering voice of a stentor, answered, " No, Sir! we have more than we want; we stand in each other's way ;" and suddenly rushed into the cabin of the ship, full armed, and found the officers, who had been disturbed by the noise upon deck, just " turning out." The intrepid Lieutenant said to them : " You are my prisoners—resistance is vain —and, if attempted, may prove fatal to you." The panic-struck enemy leaped over the gunwale of the ship, and through the cabin-windows into the water and swam to the shore, or were drowned.

Complete possession having been gained of the ship, and Lieut. Preble, being about to bear his prize out of the harbour, the batteries commenced a cannonade upon the Winthrop and the captured ship. The British troops rallied— rushed to the shore, and poured harmless vollies of musketry upon the two ships which were sailing triumphantly out of the harbour of Penobscot. Their cannon had an elevation so great, that it was fruitless to attempt to obstruct their passage out of the harbour. Neither the hulls or rigging of the Winthrop or the prize received the least injury. The "striped bunting" waved proudly over St. Georges Cross ; and the gallant Little and Preble conducted their valuable prize triumphantly into Boston harbour. The little glory which British arms acquired in taking Penobscot, was more than counterbalanced by losing this ship ; and the victors were remunerated for the loss of the Admiral Duff, which blew up after she was captured.

The contest between America and Britain was now drawing to a conclusion, by the commencement of negotiations ;
but Lieut. Preble continued to fill the station of first Lieutenant on board the Winthrop, in the active and vigilant
discharge of his duty until the treaty of Peace was ratified
in 1783.

Thus early and brilliant was the commencement of ED-
WARD PREBLE's life in the naval profession—a profession
for which he was peculiarly adapted by nature, and to
which he became ardently attached by inclination and
habit.

But the conclusion of peace with Britain, and the commanding attitude which the American Republic assumed
as a Sovereign and Independent Nation, was the annihilation of the little gallant marine force which had accomplished such wonderful effects upon the enemy. Such gallant spirits as BIDDLE, JONES, MURRAY, NICHOLSON, MAN-
LY, HARDIN, TUCKER, DECATUR the elder, and a long list
of naval heroes, who had encountered the convoys of British fleets of merchantment, or British armed ships and
fleets themselves, were now driven from their darling pursuits as naval officers.

The Republic, although independent as it regarded the
privilege of self-government, were destitute of the "ways
and means" to sustain a respectable naval force. The officers of the Army as well as those of the Navy, were compelled, while the wounds they received in the cause of their
beloved country were hardly healed, to retire, unreward-
ed—the first to their farms ; the second to the merchant-ser-
vice, as a mean of subsistence. The few little armed ships
were converted into merchantmen, to strive to regain by
commerce what the States of the Republic had lost by
war.

Lieut. Preble returned to his native town and commenced the business of a seaman in the merchant service. It would be thought by a British naval officer to be degradation itself to leave the quarter deck of a frigate, sloop of war, or any other armed ship, belonging to the government under which they had served, to enter on board an India-man, West India trader, or coaster. But Americans, at that epoch of their progress to national glory, knew well how to aid the infant Republic in any station. They knew also that individual wealth would ultimately add to the treasures of their native country, while it would furnish them with the enjoyments of individual necessaries, conveniences, and luxuries.

Lieut. Preble, at about this period of his age, entered into matrimonial life. Although a stern commander upon the ocean, he was not insensible to the fascinating and alluring charms of domestic life. His bosom companion happened to possess the noble and exalted sentiments of her husband.

He now entered, with his usual ardour, into the business of commerce,—to make provision for a family ;—knowing well that his fame as an ocean warrior, would be but a miserable support for a domestic establishment upon land. He lived in the midst of a commercial people, and was surrounded by the most accomplished and adventurous seamen. He could not endure a state of inactivity. He entered into the business of a seaman, with the same energy he did, when he entered into the contest with the enemies of his country.

He was fully aware that national wealth was the sinew of national glory. He was also sensible that individual wealth added essentially to individual consequence ; and

enabled the possessor of it to accomplish objects beyond
the reach of want and dependance.   Although but few
commercial treaties were established between the Republic and other commercial nations in the eastern continent,
yet the name of an American was a passport through the
world, for the glory his country had acquired for manfully
struggling for, and securing national independence.   Every keel that wafted from the American Republic to the
ports of Europe, Asia, or Africa, were welcomed as coming
from the most energetic and exalted race of men who ex-
isted in the eighteenth century, and were generally treated
on terms " equal to the most favoured nations."

Lieut. Preble, was one amongst the numerous American
navigators, who had aided, by his courage, in acquiring the
high rank his country sustained ; and while acquiring
wealth by commercial pursuits, he was remembered and
admired as one of the young and gallant champions of
American Independence.

From the conclusion of the war of the Revolution, the
commercial enterprise of Americans surpassed every previous example from the discovery of the magnetic needle
to that period.   The torrid, the temperate, and the frigid
zones witnessed the presence of this " New People," and
their canvas whitened every sea and ocean.   While the
kingdoms of the " Old World" were expending their treasures, and tearing from their subjects the hard-earned pittance of their labour to sustain thrones which began to totter before the majestic march of liberty which moved from
the Republic in the Western World.   While immense
standing armies covered the realms of monarchs, and vast
fleets afforded wooden walls to their shores.   While eastern empires and kingdoms were rising to the height of

glory, and sinking to the depths of corruption, Americans, better understanding the nature of true national glory,— that which produces the greatest possible happiness to the greatest number of people, were peaceably pursuing a lucrative commerce, and with unparalleled rapidity were accumulating national and individual wealth. They grew rich, not by rapine and plunder, but out of the follies, vices, and ambition of other nations.

It would be an useless waste of time, for the writer to detail, and for the reader to peruse the various pursuits of Edward Preble in the seasons of peace. However delightful peaceful scenes may be in the enjoyment of them, they are generally tame, and uninteresting in description. The biography of this energetic American, need not be protracted by expatiating upon the same events of his life, which are common with many of his humbler countrymen, whose names were never heard beyond the sound of the parish bell where they were born, and whose graves can be discovered only by the humble stone, which humble friends have erected.

The biography of Edward Preble, is vastly more fertile in incidents, than that of Samuel Johnson; yet the " Laird of Auchinleck" by detailing the little, puerile minutiæs of that giant of literature, as he was glad to be called, and as Bozzy, parrot-like, was happy to repeat, has extended his life to three huge octavos. What would the " Tars of Columbia" think, in taking up the " Life of Preble," their departed naval father, and instead of learning what he had been doing, while alive, worth reading, they should be told, that he went to the barbers upon Saturday, and dined upon fish—to church upon Sunday, and dined upon roast beef— that upon Monday he cut his nails, and drank one glass of

wine---upon Tuesday he changed his linen---upon Wednesday looked into the harbour with his spy-glass and
scoured the rust from his quadrant---upon Thursday (if it
was thanksgiving-day,) he ate turkey, plumb-pudding, and
pumpkin-pie---upon Friday (if it was " Good Friday,") he
ate no butter upon his bread, drank no cream with his
coffee, nor brandy with his water.   " Avaust there ! blind
my top-lights---stun my hearers, if I bring the first into action, to look at such blarney, or the last, to hear the report
of it." This, or something more nautical, would be their
exclamation. But badinage aside.

Thanks to the noble, daring, and gallant achievements
of our valiant countrymen, their lives are pregnant with
deeds worthy of detailing and worthy of reading.

It might be amusing to follow Preble as a master in the
merchants service through the various voyages he made
to various portions of the globe ; but there was nothing in
them to distinguish his from the voyages of other masters.
The same breeze that wafted this hero of the Revolution
from the ports of the Republic to those of foreign dominions, wafted also thousands of his own countrymen whose
names were to be found in no higher register than the ledger in the counting room ; the files of the custom-house, or
the marine list of a gazette.

While Mr. Preble was thus engaged in the unostentatious
pursuits of commerce, the government of the Republic was
preparing the only effectual safeguard for that commerce—
a NAVY.

It would illy comport with the limits of this Sketch, and
be but repeating what the writer has attempted in the Biography of Com. MURRAY, to dilate upon the immense importance of Naval Power to our Commercial Republic.

Its efficiency and its absolute necessity too, seem now to be admitted by all. But in the administration of JOHN ADAMS, who is emphatically denominated The Father of the American Navy, the question called forth the talents of the greatest men in the nation, as the Journals of Congress for 1797, and '98, will show. Our navy was commenced in the face of potent opposition—it struggled into existence—sustained itself by its early achievements, and has now fought itself into glory.

As soon as any of the frigates, or vessels of inferior rates were fitted for sea, Edward Preble was remembered as the gallant Lieutenant in the war of the Revolution, and was placed in command of the brig Pickering.

In this active craft, the Lieutenant rendered immense service in convoying American merchantmen, and protecting them from French picaroons. Such services, although they seldom call forth " Public Thanks," public applause, splendid swords, or gold medals, are neverthelss rewarded by the thankfulness and gratitude of Americans, who enjoy the protection and the independence which is thus secured to them.

Lieut. Preble, less fortunate than his senior in the revolution, Capt. George Little, had not, like him, an opportunity in this war, to distinguish himself by any brilliant achievement. Had Preble have been in command of the Frigate Boston, the La Burceau would have met with the fate she experienced.

Capt. Preble will now be presented to the reader of these imperfect sketches of his eventful life, in a capacity in which he was calculated to shine, and in which he shone most conspicuously.

After the salutary chastisement which French and Span-

22

ish picaroons received, in the administration of Mr. Adams, from Capts. Little, Truxton, Murray, the senior Decatur, and the gallant constellation of heroes in the naval
warfare, between America and France, Capt. Preble was
appointed to the command of that wonder-working ship,
the Frigate Essex, of 36 guns. ,

In 1800, it was deemed expedient to despatch an American frigate to the East Indies, to protect the immense
amount of American trade in those seas.

The presence of a single frigate in the commercial ports
of that country, immediately after the splendid victories
over Le Insurgente, Le Berceau, and other French ships,
indicated to every power that were guilty of the least en-
croachment upon American commerce, what their fate
would be.

Capt. Preble introduced into his frigate that inimitable
discipline—that nautical skill—that familiarity with naval
tactics—that skill in gunnery—that system of police in an
armed ship, which distinguished the squadron he afterwards
commanded in the Mediterranean, and which now gives
American officers and seamen, a rank above all other officers and seamen in the fleets, squadrons, and ships, of any
naval power on the earth. He finished his cruise and returned to America.

Omitting numerous incidents in the life of Preble, the
detail of which would be inconsistent with the limits of this
sketch, I now attempt briefly to narrate the events of his
life, while commanding the American squadron in the
Mediterranean.

The kingdoms, most justly denominated Barbary States,
upon the northern coast of Africa, including Morocco, Al-
giers, Tripoli and Tunis, and all owing allegiance to the

Sultan at Constantinople, the head of that vast race of human beings called Mahometans, have, for many centuries
past, mercilessly preyed upon that portion of men called
Christians, who prosecuted commerce in the Mediterranean, the largest and most renowned sea known to men.

It would be sickening to the philanthropic heart to detail,
or to read, the diabolical cruelty of these infernal descendants of Ishmael, and ferocious disciples of Mahomet, towards every portion of the Christian race, whose commercial pursuits lead them within their barbarous grasp. Too
powerful to be resisted by unarmed merchantmen, their
corsairs, for ages, have sacrificed the wealth and made
miserable slaves of the crews of merchant vessels.

If captured in the Mediterranean, they are incarcerated
in dungeons, chained to the galley, or treated like beasts of
burthen. If wrecked upon the iron-bound coast, they become still more despairing slaves to those demons incarnate,
the Wandering Arabs ; and in a state of hopeless destitution, are compelled to wander, with naked bodies, parch-
ing thirst, and famishing frames, over that vast, outspread
scene of cheerless desolation, the Desart of Zahara.

The cruelties of these children of wrath towards unfortunate Christians, whom they denominate *kellup ensaurah*,
(Christian dogs) can hardly be described in Christian language.

In hearing the pathetic and heart-rending narration of
Archibald Robbins ; (a miserable slave for about two
years, but thanks to redeeming mercy, and the smiles of
Providence, now a respectable commander in the merchant-
service) and by attempting to present, his oral communication in " Robbins' Journal," impressions were made upon the mind of the writer which nothing can eradicate, and

which may have led to the use of language, which one race
of imperfect human beings ought not to use towards another. Human, indeed they must be admitted to be, for their
origin can be traced to the most ancient race of men ; but
their principles and conduct would do credit to the character of the devil himself, if the inspired Job, and the half
inspired Milton have afforded a correct picture of that in-
vsible being.

Nations the most powerful by land and by sea, have for
ages obtained a temporary suspension from the wrath of
these Ishmaelitish pirates, whose " hands are against every
man," by paying them tribute, as the price of peace, and
ransom for the redemption of their enslaved countrymen.

It is almost invariably the practice with these detested
robbers against all mankind, to make war against other nations who are warring with each other ; especially against
that nation whom they consider the weakest. Until within
eighteen years past, these untutored barbarians, and half-
civilized hottentots, considered Americans as a mere feeble race of merchantmen. Hence in the naval warfare
with France in 1798, &c. the Tripolitan corsairs commenced a destructive war upon American commerce. When
that contest ended so gloriously for our little naval power,
these vaunting marauders were to learn the American character in a new light.

From 1801 to 1803, a small naval force, commanded the
first squadron by Com. Dale, the second by Com. Murray,
the third by Com. Morris, and the fourth by Com. Rodgers, had been in the Mediterranean ; but were barely sufficient to menace the ports of Tripoli, awe their Corsairs
and hold in check Morocco, which kingdom also had committed depredations upon Americans. This rapid sketch

was deemed expedient to prepare the mind of the reader to follow the determined, gallant, and conquering PREBLE, and his unrivalled comrades, in compelling the proud Crescent of the Turks to fall before the Stars and Stripes of America.

The American government, at peace with all the world ; with a commerce expanded over every sea and ocean— with a fine little naval force unemployed, and with officers and seamen ardently panting for an opportunity to sustain, and, if possible, to augment the glory of the American navy acquired in the contest with France, determined in 1803 to effect suddenly, what all the kingdoms of Christendom had not effected in centuries. This determination was worthy of the only real Republic on earth ; and EDWARD PREBLE as well qualified as any man on earth to execute it.

His achievements in the war of the Revolution—in the naval warfare with France—his subsequent acquaintance with navigation and commerce—his recent cruise in the Essex to the coast and ports of the East-Indies, and, to crown the climax of his high qualities, his cool determination, and dauntless courage pointed him out to his government as Commander in Chief, with an augmented force to relieve the little squadron in the Mediterranean, then commanded by the active and vigilant Com. Rodgers. This appointment was made in June 1803.

It appears from the archives in the navy department, that the government not only *felt* but *expressed* their high estimation of Com. Preble. The language of the department to him is, " *Reposing in your skill, judgment and bravery, the highest degree of confidence, the President has determined to commit the command of this squadron to your di-*

rection," &c. &c. It was in reality the most important command with which any naval officer had been invested since the adoption of the American Constitution. He was sensible of this ; and elegantly said " *I am fully aware of the great trust and responsibility of this appointment. The honour of the American flag is very dear to me ; and I hope it will not be tarnished under my command.*" I am indebted to the politeness and urbanity of Com. Macdonough for the following list of vessels, their rate, and their commanders in Com. Preble's squadron, when he entered the Mediterranean ; made from recollection.

Frigate	Constitution,	44 (flag ship)	Com. Preble.
"	Philadelphia,	44 -	Capt. Bainbridge.
Brig	Argus,	18 -	Lieut. Hull.
"	Syren,	16 -	Capt. Stewart.
Schr.	Vixen,	16 -	Lieut. Smith.
"	Nautilus,	16 -	Lieut. Somers.
"	Enterprize,	14 -	Lieut. S. Decatur.

It would be a source of the highest pleasure to the writer, and undoubtedly a gratification to the reader to be furnished with a Register of all the commissioned and warrant officers, attached to this justly renowned squadron. Many gallant young Lieutenants, and Midshipmen, till then unknown to their country and to the world, are now enrolled in the Naval Register in the temple of fame.[*]

Commodore Preble hoisted his broad pendant on board the frigate Constitution, now emphatically called " Old Iron sides." With a rapidity of sailing in squadron surpassed only by the squadron of Com. Decatur in 1815, he entered the Mediterranean Sept. 12th, 1803.

That peculiar reserve and retiring modesty, which distinguishes American naval officers, while it spreads a lus-

[*] See close of the sketch of Com. Preble.

tre over their splendid achievements, is, nevertheless, a source of regret to those who would ponder with all the rapture of delight over the record of their brilliant actions. It seems to be an invariable determination with them, never to speak in detail of gallant deeds in which they were principal actors; and, excepting their extremely brief ' official accounts' transmitted to their government, the biographical writer can learn nothing from *them*. Other sources of information must therefore be assiduously sought, and the labour of research must be endured.

As it regards that portion of Com. Preble's brilliant career, as commander of the American conquering squadron in the Mediterranean, it might well occupy a volume. If given in detail, it would be a history of American prowess in that renowned sea, which from the earliest periods of Carthage, Greece, Rome, and Syracuse, to near the close of the first quarter of the nineteenth century, has been the theatre of the most interesting and astonishing events in the civilized world.—It would be the description of the AMERICAN NAVAL SCHOOL, where the *present* brilliant constellation of naval officers obtained the first rudiments of their noble profession.

Previous to the arrival of Com. Preble with his squadron, his predecessor, Com. Rodgers, and then Capt. Bainbridge, had detained some Moorish armed ships, by way of retaliation for the Capture of American merchantmen.

The emperor of Morocco, who considers himself as a sort of Grand Sultan over the Mahometans of Africa, and feels the most sovereign contempt for the feebler Christian powers, assumed the most hostile attitude towards Americans, and detained the venerable JAMES SIMPSON, American Consul General, who received his appointment from

WASHINGTON ; and who had remained at Tangier, in Morocco until that time. As the difficulty with Morocco was so suddenly settled, it will not be minutely detailed.

Com. Rodgers, although relieved by Com. Preble, with a magnanimity and patriotism characteristic of his whole naval and official life, consented, on request, to remain in the squadron with his ships, until affairs were determined by negotiation or bombardment, with the emperor, who had repaired to Tangier with more than 5000 men.

Com. Preble, with the Constitution and Nautilus, Lieut. Somers, bore, in the most gallant style, into the bay of Tangier, and laid them within gun-shot of the extensive and powerful batteries before that city, the strongest and most important in the empire of Morocco, upon the 5th of Ocber, 1803. Com. Rodgers joined him with the frigates New York and John Adams.

He wished to communicate with the American consul ; but sentinels were placed at the door of the consular residence, and an interview between him and the commander of the American squadron, was thus inhibited.

Ambassadors, Plenipotentiaries, Ministers, and Consuls, are, by the acknowledged law of nations, considered as the representatives of the governments from which they derive their authority ; and any indignity offered to them, is considered as an insult to the nation they represent.

The American commander was aware of this ; and made every preparation in his squadron to sustain the dignity of the American Republic.

The enthusiasm of his officers, seamen and marines, corresponded with his own. They were at quarters night and day ; and, upon a given signal, were ready to perish them selves, or make the imperious Mahometans on shore bow to Christian thunder upon the waves.

A description of the batteries at Tangier, a part of which, are in the form of a crescent, and commanding the whole bay, might be amusing to the reader. But as the power of them was not tried upon the commodore's little squadron, nor the force and skill of the squadron upon them, it is omitted.

The next day, the emperor, surrounded by his numerous and splendid retinue, and at the head of his powerful army, appeared in full view of the American squadron.

Com. Preble, as is customary with civilized nations at peace with each other, saluted the Emperor from his ship— the Emperor saluted the Commodore from his batteries, and sent, as a token of peace, a few Moorish bullocks, sheep, and fowls, which were politely received by the commodore.

Previous to this, Com. Preble had ordered the ships of his squadron to bring in all Moorish vessels which fell in their way, by way of reprisal for the capture of American vessels ; and this order was still in force.

From the pacific conduct of the Emperor, amidst his warlike armaments, he was convinced that he was anxious to effect a pacification between the American government and his empire. But to effect this, was only a secondary object with the energetic Preble. His primary object was, the subjugation of the Bashaw of Tripoli, whose aggressions had been vastly more aggravating. But he saw that this was the time to prevent a protracted negotiation with Morocco, and, in conjunction with the two American consuls, James Simpson and Tobias Lear, was determined to effect a peace speedily.

He brought his squadron to within a few cables' length
of the batteries, and assumed the most warlike appearance,
upon the 7th and the 8th, in full view of the Emperor, who,
upon the 9th, relieved the American consul from his restraint, and condescended to permit him to have an interview with the American commander! Such was the sudden change of the feelings of a powerful prince, conscious
of his aggressions, when beholding the slender force of an
unoffending Republic, determined to avenge them.

The sagacious Commodore, however, was fully aware of
the faithless and perfidious conduct of the disciples of Mahomet towards all the people of Christendom ; and, in his
peculiar critical situation, resolved to prepare, as well as
he could, for the worst possible emergency.

At his interview with the American Consul, he was informed that the Emperor would give " audience" to him on
shore upon the 10th.*   This dauntless son of the ocean
could speak more audibly from his squadron than from his
lips ; but as the potent prince had invited him to a *tete a
tete*, he was resolved *to be heard*, in human language, and
be a pacificator on shore for once.

Upon the 10th, in the morning. Com. Preble prepared
to go on shore with only four attendants.†   Before leaving

* In a London paper in 1779, is found this article—
Gibraltar, Sept. 18—We hear that the Emperor of Morocco hath
refused to give an audience to Mr. Logie, the English Consul, and
that he will neither admit him into his presence, nor receive the presents from his court."
Little did the imperious court of Britain suppose that a young Lieutenant in the then " rebel marine," would, twenty-five years after,
awe the Emperor, and be " admitted into his presence," full armed,
and compel him to respect "American Rebels."

† Consul Simpson, his Secretary, Charles Morris, and two midshipmen.

the Constitution, he addressed the officers of his squadron, as near as could be recollected, in these energetic terms : " Comrades—The result of the approaching interview is known only to God. Be it what it may, during my absence, keep ships clear for action—let every officer and seaman be at his quarters :—and, if the least injury is offered to my person, immediately attack the batteries, the castles, the city, and the troops, totally regardless of me or my personal safety."

As represented by a spectator, and actor in this scene, (Mr. Morris) it was one of the most solemn and interesting that can be conceived, and the efforts of the pen and the pencil would equally lag behind reality in the description.

The mosques, towers, terraces, and dwellings of Tangier were crowded with spectators. Five thousand full armed Moorish troops were drawn up in double files, forming a lengthened vista, rendered brilliant by burnished muskets, sabres, and scimetars. The Emperor, in the splendid costume of Eastern monarchs, surrounded by a numerous retinue of princes, courtiers, alcades and guards, was seated upon a spangled carpet spread out in his castle.

The bay presented a view, less variegated, but no less interesting. The frigates Constitution, New-York, and John Adams, and brig Nautilus, with colors hoisted, were arranged with all the masterly skill of naval tacticians.

Com. Preble and his attendants descended from the quarter deck of the Constitution, upon which his broad pendant was proudly waving, into his barge, and was rowed to the shore.

Full dressed and full armed, he landed, near the fortress. The Emperor's officer requested him to lay off his arms. With manly dignity, he promptly declined it.   With a firm and dignified step, he approached towards the Emperor, through the double files of Moorish troops, viewing them as calmly as he passed along, as a general would review a regiment in time of peace. Upon reaching the Emperor, he was requested to kneel, pursuant to custom. Upon declining it, the ceremony was dispensed with. The Emperor demanded of the Commodore—" If he was not in fear of being detained ?" " No ! Sir," said he—" you dare not detain me. But if you should presume to do it, my squadron, in your full view, would lay your batteries, your castles and your city in ruins in one hour ! !"

The Emperor, who had always been accustomed to receive the humble submission of subjugated men, was awe-struck by the presence and firmness of the American commander.

He immediately gave orders to his marine officers to restore all American vessels that had been taken, and formally renewed the treaty made with America in 1786. Com. Preble revoked his orders to capture Moorish ships, and restored those that had been taken.   Happy had it been for the blood-stained *Jussuff*, the Bashaw of Tripoli, if he had followed the example of *Moolay Solimaan*,* the Emperor of Morocco.

The memory of Com. Preble, ought to be venerated, and the characters of Commodores Rodgers and Bainbridge duly estimated, for having *first* compelled the Emperor of Morocco to respect the American Republic. From 1803 to this time, Americans have suffered no obstructions in their commercial pursuits from the Moors.

* The writer of these Sketches is not certain that this was the name of the Emperor of Morocco in 1803 ; but he knows it to be the name of the emperor in 1817, when Archibald Robbins passed through his dominions from Zahara Desart.

From the decision. firmness, and energy of Com. Preble,
in his transactions with the Emperor of Morocco, his officers and seamen were readily enabled to anticipate their
duty when they reached their ultimate destination before
Tripoli.

He had declared Tripoli to be in a state of blockade,
and had given formal notice of it to all the American Consuls in the Mediterranean. It was not like the " Decrees
of Berlin and Milan," without power to enforce them—it
was a blockade with a competent naval force to carry it
into execution.

The writer of this sketch, having recently offered to the
public, the second edition of the " Life of Com. Stephen
Decatur ;" and having in that volume attempted to give a
succinct account of the operations of Com. Preble's squadron in the Mediterranean, derived from sources of unquestionable authenticity ; and being under the necessity of
connecting the actions of the gallant Commander in Chief,
with that of his favorite officer, Capt. Decatur, the detail of
some events, of Com. Preble's Life, while in the Mediterranean, is adopted from that volume, with such additions
and corrections as recent information suggested.

While Com. Preble had been thus engaged, Captain
Bainbridge, in the frigate Philadelphia, Lieut. Smith, with
the Vixen Sloop of war, laid before Tripoli, and, with this
small force, completely blockaded that important port.

On the last day of October, the Philadelphia, lying about
fifteen miles from Tripoli, Captain Bainbridge discovered
a large ship, with Tripolitan colours, under sail, between
him and the shore. He immediately gave chase to her,
and continued the pursuit until the ship entered the port
for safety. In beating out of the harbour his noble frigate

struck violently upon an unseen and hitherto undescribed rock.

It is wholly impossible to conceive what must have been the feelings—the distress—the agony of the gallant Bainbridge, and his no less gallant officers and crew, upon the happening of this dreadful disaster.

Capt. Bainbridge and his crew, while the frigate floated would have fought at sea, all the Tripolitan marine, single handed. But his irreversible fate was decided—the ship could not then be moved, and he was compelled, when an overwhelming Tripolitan force assailed him, to strike the banner of his country, to the crescent of Mahomet, and, with his truly American crew, to be reduced to the most abject slavery, which the most merciless of human beings, can inflict upon civilized man.

The whole crew exceeded three hundred Americans ; and they were immediately immured in a dungeon. In this crew were Bainbridge, Porter, Jones, Biddle,—names familiar to every American, who knows or appreciates the glory of their country.

And here I have the infinite satisfaction of recording an instance of mutual attachment, perhaps without a parallel in the history of the most romantic affection. Captain Bainbridge, his officers and crew, now reduced, in a degree, to equality, by common misery, pledged themselves to each other, never to separate alive ; but to endure one common bondage, or enjoy together, one general emancipation. The friends of the accomplished Biddle, offered the sum demanded for his ransom, which he decidedly refused to accept.

This noble crew were confined in a tower which overlooked the bay of Tripoli.   They beheld their gallant

countrymen, wafting triumphantly in their floating bulwarks, and knew that the day of their redemption would
one day come. They knew that a Preble, and a band of
unconquerable warriors from the ' land of their home'
would not forget them. They knew what they *had* done,
in Morocco, and what they *could* do in Tripoli. They
nevertheless could not help thinking of their country,—
their friends ; and, what to an ocean-warrior, perhaps,
is dearer than all, the laurels they wished to gain in chastising the diabolical wretches, who, by an unavoidable disaster, and not by their courage, now held them in degraded subjugation.*

* The following pathetic lines are extracted from a poem originally
published in the " Analectic Magazine." They apply with peculiar
force to the captive crew of the Philadelphia frigate in a Tripolitan
dungeon. I should be happy to give the author's name.

> Blest country of freedom ! no longer my home !
> In my boyhood I lov'd o'er your green fields to roam ;
> Columbia ! still sweet to my ear is the sound,
> Though now I'm a captive dishonour'd and bound.
>
> Dear land of my birth ! where my kindred all dwell,
> Couldst thou see thy lost son in this comfortless cell,
> Pale, starving, a slave, and with irons compress'd,
> Thy vengeance would rise, and his woes be redress'd.
>
> While millions thy bloom-scented breezes inhale,
> And on thy rich harvests of plenty regale ;
> Here, far from the shores of abundance and health,
> My *wretchedness** adds to a rude tyrant's wealth.
>
> When night o'er the world drops her curtains of gloom,
> I am plung'd in the damps of this horrible tomb ;
> Where nought can be heard but the clanking of chains,
> And moaning of slaves that give vent to their pains.

* It is the practice of Mahometans, to aggravate the miseries of
Christian slaves to extort a higher ransom.

But we turn from a picture coloured in the darkest shades of human calamity, to some of the brightest ornaments of the human race. Com. Preble despatched Lt. Decatur, on the 14th of December from Malta with the schooner Enterprise, and he laid his course for Tripoli. The Tripolitans had seen this little schooner *before*, and the reader already knows what was the result of the interview.†

On the 23d, in full view of Tripoli, he engaged an armed Tripolitan vessel ; and, in a few minutes, made her his own. She was under Turkish colours, and manned principally with Greeks and Turks, and commanded by a Turkish Captain. Under these circumstances, the Lieutenant hesitated for some time, whether to detain or release the captured vessel. Upon investigation, he found that there was on board two very distinguished Tripolitan officers, and that the commander of her, in the most dastardly manner, had attacked the Philadelphia frigate, when driven on a rock. He farther learned from unquestionable authority, that on this occasion he fought under false colours ; and that when the heroic but unfortunate crew of the Philadelphia, could no longer resist the immense force brought against her, he boarded her ; and with the well known ferocity of a Mahometan, plundered the officers of the captured frigate. Here the exalted character of Com. Preble's favorite officer Lieut. Decatur, began to be developed. He was then, as he ever was, a lamb to his friends—a lion to his enemies. He had before his eyes the beloved frigate, which had fallen a victim to misfortune and to demons. But, adhering rigidly to the rights of war, he man-

---

* Alluding to the victory of Lieut. Sterrett.

ifested no resentment against the humbled and trembling wretches now in his power. His great spirit scorned to make war upon weakness, or triumph over a fallen foe. He indignantly disposed of the crew—handed the papers of the vessel, to Com. Preble, who took her into the service of his own country, and gave her a name which she afterwards so well supported, The Ketch Intrepid.

Notwithstanding the loss of the fine frigate Philadelphia, and the bondage of her accomplished crew, which very materially reduced the force of Com. Preble's little squadron, that veteran officer was not to be deterred from attempting to accomplish the great object of his government, in sending him to the Mediterranean.

Fortunately for his own fame, and for the lasting glory and benefit of his beloved country, he united the most cool deliberation, with the most dauntless courage. The first, enabled him to prepare well for the tremendous contest which lay before him. He might have exclaimed, in the language of an inimitable, although not a very modern bard—

" The wide, the unbounded prospect lies before me,
But shadows, clouds, and darkness rest upon it."

The second quality enabled him, when entered into the dreadful brunt of devastating warfare, to brave death in its most appalling and horrid forms. In his officers and seamen, he recognized chivalrous warriors, who, amidst a host of dangers, and the strides of death, thought less of themselves than they did of their country.

Fortunately, was it, I may again say, that there was such a man as Preble at such a time, to command such men. He wanted nothing to stimulate him to the most daring attempts.

As commander of the little squadron in the Mediterranean, he was in some measure situated as Jackson was,
when commanding his little army at New Orleans. His
language to Mr. Monroe, then secretary of war, was, " as
the safety of this city will depend upon the fate of this army.
it must not be incautiously exposed." The gallant Commodore might have said—" As the glory of my country,
the safety of her merchants, and the redemption of my
countrymen depend upon my small force, it must not rashly be carried into a contest where so many chances are
against its success."

He selected the harbours of the cities of Syracuse and
Messina for his general rendezvous in the Mediterranean
—occasionally laid off the island of Malta, and sometimes
carried his squadron into the bay of Naples.

No portion of this globe could afford the ardent hero.
and the classical scholar a more sublime subject for contemplation. Excepting some sections of the immense
American Republic, no part of our world seems to have
been created upon a scale so wonderfully grand. It is
calculated to inspire the most exalted views of the boundless greatness, incomprehensible wisdom, and resistless
power of the Creator.

Com. Preble, his accomplished officers, and intelligent
crews, in different ships, and in different positions, were in
view of three of the four quarters of the globe—Of *Asia*,
whence issued the Law from Sinai, and Grace from Bethle-
hem, and where Mahometans and heathen now bear sway.
Of *Africa*, once the seat of Egyptian power and science,
and now the region of superstition. Of *Europe*, the smallest,
and yet more powerful than all the three other quarters of
the globe. They were in view of Vesuvius and Etna.

which, for ages have spread desolation over the cities at their bases. The gulph of Charybdis, which long swallowed up mariners who escaped from Scylla—the place where Euphemia once was, and where the hideous desolation of earthquakes are yet visible throughout Calabria, were within his view.

In addition to this, it has been the theatre of the most important events recorded in ancient or modern history. The minds of the historian, the scholar, the poet and the warrior, seem to be irresistably hurried back to the days of antiquity, and traces the events and the works which have so astonishingly developed the moral, physical, and intellectual faculties of man in this region.

Com. Preble had in his squadron many scholars of the first water, as they were all heroes of the first stamp. The region in which they moved, and the object they had to accomplish, were both calculated to stimulate them to that pitch of unparalleled enthusiasm which led them to the achievement of such unparalleled deeds.

The renowned city of Syracuse is situated upon the island of Sicily. The historian will readily recollect its former grandeur and importance ; but the writer has enjoyed the desirable satisfaction of learning its present state from some of the accomplished officers of Com. Preble's squadron, and other American gentlemen who have recently explored the island of Sicily, and who have resided in the city of Syracuse.

This island was once the region of fertility ; and while the Roman legions were striding on from conquest to conquest, over what was then called " the whole world," this island was literally their granary.

The climate is altogether the finest that can be imagined.

The soil produces not only all the necessaries but all the luxuries of life. The ancient Syracusans carried their city to a pitch of grandeur, second only to that of Rome.

It can hardly be believed in the nineteenth century, that this single city in ancient days, furnished one hundred thousand foot soldiers, and ten thousand horsemen, but such was the fact. And, when it is mentioned that her navy amounted to four hundred vessels, the assertion would almost seem to be incredible ; but it is no less true.

At that period of their history, the Syracusans flourished by war—they afterwards became degenerated by peace.

Rome conquered Greece by arms, and was herself conquered by the refinements of Greece. It was easy for the clans which composed what is generally called the " Northern Hive" in the fifth century of the Christian era, to conquer them both. They only had to conquer a people by *arms*, who had conquered themselves by *effeminacy*.

The Saxons, from whom Englishmen and Americans principally derive their origin, were in that myriad who precipitated themselves upon the ancient nations of Europe, and established those which now so completely eclipse their former splendour. The Gauls, Franks, and other clans followed in their train, and European nations are *now*, what the Grecians, Carthagenians, Romans and other ancient nations were about the commencement of the Christian era ; and London, Paris, and other cities, are what Rome, Syracuse and other cities were then.

While at anchor in the harbour of Syracuse and other places, Com. Preble and his brother officers frequently went on shore and explored these places of ancient wealth, refinement and grandeur.

Syracuse is twenty-two miles in circumference ; although its limits could then be discovered only by the mouldering ruins of its ancient boundaries.

Although the natural charms of the country remain the same as they were when the fiat of creative power brought the universe into existence, yet the miserable, degenerated, and vitiated descendants of the ancient Syracusans, had so scandalously degraded the noble and glorious ancestors from whom they descended, that the officers of Commodore Preble's squadron saw nothing in them to excite their respect—much less their admiration.

But Com. Preble was not designated by the American government to conduct a squadron into the Mediterranean for the purpose of visiting the tombs of Archimedes, Theocritus, Petrarch, and Virgil, in the adjoining regions of that sea, and then to return home and amuse his countrymen with the present state of the "classic ground" which their splendid geniuses have rendered sacred.

His business was to conquer a barbarous foe bordering upon another portion of the Mediterranean who never had any more pretentions to the productions of genius, than they have to the exercise of humanity.

He perfectly well understood the ancient character of the Syracusans, and from occular demonstration had plenary evidence of their modern degeneracy.

As the squadron rendezvoused there to obtain water and fresh provisions, the officers and seamen had occasion frequently to be on shore within the city by night and by day.

Although the American Republic was at perfect peace with the Neapolitan government, yet there was no individual safety when intercourse became necessary with its vindictive and sanguinary subjects.

From many interesting narrations of many of the accom-

plished officers of Com. Preble's squadron, the fact may
be asserted, that the Syracusans, who were amongst the
most noble of the ancients, are amongst the most degraded
of the moderns.   Their sordid and mercenary rulers exercise a boundless, undefined, and unrestrained power, over
the miserable and degraded people.   They, in hopeless
despondence, prey upon each other, and like Macbeth,
having long waded in blood, may as well advance as to re-
cede: and, as if blood was their aliment, they make a business of assassination.

Armed with concealed daggers, stilettoes, and knives,
our unsuspecting officers and seamen were assailed when
the earth was shrouded in darkness, and sometimes escaped with their lives by putting their assailants to death.

This is no place for grave and prolix reflections—they
belong to the writers of ethics, and not to the biographer;
but it is utterly impossible to avoid the inquiry, how the
human heart can become so completely divested of the
feelings of humanity, and be metamorphosed into those of
beasts of prey? and how those portions of the world where
the arts and sciences not only once flourished, but may be
said almost to have originated, should now be reduced to a
state far worse than that which is naturally savage?

Many portions of Asia, Europe, and Africa, bordering
upon the renowned Mediterranean sea, are now inhabited
by races of men far less magnanimous, and little less ferocious, than the aborigines who roam through the boundless
wildernesses of America, where science never diffused its
lights, and where civilization never imparted its refined
blessings.

While at Syracuse, Com. Preble was incessantly employed in preparing his crews for the unequal, the daring, and desperate contest into which he was shortly to enter.

His arduous and impatient soul panted for an opportunity to avenge the injuries of his country, and above all to relieve his countrymen from the dreadful state of wretchedness to which they were reduced by their slavery, under Jussuff, at that time reigning Bashaw of Tripoli.

It will not, I trust, be deemed a digression—indeed, upon second thought, it is no digression at all, to make a brief allusion to the blood-thirsty demon, who sat upon the blood-stained throne of Tripoli, while Preble and his associates were pouring out the vindictive wrath of an injured and indignant Republic upon his no less blood-thirsty subjects.

Jussuff was to the reigning family of Tripoli, what Richard III. once was to the reigning family of England. He was a remote heir to the throne of the Bashaw, filled by his father. The certain progress of the king of terrors, or the sanguinary hand of some other assassin, might have placed him upon the throne according to the laws of succession, (if they have any in Tripoli) without ascending it with his hands reeking in the blood of his father and his eldest brother. Both of these he had murdered ; and his next eldest brother, Hamet Caramalli, apprehending the same fate, sought a refuge from unnatural death by fleeing into Egypt.

Having no other rival, this modern Cain mounted the throne of his father and his brother ; and, as he had acquired it by violating the laws of God, of nature, and of man, he endeavoured to support himself upon it by re-acting the same tragical scenes which carried him to it. The " compunctious visitings" of conscience ; the monitor in the human breast, excited no horrors in his callous and reprobate heart.

A gleam of horrid triumph seemed to shed a baleful and blasting illumination over his blackened and bloody soul. He " grinned horribly a ghastly smile" at the fate of his innocent and exiled brother; and gnashed his teeth at the gallant Bainbridge, his incarcerated crew, and the rest of the American prisoners, then in his dungeons

It was in vain for Mr. Lear, then American consul, by all the melting and impassioned appeals he could make to the obdurate heart of this demon incarnate, to obtain the least mitigation of the indescribably wretched bondage to which his beloved countrymen were reduced. As well might the lamb bleat for mercy in the paw of a tiger, or the child attempt to demolish the bashaw's castle with his wind-gun.

Mr. Lear was compelled to be an agonized spectator of the accumulated and accumulating miseries of gallant Americans, who had left the regions of happiness—the arms of fathers, mothers, brothers, and sisters—of wives and children, to redeem, by their courage, their own countrymen, who had previously been enslaved.

The powerful arms of Bainbridge and his crew, which, at liberty, would have scattered death amongst a host of Turks, were pinioned and lashed together, they driven to the shore; and, in taunting derision, commanded to cast their swimming eyes upon their shipmates, then wafting in the bay of Tripoli ; and to heave forth the sighs of hearts already bursting for the land of their homes.

But I must retract—not a tear was dropped ; not a sigh was heard ; for revenge had closed the flood-gates of grief ; and American hearts, beating in bosoms truly American, panted for nothing but vengeance upon their demoniacal oppressors.

The bashaw, who might well be compared to the toad which wished to swell to the size of the ox, reposed in fancied security. He cast a malignant glance at the little squadron in which Preble was the commander. He saw in the bay, spreading before the city, his batteries, and his castles, a noble American frigate, (the Philadelphia,) once the pride of the American navy—upon which the " Star-spangled banner" once triumphantly waved, now added to *his* naval force—manned by a double crew of Tripolitans ; and, with the Turkish crescent waving on its mast. He saw its once gallant crew, miserable slaves in his own gloomy dungeons ; and, in anticipation, feasted his cannibal appetite upon all the victims which the American squadron could add to his list of Christian slaves.

Com. Preble's fearless and noble soul, was not only aroused to the highest pitch of enthusiastic courage, but it was absolutely inflamed with desperation to behold his former companions in the navy, thus degraded—thus humiliated—thus subjugated. But, like a lion, growling at a distance, and indicating to his foe their future fate, he was restrained, from rushing too precipitately upon the barbarous enemy, he wished instantly to encounter.

All personal considerations, were completely merged and lost, in the agony he felt for his brother officers and seamen in slavery. He had taken his life in his hand, and seemed anxious to offer it up, if so decreed by the God of battles, for the redemption of his endeared countrymen. But the cool and yet cautious Preble, knew full well that the means in his hands, must be directed with the utmost caution, to accomplish the end he had in view.

25

To recapture the Philadelphia, was absolutely impracticable, as the writer has been assured by some of the experienced and accomplished officers of Commodore Preble's squadron. She was moored under the guns of the Bashaw's castle, and his extensive and powerful batteries, and was herself, in her present hands, completely prepared to join them in repelling any assailants that should approach her. There were these alternatives—she must either be destroyed—constantly blockaded—or suffered to escape, and commit depredations upon the commerce, and outrage upon the citizens of the country who built, equipped, and manned her.

Lieut. Stephen Decatur, with the most impassioned and fervent appeals to the Commodore, entreated him to permit an attempt to destroy her, as she lay at her moorings. It was an attempt so pregnant with danger, and approaching so near to certain destruction, that the heroic, though cautious Preble, hesitated in granting the request. The imminent hazard of the enterprise was pointed out in such a manner as was calculated to allay the ardour of the most romantic heroism. But Decatur, rising above the ordinary calculations of chances—retiring into his own bosom, and forming his judgment from his own exalted gallantry, took no counsel from fear, but volunteered his services to his Superior officer, to command the desperate expedition. At length,

" He wrung from him his slow leave"—

and immediately commenced his preparations for the awful undertaking. The ardour of the Lieutenant was increased as the danger of the attempt was magnified. At this early period of his life, he seemed to have revived the spirit which pervaded the hearts of men in the " age of

chivalry," and to have adopted the ancient axiom " the
greater the danger the greater the glory." But let it be
remembered that Decatur sought for *glory*, only by the
discharge of *duty*.

Uniting the most consummate sagacity with the most
daring courage, he selected the little ketch Intrepid, which,
as previously mentioned he had himself captured, in full
view of the bay where the Philadelphia was moored. He
was aware that if the expedition should prove successful,
it would render the mortification of the insolent Bashaw
doubly severe, to see a little vessel which lately belonged
to his own marine force, boldly approach to the guns of
his battery and castle, and destroy the largest ship that belonged to his navy. A ship, too, which he neither built
nor honourably captured, but which became his by the irresistible laws of the elements.

No sooner was it known that this expedition was to be
undertaken, than the crew of Lieutenant Decatur volunteered their services—ever ready to follow their beloved
commander to victory or to death. Other seamen followed their example. Nor was this the most conclusive evidence of the unbounded confidence placed in his skill and
courage. Lieut. CHARLES STEWART, also volunteered under Decatur; and for the expedition took the brig Syren
and a few boats ; and, to show still farther the high estimation in which he was holden—Lieut. JAMES LAWRENCE,
and CHARLES MORRIS, and THOMAS MACDONOUGH, then
midshipmen, entered on board the Intrepid with Decatur.
What a constellation of rising ocean heroes were here associated! They were then all young officers, almost unknown to fame. Now their names are all identified with
the naval glory of the American Republic.

As soon as the crews of the ketch Intrepid and the brig Syren were made up, the utmost despatch was used in preparing them for the expedition. The Ketch was fitted out as a fire ship, in case it should be necessary to use her as such. The Brig, with the boats accompanying her, were to aid as circumstances rendered it necessary, and to receive the crew of the Ketch if she was driven to the necessity of being blown up.

Upon the 3d day of February, Decatur weighed anchor in the little Intrepid, accompanied by Lieutenant Stewart in the Syren, who was also accompanied by the boats. A favourable wind would have wafted them to their destined port in less than five days ; but for fifteen days, they encountered the most boisterous and tempestuous weather. Instead of encountering a barbarous enemy, they were buffeting the waves and struggling for life with a tumultuous and agitated sea. Nothing could be better calculated to repress the ardour of Decatur and his little band. His provisions were diminished and almost expended, and although not a murmur escaped the lips of the humblest seaman, it may well be imagined what must be their reflections, when liable every hour to be swallowed up by the waves ; and, if they escaped them to be famished with hunger ! Men of the stoutest hearts, who would undauntedly rush to the cannon's mouth, become even children at the prospect of famine.

At length upon the memorable 16th of February, 1804, a little before sunset, Decatur hove in sight of the bay of Tripoli, and of the frigate Philadelphia, with the Turkish Crescent proudly waving at her head. The apprehensions arising from storms and famine were suddenly banished by the prospect of a glorious victory or a glorious death.

It had previously been arranged between Decatur, and Lieutenant Stewart, that the Intrepid, accompanied by the boats which had been attached to the Syren, should enter the harbour at 10 o'clock at night, with the utmost possible silence, bear down upon the Philadelphia, and take her by boarding. But, as if fate had entered its *veto* against the success of the expedition, the Syren, with all the boats, by a change of wind, were driven from five to ten miles from the Intrepid, leaving Decatur, with only seventy volunteers in this small Ketch.

The moment of decision had come. His provisions were nearly expended, and the expedition must have been relinquished for that season, unless the object of it was now accomplished.

He knew that her gallant little crew were as true to him, as the needle by which he directed his ketch to Tripoli, was to the pole. Wherever he would lead, he knew they would follow. Having a Maltese pilot on board the Ketch, he ordered him to answer the hail from the frigate, in the Tripolitan tongue ; and, if they were ordered to come to an anchor, to answer, that they had lost their anchors upon the coast in a gale of wind, and that a compliance with the order was impossible.

He addressed his gallant officers and men in the most animated and impassioned style—pointed out to them the glory of the achievements which would redound to themselves, and the lasting benefit it would secure to their country,—that it would hasten the redemption of their brother seamen, from horrible bondage, and give to the name of Americans, an exalted rank even amongst Mahometans. Every heart on board swelled with enthusiasm, and responded to the patriotic sentiments of their beloved

leader in this expedition, by wishing to be led immediately
into the contest. Every man was completely armed—not
only with the most deadly weapons, but with the most
dauntless courage.

The reader may form some faint conceptions of the tremendous hazard of this engagement by learning that the
Philadelphia was moored near the Bashaw's extensive and
powerful batteries, and equally near to what he deemed
his impregnable castle. One of her full broadsides, of
twenty-six guns, pointed directly into the harbour, and
were all mounted and loaded with double headed shot.
Two of the Tripolitan's largest corsairs were anchored
within two cables' length of her starboard quarter, while a
great number of heavy gun-boats were stationed about the
same distance from her starboard bow.

As the Bashaw had reasons daily to expect an attack
from Com. Preble's squadron, the Tripolitan commander
of the Philadelphia, had augmented her crew to nearly a
thousand Turks. In addition to all these formidable,—
yea, appalling considerations, Decatur and his noble crew,
knew full well that after having entered into this dreadfully unequal combat, there was no escape. It was a " forlorn hope"—it was victory, slavery, or death—death perhaps by the hands of the Turks—perhaps by the explosion
of the Intrepid.

As soon as darkness had concealed the Ketch from the
view of the Tripolitans, Decatur bore slowly into the harbour, and approached the numerous magazines of death
which were prepared to repel or destroy any assailant that
should approach.

The light breeze he had when he entered the harbour
died away, and a dead calm succeeded. At 11 o'clock he

had approached within two hundred yards of the Philadelphia. An unbroken silence for the three preceding hours had prevailed; reminding the poetical reader of the expressive couplet—

> " A fearful silence now invades the ear,
> And in that *silence* all a *tempest* fear."

At this portentous moment, the hoarse and dissonant voice of a Turk hailed the Intrepid, and ordered her to come to anchor. The faithful Maltese pilot answered as previously directed, and the sentinel supposed " all was well." The Ketch gradually approached the frigate ; and when within about fifty yards of her, Decatur ordered the Intrepid's small boat to take a rope and make it fast to the fore chains of the frigate, and the men to return immediately on board the Ketch. This done, some of the crew with the rope began to warp the Ketch along-side the Philadelphia.

The imperious Turks at this time began to imagine that " all was *not* well." The Ketch was suddenly brought into contact with the frigate—Decatur, full armed, darted like lightning upon her deck, and was immediately followed by midshipman Morris. For a full minute, they were the only Americans on board, contending with hundreds of Turks. Lieutenant Lawrence* and midshipman Macdonough, as soon as possible followed their leader, and were themselves followed by the whole of the little crew of the Intrepid.

A scene followed which beggars description. The consternation of the Turks increased the wild confusion which the unexpected assault occasioned. They rushed upon

* Lawrence at this time was a midshipman; but was acting lieutenant in the schooner Enterprise.

deck from every other part of the frigate ; and, instead of
aiding, obstructed each other in defending her.   Decatur
and his crew formed a front equal to that of the Turks, and
then impetuously rushed upon them.   It was the business
of the Americans to slay, and of the Turks to die.   It was
impossible to ascertain the number slain ; but it was estimated at from twenty to thirty.   As soon as any Turk was
wounded, he immediately jumped overboard ; choosing a
voluntary death, rather than the disgrace of losing blood
by the hand of a " christian dog."   Those who were not
slain, or who had leaped overboard, excepting one, escaped in a boat to the shore.

Decatur now found himself in complete possession of
the Philadelphia, and commanded upon the same deck
where his gallant father had commanded before him.   But
in life, he was in the midst of death.   He could not move
the frigate, for there was no wind—he could not tow her
out of the harbour, for he had not sufficient strength.   The
Bashaw's troops commenced a tremendous fire from their
batteries and the castle upon the frigate.   The gun-boats
were arranged in the harbour; and the two corsairs near
her were pouring their fire into her starboard quarter.   Decatur and his gallant companions remained in the frigate,
cool and collected, fully convinced that that was the only
place where they could defend themselves.

Finding it totally impossible to withstand, for any length
of time such a tremendous cannonade as was now pouring
in upon him, he resolved to set the frigate on fire in every
one of her combustible parts, and run the hazard of escaping, with his officers and seamen, in the little Intrepid,
which still lay along side of her.   It was a moment, pregnant with the most awful, or the most happy consequences
to these gallant heroes.

After the conflagration commenced, Decatur and his associates entered the ketch as it increased; and for some time were in imminent danger of being blown up with her.

As if Heaven smiled upon the conclusion of this enterprise, as it seemed to frown upon its beginning, a favourable breeze at this moment arose, which blew the Intrepid directly out of the reach of the enemy's cannon, and enabled Decatur and his officers and seamen to behold, at a secure distance, the furious flames and rolling columns of smoke which issued from the Philadelphia.

As the flames heated the loaded cannon in the frigate, they were discharged, one after the other—those pointing into the harbour without injury; and those pointing into the city of Tripoli to the great damage and consternation of the barbarous wretches who had loaded them to destroy our countrymen. One of the shot entered the dungeon where Capt. Bainbridge and his crew were confined!

It is wholly impossible for those unaccustomed to scenes like this, to form a conception of the feelings of Decatur and his comrades upon this occasion. Their safe retreat was next to a resurrection from the dead. Not an American was slain in the desperate rencontre, and but four were wounded.

Com. Preble might well have exclaimed to Lieut. Decatur upon joining his squadron, as an ancient Baron did to his favourite knight—

"Welcome to my arms; thou art *twice* a conqueror,
"For thou bringest home *full* numbers."

Equally impossible is it to imagine the feelings of Captain Bainbridge and his companions in bondage upon this almost miraculous event. They heard the roar of cannon

26

in their gloomy dungeon, and saw the gleaming light of the flames, but knew not the cause. Upon learning the cheering tidings, joy converted their chains and cords to silken threads. It was a presage of there deliverance, and foretold to them a glorious jubilee. They might have said of the Commodore, " Better is a friend that is nigh, than a brother that is far off."

Com. Preble, fully sensible of the deficiency of his squadron in vessels of a smaller class, negotiated with the king of Naples for the loan of two bombards, and six gun-boats. Nelson, when commanding immense squadrons of ships of the line declared that " Frigates were the eyes of a fleet ;" and gun-boats were to Preble, what frigates were to him.

This great man, and veteran officer had the scantiest means to accomplish a most important end. But as the gallant Henry V. with his little army before Agincourt " wished not for another man from England," so Preble wished not for another keel, another gun, or another man from America. His noble soul converted his little squadron into a powerful fleet; and, surrounded by such officers as Decatur, Hull, Stewart, Smith, Somers and others, then less known, and perhaps equally gallant, his comrades were magnified into a mighty host.

While Com. Preble was thus preparing to negotiate with the tyrannous and murderous Jussuff at the mouth of his cannon, and to send *his ultimatum* in powder and ball, Mr. William Eaton, who had previously been a consul from America up the Mediterranean, conceived the daring and romantic project of restoring Hamet Caramalli to the throne of Tripoli which had been usurped by the reigning Bashaw.

Hamet had relinquished all hopes of regaining a throne which had always been acquired and sustained by blood and assassination. Like a philosopher, he had retired to Egypt, where the beys of that ancient kingdom extended to him their protection and their hospitality. To use his own language, as translated into ours he " reposed in the security of peace—had almost ceased to repine for the loss of his throne, and regretted only the lot of his unhappy people, doomed to the yoke of his cruel and tyrannical brother."

Novel language this, to be sure in the mouth of a Mahometan! How much his " unhappy people" would have been benefited by his reign, cannot now be determined ; as he is not amongst the " legitimate sovereigns" who have, in later times, waded through the blood of their own subjects to thrones from which they were driven by the public voice. Thrones which tremble beneath them, and which they maintain only by the strong arm of power.

Some few Americans from the American squadron, joined Eaton, and, many natives of various tribes, languages and colours flocked to his standard. A motley sort of an army was thus formed, and Eaton placed himself at their head as a general. He repaired to Alexandria, and found the feeble Caramalli, as just mentioned " reposing in security and peace."

Fortunate indeed had it been for him, if he had remained in safety by continuing in obscurity. Few instances are left us upon record of princes who have been exiled from their thrones and kingdoms, who have enjoyed either of them upon their restoration. The houses of Stuart, Bourbon, and Braganzi furnish the commentary.

The expiring hopes of Caramalli, were brightened up by the ardent and romantic Eaton, as a sudden gust elicits a spark from the faint glimmering light in the socket. He cast a longing eye towards the dangerous throne of Tripoli, more than half a thousand miles distant, between which and himself stretched an immense desart second only in barrenness and desolation to that of Zahara.

But nothing could repress the ardour of Eaton. The idea of an American, taking from the land where Pharaoh once held the children of Israel in captivity, an exiled prince, and placing him upon the throne of a distant kingdom, had something in it so outrageously captivating, that the enthusiastic mind of the chivalrous Eaton was lost to every other consideration.

The grateful Caramalli, if an Ishmaelite can be grateful, took leave of his Egyptian friends, and placed himself under the banner of Eaton. He entered into a Convention with the general, by which he promised immense favours to the Americans, and to make the engagements reciprocal, the general promised to restore him to his throne. This diplomatic arrangement was doubtless mutually satisfactory to the parties, although the American and Tripolitan governments had no hand in this negociation.

Caramalli, his general, and a great assemblage of incongruous materials called an army, moved across the desarts ; and endured every thing which they might have anticipated from the nature of the country. After passing about six hundred miles they reached the city of Derne, which they triumphantly entered, and at least found some repose and a supply of their immediate wants.

The reigning Bashaw in the mean time had augmented his garrisons to three thousand Turkish troops, and an army of more than twenty thousand Arabs were encamped in the neighbourhood of the strong city of Tripoli. However contemptuously he might smile at the force which surrounded his approaching brother by land, and however

little he cared for the loss of the little city of Derne, a
" fearful looking for of judgment" harrowed his guilty soul
when he beheld the whole of Commodore Preble's squadron, upon the first week of August, approaching the harbour of Tripoli.

He had seen the gallant Capt. Decatur, in his bay capture one of his corsairs—he had seen the same warrior with
the same corsair destroy his heaviest ship of war, under the
very guns of his batteries and castle, surrounded also by
his marine force. The name of DECATUR sounded in his
ear, like the knells of his parting glory ; and when he saw
the broad pendant of PREBLE waving upon that wonder-
working ship the Constitution, and surrounded by brigs,
bombards, and gun-boats, he almost despaired. He had
the crew of the Philadelphia and many other Americans in
wretched bondage. Determining to extort an enormous
ransom for the prisoners from the American government to
enable him to support the vain and gorgeous pageantry of
royalty, he demanded the sum of six hundred thousand dollars for their emancipation, and an annual tribute as the
price of peace. This Mr. Lear indignantly rejected. He
left it with such negociators as Com. Preble, Decatur, &c.
to make the interchange of powers, and to agree upon the
preliminaries of a treaty.

After having stated that the whole of Com. Preble's
squadron laid before Tripoli, the reader may have been
led to suppose that it was a very formidable force. But to
prepare the mind to follow him and his comrades into the
harbour, and to pursue him to the very mouths of the Bashaw's cannon upon his batteries, in his castle, and on
board his corsairs, gun-boats, and other marine force,
mounting little less than three hundred cannon—let it be

remembered that *his* whole squadron, including the Neapolitan bombards and gun-boats, mounted less guns than
one completely armed seventy-four, and one frigate !! His
squadron consisted of one frigate, three brigs, (one of which
had been captured from the enemy) three schooners, two
bombards, and six gun-boats. His men amounted to a
very little over one thousand ; a considerable number of
whom were Neapolitans, upon whom he could place but
little reliance in a close engagement with Turks. But *he*
felt like a warrior, and knew that Americans were heroes.

    "* * * * * * * From hearts so firm,
    " Whom dangers fortify, and toils inspire,
    " What has a leader not to hope ?"

Com. Preble had made the best possible preparations he
could, with his limited means, to effect his ultimate object.
The four preceding squadrons sent to the Mediterranean
under Coms. Dale, Murray, Morris and Rodgers, had
gone but little beyond mere blockading ships—for this was
all they could do. The American government, in the season of 1803, used every exertion to prepare a respectable
augmentation to Com. Preble's squadron, and in the mean-
time he was preparing to make " demonstrations" upon
Tripoli rather more impressive than those made by ten
times his force upon fort M'Henry, fort Bowyer, and fort
St. Phillip by immense British squadrons in the war of 1812
in America.

After having been baffled for a long time by adverse
winds, he reached the harbour of Tripoli in the last week
of July. The Bashaw affected to disguise the real apprehensions he felt by exclaiming to his courtiers—" They
will mark their distance for tacking—they are a sort of
Jews who have no notion of fighting." He had not yet

sufficiently studied the American character; and needed
a few more lessons from Preble, Decatur, &c. to enable
him thoroughly to comprehend it. He was soon to learn
that Americans upon the ocean were not like the children
of Israel, or the descendants of Ishmael.

Captain Decatur was selected by Commodore Preble to
command one division of the gun-boats, and Lieut. Somers
the other. The duty imposed upon them was of a nature
the most hazardous; as from the little water they drew,
they would come almost into contact with the Bashaw's
batteries and castle where the numerous gun-boats of the
Tripolitans were stationed. As this was one of the most
desperate engagements amongst the numerous ones in
which Americans were ever called to display their nautical skill and desperate courage, the reader will indulge
the writer in detailing it particularly as related to him by
one of the officers on board the Constitution, lying in full
view of the bloody scene.

The bombards, each carrying a mortar of thirteen inch-
es were commanded, one by Lieut. commandant Dent, and
the other by first Lieut. Robinson, of the Constitution.
The gun-boats were thus arranged, mounting each a brass
twenty-six pounder.

FIRST DIVISION.	SECOND DIVISION.
No. I. Lieut. Somers.	No. IV. Capt. Decatur.
No. II. Lieut. J. Decatur.	No. V. Lieut. Bainbridge.
No. III. Lieut. Blake.	No. VI. Lieut. Trippe.

The Constitution, Com. Preble's flag ship, the brigs and
the schooners were to be situated to cover them from the
fire of the batteries and the castle, and to silence if possible
the tremendous cannonade expected from more than two
hundred pieces of heavy ordnance mounted on them and
in the marine force of the enemy.

Although the squadron had been long in the Mediterranean, the unceasing vigilance and assiduity of Com. Preble,
and the rest of the officers and seamen, had kept it in the
most complete preparation for any service.

The bashaw was also prepared to receive them, and,
as he confidently expected, to repulse them. Com. Preble had not the most distant wish to enter the city with his
small force. He was determined, if possible, to destroy
the naval force, the batteries, and the castle of the enemy,
and conquer them into peace upon his chosen element.

Upon the 3d of August, the gales subsided, and the Commodore resolved to commence an attack. The disparity
of force between Preble and the Bashaw of Tripoli, was
much greater than that of Nelson and the King of Den-
mark at Copenhagen.

At half past ten o'clock, the bombards, from signals previously arranged, stood in for the town, followed by the
whole squadron, in the most gallant style.

More than two hundred of the Bashaw's guns were
brought to bear directly upon the American squadron.—
Included in this force of the enemy, were one heavy armed
brig—two schooners—two large gallies, and nineteen gun-
boats ; each of superior force to those commanded by Captain Decatur and Lieutenant Somers ; as they mounted
each a brass twenty-four pounder, in the bow, and two
smaller guns in the stern.

The number of men in each boat of the enemy, were
forty. In the six boats of Com. Preble's squadron, were
twenty-seven Americans, and thirteen Neapolitans each ;
but, as the latter, in close engagement, remained aghast—
in awe-struck astonishment, and declined boarding, they
were of but little service, but rather a detriment. They

huddled together, and, instead of aiding the Americans, were praying for their own *souls*, while they ought to have been destroying the *bodies* of the Turks.

Thus, at the commencement of the engagement between the rival gun-boats, the different forces stood—

American.	*Tripolitan.*
Gun-boats 6 guns 6	Gun boats 19 guns 57
Americans 162	Officers and seamen 760
Neapolitans 78	
Officers and seamen—240	

To "make assurance doubly sure," the enemy's gun-boats were stationed directly under cover of the Bashaw's batteries, and within gun-shot of them.   So perfectly confident were their commanders of a decisive victory, that the sails of every one of them had been removed, being determined to conquer or to sink.

Com. Preble had so arranged his squadron as to afford every possible aid to his two bombards, and his six gun-boats ; but his ulterior object was to pour his heaviest shot into the batteries, the castle, and the town—knowing that if he dismayed the boasting Bashaw in his den, his affrighted slaves would flee in promiscuous consternation.

The elevated roof of the palace,—the terraces of the houses, and every building capable of sustaining spectators were crowded to overflowing, to behold the triumph of Mahometans over Christians.

At a little before 3 o'clock, August 3d, the gallant Commodore made signal for general action.   The bombards led in ; and, with a precision and rapidity, perfectly astonishing, poured their shells into the city.

The immense force of the Bashaw immediately opened their whole batteries upon the squadron, from the land and

in the harbour. The Constitution, the Brigs, and Schooners, approached within musket shot of them, and answered
the fire of the enemy. Every soul was inspired by the fearless example of Com. Preble.

Captain Decatur, in the leading Gunboat of his division,
followed by Lieutenants Bainbridge, and Trippe, in Nos.
5, and 6, bore impetuously into the midst of the enemy's
windward division of nine Gunboats, consisting of the men
and guns before mentioned.

He had previously ordered his three boats to unship
their bowsprits ; as he and his dauntless comrades resolved to board the enemy. Lieutenant Somers and his division, were to follow and support Captain Decatur's ; but
his and Lieutenant Blake's boats had fallen so far to leeward that it was rendered impossible. Lieutenant James
B. Decatur, of No. II. however, brought his boat into his
intrepid brother's division, and entered into the engagement
nearly at the same time with him.

A contest more unequal and more desperate cannot be
imagined. As soon as the contending boats were brought
into contact with each other, the discharge of the cannon
and musketry, on board of them, almost entirely ceased,
and the more bloody and destructive struggle with swords,
sabres, espontoons, spears, scimetars, and other deadly
weapons succeeded.

Captain Decatur grappled an enemy's boat, full armed
and full manned—leaped on board of her—was followed
by only fifteen Americans, (little more than one third of
the Tripolitans in number,) and, in the space of ten minutes made her his prize.

At this moment the American Gunboats were brought
within range of the Bashaw's batteries which opened a tremendous though harmless cannonade upon them.

Com. Preble, perceiving the imminent danger, and the almost inevitable destruction of Captain Decatur's division of boats, immediately ordered the signal for retreat to be made.

Amongst the numerous signals on board the Commodore's ship, that for the retreat of the boats had been accidentally omitted. The dauntless Preble determining to support them, or perish with them, brought the Constitution, the Brigs, and the Schooners, to within three cables length of the batteries—completely silenced them by a few broadsides, and covered the retreat of the Gunboats with their prizes. Had he left them to their fate, their fate would have been inevitable.

But a duty, encircled with peril without a parallel—an achievement to be performed without an equal—a display of affection surpassing the tales of romance—and the sudden execution of vengeance upon transgression remained for Captain Decatur, before he left the blood-stained harbour of Tripoli.

His gallant brother, Lt. James B. Decatur, no less daring than himself, had captured a Tripolitan gun-boat ; and, after it was surrendered to him, its commander, with diabolical perfidiousness, combined with dastardly ferocity, shot him dead, just as he was stepping upon deck ! While the Americans were recovering the body of their commander, the Turks escaped with the prize boat.

As Captain Decatur was bearing his prize triumphantly out of the harbour, this heart rending catastrophe was communicated to him.

Instinctive vengeance, sudden as the electric shock, took possession of his naturally humane and pailanthropic soul. It was no time for pathetic lamentation.   The mandate of nature, and nature's God, cried aloud in his ear—*Avenge a brother's blood.*

With a celerity, almost supernatural, he changed his course—rushed within the enemy's whole line, with his single boat, with the gallant Macdonough and eight men only for his crew ! !

His previous desperate rencontres, scarcely paralleled, and never surpassed in any age or country, seem like safety itself when compared with what immediately followed.

Like an ancient knight, in the days of chivalry, he scorned, on any occasion like this, to tarnish his sword with the blood of vassals. His first object was to board the boat that contained the base and perfidious commander, whose hands still smoked with the blood of his murdered brother. This gained, he forced his way through a crew of Turks, quadruple the number of his own ; and, like an avenging messenger of the King of Terrors, singled out the guilty victim. The strong and powerful Turk, first assailed him with a long espontoon, heavily ironed at the thrusting end. In attempting to cut off the staff, Captain Decatur furiously struck the ironed part of the weapon, and broke his sword at the hilt. The Turk made a violent thrust, and wounded Decatur in his sword arm and right breast. He suddenly wrested the weapon from the hand of his gigantic antagonist ; and, as one " doubly arm'd who hath his quarrel just," he closed with him ; and, after a long, fierce, and doubtful struggle, prostrated him upon the deck.

During this struggle, one of Decatur's crew who had lost the use of both arms by severe wounds, beheld a Turk, with an immense sabre, aiming a fatal blow at his adored commander. He immediately threw his mutilated body between the falling sabre and his Captain's head—received a severe fracture in his own, and saved for his country, one of its most distinguished champions, to fight its future battles upon the ocean* While Decatur and the Turk were struggling for life in the very throat of death, the exasperated and infuriated crews rushed impetuously forward in defence of their respective captains. A scene terrific and horrible beyond description followed. The Turk drew a concealed dagger from its sheath, which Decatur seized at the moment it was pointed at his heart— drew his own pistol from his pocket, and instantly sent his furious foe,

" To his long account, unanointed, unanneal'd,
" With all his sins and imperfections on his head."

Thus ended a conflict, feebly described, but dreadful in . the extreme. Captain Decatur and all his men were severely wounded but four. The Turks lay killed and wounded in heaps around him. The boat was a floating Golgotha for the dead, and a bloody arena for the wounded and dying.

Captain Decatur bore his second prize out of the harbour, as he had the first, amidst a shower of ill-directed shot from the astonished and bewildered enemy ; and conducted them both to the squadron.

On board the two prizes, there were thirty-three officers and men killed ; more than double the number of

---

* This was an instance of affection which has but few parallels. To sacrifice property for a companion and a friend, is no uncommon occurrence. But, for a common seaman, to offer his life to save his commander, with whom, perhaps, he never spoke, shows a trait of character, equally admirable in the offered victim, and in him whose manly virtues attracted such romantic affection. The lamented Decatur afterwards distinguished this seaman with something more than mere notice—he gave him money.

Americans under Decatur at any one time in close engagement. Twenty-seven were made prisoners, nineteen of whom were desperately wounded—the whole a miserable off-set for the blood of Lieutenant Decatur, treacherously slain. The blood of all Tripoli could not atone for it, nor a perpetual pilgrimage to Mecca wash away the bloody stain.

The gallant and lamented Lieut. Somers, as he could not join Decatur, as ordered, with his single boat No. 1. attacked five full armed and full manned Tripolitan gunboats—committed dreadful slaughter amongst them, and drove them upon the rocks in a condition dreadfully shattered.

Lieut. Trippe, whose name will forever be associated with courage, as well as that of midshipman Henly, with only nine men besides themselves, rushed on board an enemy's gun-boat—slew fourteen, and made twenty-two prisoners, seven of whom were badly wounded. Lieut. Trippe received eleven sabre wounds. Lieut. Bainbridge, also distinguished himself for saving his disabled boat and gallant crew from almost certain destruction, and beating off the enemy.

The bombards, by the rapid and accurate directions of shells, spread as much consternation in the city as the squadron did in the harbour.

The skilful and fearless Com. Preble, in the frigate Constitution, keeping his ship in easy motion, was found wherever the greatest danger threatened ; and by frequently wearing and tacking, gave perpetual annoyance to the enemy, and afforded to the smaller vessels of his squadron, constant protection.

The enemy, driven to desperation, by the loss of their

boats, and by the numerous hosts of their comrades slain upon land, as well as those who fell under their immediate view, attempted to rally, and regain what they had lost. They were suddenly foiled by the brigs and schooners, who acted a no less gallant part in this desperate ocean-affray than did all the rest of this immortalized squadron. They attempted a second time ; and met with a second repulse. Finding that no naval power in the Mediterranean could withstand Com. Preble's squadron, they sought a covert under rocks, a natural, and under batteries and castles, artificial defences.

At a little before 5 o'clock, Com. Preble, with the whole squadron, and their prizes, and prisoners, moved majestically out of the harbour ; and left the Bashaw to examine and reflect upon the consequences of the third visit which the vessels of his squadron had made.

The reader who has past his early, advanced, and closing years of life in the tranquil scenes of retirement, can form but a faint idea of the sensations of the officers and seamen of Com. Preble's squadron when they met each other after this desperate and most unequal combat.

Every one would naturally inquire—" How many were killed and wounded in the frigate—how many in the different brigs, schooners, bombards and gun-boats." It was for Captain Decatur to make the answer. " Many are wounded, my comrades, but not one is slain, but my brother." He might have said—" If you have tears to shed, shed them now." Well might the tears of grief be mingled with the smiles of triumph, upon this saddening intelligence. " Death loves a shining mark," and when James B. Decatur fell, the American navy lost a brilliant ornament— Com. Preble a favourite officer, Capt. Decatur a brother, he loved as he did himself, and our Republic a most gal·lant and accomplished ocean warrior. But, like Nelson, he died in the arms of victory, and his death was most signally avenged.

As represented by an officer of the Constitution, when Captain Decatur, Lieutenant Trippe, Macdonough, Henly, and most of the officers and seamen belonging to the gun-boats, joined the squadron, they looked as if they had just escaped from the slaughter-house. Their truly noble blood was mingled with that of Mahometans, and the garb of those whose hearts or hands would never be stained with dishonour, were crimsoned with barbarous blood.

The injury sustained by Com. Preble's squadron sinks into nothing when the danger it was exposed to is considered. This was owing to the consummate nautical skill and coolness of the Commodore and his officers and seamen ; and to the stupid, sullen ignorance and consternation of the enemy.

To them the 3d of August was a day of dreadful retribution. A furious tornado not more suddenly drives the feathered race to their coverts, than did the first discharges from our squadron, the frenzied Turks, who came to witness its discomfiture.

From the representation of an intelligent officer, once of the Philadelphia, then a prisoner to the bashaw, it is learned that every one in the city fled who could flee. Even the troops in the batteries and castle dared not mount the parapet to discharge the cannon. The affrighted Bashaw, with a Mahometan priest concealed himself in his bomb-proof room ; and undoubtedly responded to the roar of christian cannon, by pitiful orisons to the Prophet of Mecca. They were as fruitless as the prayers of the Philistines to

Dagon or Ashdod.   His slaves who had no covert, buried themselves in sand to escape the bursting bombs.   Although it was a scene of blood and carnage, there is enough of the ludicrous in it to excite a smile in the American reader.   It clearly evinces that those who are most boastful and imperious, when possessed of real or supposed power, are the most mean, pusillanimous, and contemptible when convinced of their weakness.

I will here present the reader with the sentiments of a distinguished Turk in the language of an American officer, then a prisoner.   He asked the officer—" If those men that fought so were Americans, or infernals in Christian shape sent to destroy the sons of Mahomet the prophet ?   The English, French, and Spanish consuls have told us that they are a young nation, and got their independence by means of France.   That they had a small navy, and their officers were inexperienced ; and that they were merely a nation of merchants ; and that by taking their ships and men we should get great ransoms.—Instead of this, their Preble pays us a coin of shot, shells and hard blows ; and sent a Decatur in a dark night, with a band of christian dogs, fierce and cruel as the tiger, who killed our brothers and burnt our ships before our eyes."

By this first attack, the city of Tripoli suffered considerable damage.   Many of the guns were dismounted, and many Turks were slain.   But it was in the Bashaw's marine force, where the most destructive blow was struck. In the two prizes taken by Capt. Decatur, and the one by Lieut. Trippe, there were originally one hundred and twenty men.   Forty-seven were killed, twenty-six wounded, who, with the remainder, were taken prisoners. Three full manned boats were sunk with every soul on board ;

28

and almost every deck of the enemy's vessels within the range of American cannon were swept of their crews.

In consequence of the destruction of the Philadelphia frigate, the barbarism of Jussuff, the bloody Bashaw, was increased against Captain Bainbridge, and his officers and seamen in bondage. But Com. Preble and Capt. Decatur, aided by the magnanimous and patriotic exertions of Sir Alexander Ball, once a favourite officer with Nelson, and then at the island of Malta, found means to alleviate the dismal gloom of their bondage. A gallant naval commander, like Sir Alexander Ball, could not endure the thought that a gallant hero like Bainbridge and his valiant crew, should suffer indignity or abuse from such a sanguinary wretch as Jussuff and his slaves.

After the 3d of August, the humbled Bashaw began to relent. But his conviction was more the result of alarming fears, than of a consciousness of guilt.

The noble hearted Preble treated his wounded prisoners with the greatest humanity. Their wounds were dressed with the utmost care ; and, upon the 5th, he sent fourteen of them home to their friends.

In a generous bosom, although an enemy, such an act would have excited inexpressible admiration ; and although a species of revenge calculated to " heap coals of fire upon the head" of a subdued enemy, yet it should have melted a heart of adamant. The Bashaw knew that one of his officers had basely slain Lieut. Decatur, and could not comprehend the motives of *his* humanity. His savage subtilty augured evil, even from an act of pure benevolence. But when he heard the wounded and restored Tripolitans exclaim in the rapture of *enforced* gratitude, " the Americans in battle are fiercer than lions, and after victory, kinder than Mussulmen," his savage heart began to soften.   But, without a great ransom, he would not release a single prisoner who belonged to the Philadelphia frigate.

From the 3d to the 7th of August, Com. Preble, and the rest of the officers and seaman had but little time for repose after their arduous toils in reaching the harbour of Tripoli, and administering to the Bashaw a portion of American vengeance.   They were all incessantly engaged in preparing for another visit.   They had become perfectly familiar with the theatre of action on which the American squadron was now acting its various parts.   Every scene was drawing towards the developement of the tragedy.   The imperious tone of the Bashaw was lowered as his hopes of safety diminished.   He however would surrender no prisoners without a ransom beyond what Com. Preble thought himself authorised by his government to offer.   He rather preferred to have consul Lear negotiate upon land ; and he felt confident of his powers to negotiate with his invincible squadron.

All the officers of every grade, and every seaman, exerted every nerve to aid Com. Preble.   They stood around him like affectionate and obedient children around a beloved and dignified parent, anxious to learn his precepts, and prompt to obey his commands.   He stood in the midst of them in the double capacity of their father, and a representative of his and their country.   He knew they would follow wherever he would lead, and would lead where necessary prudence would prevent him from following.— Well might the astonished Turks compare them to lions ; for they had proved themselves irresistible in battle—generous and noble in victory.

Com. Preble could bestow nothing upon his officers and

seaman, but his highest and most unqualified commendation. This was not the mere effusion of an admiring commander, surrounded by his victorious comrades around
the festive board, after a signal victory, but it was official-
ly announced to the whole squarron in a " general order"
upon the 4th. The Commodore knew well where to bestow applause, and when to make, or rather to recommend
promotion. His general order is in the Navy Department.

Amidst the congratulations in the squadron for the successful issue of the first attack upon Tripoli, a silent gloom
irresistibly pervaded the hearts of the officers and seamen.
It was not caused by contemplating upon the arduous and
yet uncertain contest which they were directly to renew.
Inured to duty and familiar with victory, they were total
strangers to fear. But Lieutenant JAMES B. DECATUR
" was dead !" While they were floating triumphantly upon the waves of the Mediterranean, his body was reposing
in death upon its bed ; and his gallant spirit had flown to
heaven. The shouts of joy over all Britain for the victory
of Trafalgar, were mingled with groans of grief for the
death of Nelson. No less pungent was the sorrow of intrepid Americans at the fall of Lieutenant Decatur.

He had unremittingly pursued the duty of the naval profession from the time he entered the navy, until the day
he was basely and treacherously slain. It is inconsistent
with the design of this sketch, to go into a minute detail of
his life. Suffice it then to say, that by a long course of
assiduous duty in various ships of the American navy, and
under different commanders, he secured to himself the confidence of his superiors, and the approbation of his government. The post assigned him upon the 3d of August,

evinced the high estimation in which he was holden by the discerning and penetrating Com. Preble. The manner in which he discharged the duty imposed upon him, and the manner in which he fell, have already been mentioned. His memory is embalmed with those of Somers, Wadsworth, and Israel, who followed him into eternity thirty days after he left the world, and who made their exit from the same sanguinary theatre upon which he fell.

The fearful, yet temporising Bashaw, through the medium of a foreign consul, offered terms to Com. Preble which he indignantly rejected, as degrading to his government.

Upon the 7th, another attack was resolved upon ; and the squadron arranged in order to execute it. The effect desired was produced. A heavy battery was silenced— many bomb shells and round shot were thrown into the town—and, although the damage to the enemy was not so essential as the attack of the 3d, it increased the dismay of the Bashaw.

Amongst the Gun-boats engaged in this second attack, was one taken from the enemy by Capt. Decatur. She was blown up by a hot ball sent from the batteries ; and Lieutenant Caldwell, Midshipmen Dorsey, and eight seamen were killed ; six were wounded ; and Midshipman Spence with eleven seamen were rescued unhurt from the waves.

Two days afterwards, Com. Preble took a deliberate view of the harbour in one of the Brigs, in order to determine the best mode of commencing a third attack. He gave " no sleep to the eyes nor slumber to the eyelids" of the sullen and incorrigible wretch who wielded the sceptre of blood-begotten power over his subjects, the wretched and degraded race of beings who were dragging out a miserable existence in Tripoli. The hopes of the American prisoners increased, as those of the Bashaw and his troops diminished.

The terms for ransom were lowered more than two thirds, from the original enormous sum; but Com. Preble had become a stern negotiator; and Mr. Lear chose to let him continue to display his diplomatic skill, upon his chosen element.

The prospect of a long protracted warfare, at an immense expense to the American government—the tedious and gloomy imprisonment of nearly half a thousand of Americans, in the dungeons of a barbarian, amongst whom were some of the noblest hearts that ever beat in human bosoms—the probability that more American blood must be shed in effecting a complete subjugation of the yet unyielding Bashaw, induced Commodore Preble to offer the sum of eighty thousand dollars, as ransom for the prisoners, and ten thousand dollars as presents, provided he would enter into a solemn and perpetual treaty with the American government, never to demand an annual tribute as the price of peace.

The infatuated and infuriated Bashaw rejected these proposals with affected disdain mingled with real fear. Com. Preble, had nothing now to do but to renew his naval operations.

To repel the idea that the pacific offer of the Commodore arose from apprehensions of defeat, the bombards occasionally disgorged their destructive contents into the city, to the dire consternation of the bashaw and his slaves.

Upon the 27th of August, another general attack was made with such effect as to induce the Bashaw to renew negotiations for peace, but nothing definitive was effected ; and Com. Preble took every advantage of his horrid fears. Upon the 3d of September, another attack was made to the very great injury of the Bashaw's batteries, castle and city ; the particulars of which would too much swell this sketch.

Although but few Americans had lost their lives in the various battles, yet the vessels of the squadron had suffered very considerable injury from incessant service.

It was proposed that the ketch Intrepid should be converted into a fire ship, and sent into the midst of the enemy's galleys and gunboats to complete their destruction. To this the Commodore acceded—loaded her with one hundred barrels of powder, and one hundred and fifty shells ; and fixed upon the night of the memorable 4th of September for the daring and hazardous attempt.

Capt. Somers volunteered his services and was designated as the commander. He was immediately joined by Lieutenants Wadsworth and Israel, and a sufficient number of gallant seamen.

Of the awfully tremendous scene that followed, the reader may be gratified by a succinct account, as related by an accomplished eye-witness, to the writer; but any description by the pen or the pencil is tame and dull, compared with the animated narration of Capt. ———.

The evening was unusally calm ; and the sea scarcely presented the smallest wave to the eye. That part of the squadron which was not designated as a convoy to the Intrepid, lay in the outer harbour. Two swift-sailing boats were attached to the Intrepid, and the Argus, Vixen, and Nautilus, were to conduct them to their destination, and receive the crew after the match was applied to the fatal train.

At a little before 9 o'clock the Intrepid, followed by the convoy, moved slowly and silently into the inner harbour, watched with the deepest solicitude by the Argus, &c.— Two of the enemy's heavy galleys, with more than a hundred men each, encountered the fire-ship, unconscious that she was pregnant with concealed magazines of death. They captured her of course, as the little crew could not withstand such an overwhelming force for a moment.

It being the first prize the Tripolitans had made, the exulting captors were about bearing her and the prisoners triumphantly into port. The crew were to be immured in the same dungeon with Capt. Bainbridge and his crew, who had worn away eleven tedious months in dismal slavery.

To Somers, Wadsworth and Israel,

"*One hour* of virtuous *liberty*, was worth
"A *whole eternity* of *bondage.*"

and, instant death, far preferable to Turkish captivity. It is still left to conjecture, and must always be so left, by whom their instantaneous release from slavery and from mortality was occasioned.

It is with an agitated heart and a trembling hand that it is recorded, that the Intrepid suddenly exploded, and a few gallant Americans, with countless numbers of barbarians, met with one common and undistinguished destruction.

It is generally understood by American readers that Capt. Somers, his officers and crew, after being captured, mutually agreed to make voluntary sacrifices of themselves to avoid slavery and to destroy the enemy. In support of this, the writer is authorised to state that Capt. Somers directly before entering into this enterprise, declared that " he would never be captured by the enemy or go into Turkish bondage."

It is entirely beyond the reach of the most fertile imagination to form an adequate conception of the reality of this awful scene. The silence that preceded the approach of the Intrepid, was followed by the discharge of cannon and musketry, and ended by the fearful and alarming shock of the explosion. Every living Christian and Mahometan within view or hearing, stood aghast and awe-struck.

Thus barbarous Turks and gallant Americans met with one common destiny, and all was an outspread scene of desolation. The remaining part of the night was as silent as the season that immediately succeeds some violent convulsion of nature.

Com. Preble, who had the preceding day enjoyed an animated interview with this *trio* of heroes, found an awful chasm made in the catalogue of his associates.

If the biographical writer could be allowed to blend his own " reflections and remarks" with the incidents and events he records, this momentous occurrence might justify them. It will, however, only be observed, that Captain Somers's memory has sometimes been assailed by those whose contracted and scrupulous system of morals evinces a " zeal without knowledge."

Admitting that he made a voluntary sacrifice of himself, his officers and his crew, to avenge the injuries of his country, and rescue his numerous countrymen, in his full view, from bondage ; let the severest casuist that ever perverted the plain dictates of conscience, by metaphysical subtlety, be asked if every man who enters the navy or army of his country does not voluntarily expose himself to death in de-

29

fending its rights, its honour, and its independeuce? No matter in what manner death is occasioned, so be it the sacrifice adds to the security and advances the glory of his country. Whether it happens in the midst of opposing hosts, in single combat, or as that of Somers and his comrades did by voluntary sacrifice, it equally redounds to their glory and their country's weal. To those who form their systems exclusively from the records of inspiration, examples from them might be quoted; and the instance of Sampson alone, who fell with a host of his enemies, will not, by them, be denied as being analogous. The classical reader will immediately recollect that Rome herself was twice saved from destruction by the voluntary sacrifice of the Decii.

The writer hopes to be indulged in a brief allusion to the gallant, the accomplished, the lamented Lieutenant WADS-WORTH, with whom he had the honour, and enjoyed the pleasure, of some acquaintance. His birth-place and residence was in Portland, the metropolis of the state of Maine, and in the immediate neighbourhood of the great PREBLE. To a very elegant person, he added the captivating charms of a mind highly refined. His situation placed within his reach all the fascinating enjoyments of fashionable life; but a participation in them could not render him effeminate. The previous examples of Stephen and James B. Decatur inspired his ardent bosom with a thirst for naval glory, and this was enhanced by the renown acquired by his distinguished townsman, and *naval* father, Com. Preble. He repaired to the renowned sea, whose waves are bounded by three of the great quarters of the globe, and almost in the sight of which the American squadron was triumphantly wafting. He did not *envy*, for envy found no place in his noble heart; but he wished to *emulate* the gallant deeds of his brother officers. The disastrous, yet splendid affair of the 4th of September, has been briefly detailed. Wadsworth upon that fatal, awful night, left the world in a blaze of glory—gave his mangled corse to the waves—his exalted spirit to heaven—and his immortal fame to his country. Although his precious manes are "far away o'er the billow," his virtues and gallantry are commemorated by a monument in his native town, the voluntary tribute of his admiring friends to his inestimable worth.

While the American squadron was achieving such unparalleled deeds in the Mediterranean, the American government yet unadvised of its splendid success, despatched an additional squadron to that sea. From the state of the naval register, and the rank of the post-captains, the new squadron could not be supplied with officers without designating one who was senior to Com. Preble. This devolved upon Com. James Barron, who arrived upon the 9th of September, 1804.

To an aspiring hero just entering the path of fame, and anxious to reach its temple, a sudden check to his progress is like the stroke of death. It was not so with Com. Preble when he was superseded by Com. Barron. His work was "done, and well done;" and he surrendered the squadron to his senior as, Gen. Jackson did his army to Gen. Pinckney, when there was nothing to do but to enjoy the fruits of victory.

He immediately gave the command of his favourite frigate, the Constitution, to his favourite officer, Captain Decatur, and obtained leave to return to America.

It has been barely mentioned that the government of the Republic were unadvised of the splendid achievements of

Com. Preble, when the additional force was sent out from America to Tripoli. The slightest recurrence to dates will place this subject beyond all doubt.

Nothing but the intervention of contrary winds for a long period, had spared the boasting Bashaw of Tripoli, from the accumulated stores of vengeance, and the red artillery of Preble's squadron, which were in reserve for the chastisement, the consternation, and all but the annihilation of this diabolical representative of the Sultan of Turkey, and the vicegerent of Mahomet on earth.

The first general attack upon the strong city of Tripoli, was made upon the third of August, when the terrible battle of the gun-boats took place. Upon the 7th another general attack was made ; and for a number of days in succession, the alarmed and affrighted Bashaw was coiled up like a venomous reptile in his bomb-proof castle,—gnashing his teeth like a " serpent biting a file," and, like the enraged lion in a cage, lacerating himself by his own tail, he was torturing his own horrid and blood-guilty soul, by the agonizing contortions of his blood-stained body.

He occasionally

———" grinn'd horribly a ghastly smile,"

at half a thousand Americans incarcerated in his dungeons near at hand. Amongst them, he recognized the exalted spirits of Bainbridge, Porter, Jones, Biddle, and about four hundred other noble American ocean-champions whose bodies only were held in " durance vile" by a detested power which they could not then resist, or escape, but which they despised with ineffable contempt.

Upon the 4th of September, as the reader will recollect, the truly awful explosion of the fire-ship " Intrepid" convinced the astonished Bashaw, that his whole marine was to be destroyed, unless he hastened to make peace with the veteran Com. Preble, and Preble's indignant government, whose energy he had so sorely felt.

During the whole of the memorable month of August, 1804, Com. Barron and his vessels were as peaceably wafting over the Atlantic, and the Mediterranean as American ships are now, 1823. As mentioned, his vessels appeared before Tripoli upon Sept. 9th, when the echo of Com. Preble's cannon had scarcely ceased ; and when the commotion of the waves from the explosion of Capt. Somers' fire-ship, had hardly subsided.

He had the good fortune to enjoy the fruits of the conquest, without hazarding any " hair breadth 'scapes" or attempting any " imminent deadly breach." The Bashaw's immense batteries were silenced—negotiations were just commencing, and Com. Barron, without any opportunity to show his skill and prowess, had nothing to perform but the manœuvrings of his squadron—standing off and on—and blockading Tripoli, which Capt. Bainbridge* in the Philadelphia, and Lieut. Smith† in the little Vixen had done before him. His duty, compared with what Com. Preble had performed, was as different as a regimental review in time of peace is from a sanguinary battle in field fight.

The admiring comrades of Com. Preble were now to perform a duty more affecting to the hearts of noble and high-minded men, than danger, battles, bondage, wounds, and death itself—it was to bid adieu to their beloved, venerated, and almost adored commander, EDWARD PREBLE.

The parting scene, as described by one who painfully witnessed, and who was sensibly penetrated with it, was one of the most interesting that the mind can conceive.

* Now Com. Bainbridge.   † Now Capt. Smith.

For more than a year, the Commodore, and his gallant comrades, had been absent from their friends and their country—a *year* that may well be denominated an *age* in the callendar of American Naval skill, prowess and glory —a period of splendid and " successful experiment" with our ships, and of naval instruction and experience to our officers and seamen.

Their mutual attachment had become strongly cemented by common toils and privations—common dangers and disasters, and by fighting the common enemy of the civilized world, and forcing Mahometans to crave mercy of the same Christians, whom, a few months before, they affected to despise.

The war-worn and veteran Preble, gave the parting hand to his officers, as the father would extend the hand of parental affection to his children, who were about to depart into a world beyond his immediate care, but never out of his remembrance and solicitude.

His officers manifested a dignified regret, mingled with a consciousness of untarnished honour, rectitude of conduct, and unsurpassed courage.

His noble tars, who always sought the post of duty and of danger, and whose natural heroism was augmented by the fearless example of their noble commander, gazed at a respectful distance upon their Patron, their Friend, and their Commodore. With swelling, but with manly grief, they cast their moistened eyes upon the last visible piece of canvas that wafted their once beloved commander in chief from their anxious view.

Although all were affected, none could be more so than Charles Morris* his midshipman and his faithful secretary

* Now the highly respected and accomplished Capt. Morris, commissioner of the navy.

on board the Constitution. This gallant son of Connecticut was born in the vicinity of the writer of this imperfect sketch of his matchless commander's life.

It is a sentiment entirely paramount to local attachment, which excites his esteem and respect for this excellent man and excellent officer. His father was an officer in the naval warfare with France in the administration of Adams. His son Charles, as soon as requisite years and suitable acquirements rendered him fit for the station of a Midshipman, repaired to the Mediterranean, the American Naval School.

The correct discernment of Com. Preble selected him as his confidant and his secretary. He was one of the four who landed at Tangier with him, amidst Moorish hosts, and accompanied him to his interview with the emperor of Morocco, previously described. He sailed with him to Tripoli. He was one of the first who volunteered, with Lawrence and Macdonough, under that unequalled, that universally lamented hero, Decatur, for the destruction of the Philadelphia frigate. He was the first who gained the deck of that ill-fated ship, after his dauntless leader reached it. He was in the Constitution in all her attacks upon Tripoli.

In the war of 1812 with Britain, he was first Lieutenant of the same wonder-working ship, in the first wonderful escape from a British squadron. He was in the same capacity when the same ship sent the Gurriere to the bottom.

Morris was the favourite of the gallant Hull, the favourite of Connecticut and his country. In the action with the Gurriere, as a native poet elegantly says,

"Where virtue, skill and bravery,
With gallant Morris fell ;—

That heart so well in battle tried
Along the Moorish shore."

He long languished, but survived to advance still farther
in the dangerous path to fame.

He became commander of the frigate Adams—entered
Penobscot bay, (where his patron, Com. Preble signalized
himself in the war of the Revolution,) ascended the Penobscot river, defended his ship against an immense force, until, to use his own language, " he had no alternative but
precipitate retreat or captivity." He destroyed his own
ship, and, with his noble crew, wandered over the wilds of
Maine, in a state of destitution, to Portland, once the home
of the then sleeping Preble, whose tomb he bedewed with
manly tears.* Morris still lives ; and lives the ornament of

---

* Although this volume professedly relates to the Naval Heroes of
the Revolution, yet, as Com. Preble's young officers in the Mediterranean acted such signal parts in the second War with Britain, and
as Capt. Morris, after he left the Constitution and took the command
of the Adams, had not the good fortune again to meet the enemy in
equal contest, I give the following extract from his official letter,
shewing his conduct in the hour of disaster. Although overwhelmed,
he did not " give up the Ship" to the enemy.—

Boston, September 20, 1814.

Sir---I have the honour to forward a detailed report of the circumstances attending the destruction of the United States' ship Adams, at
Hampden, on the 3d instant.

On the first instant, at noon, I received intelligence by express
that the enemy with a force of sixteen sail were off the harbour of Castine, 30 miles below us. This intelligence was immediately forward-
ed to brigadier general Blake, with a request, that he would direct
such force as could be collected to repair immediately to Hampden.
As our ship, prepared for heaving down, was in no situation to receive
her armament, our attention was immediately directed to the occupa-
tion of such positions on shore as would best enable us to protect her.
By great and unremitted exertions, and the prompt assistance of all
the inhabitants in our immediate vicinity, during the 1st and 2d inst.

of the navy, the delight of his friends, and the pride of his
country.   This brief digression will be excused in the wri-

nine pieces were transported to a commanding eminence near the ship,
one to the place selected by general Blake for his line of battle, fourteen upon a wharf commanding the river below, and one on a point
covering the communication between our hill and wharf batteries;
temporary platforms of loose plank were laid, and such other arrangements made as would enable us to dispute the passage of a naval force.
Want of time prevented our improving all the advantages of our position, and we were compelled to leave our rear and flanks to the defence of the militia in case of attack by land troops.   Favoured by a
fresh breeze, the enemy had advanced to within 3 miles of our position at sunset on the 2d with the Sylph mounting 22, and Peruvian 18
guns, and one transport, one tender and ten barges manned with seamen from the Bulwark and Dragon, under command of Com. Barrie.
Troops were landed under command of Col. John, opposite their shipping without opposition, their number unknown, but supposed to be
about 350.   To oppose these troops, about 370 militia were then collected, assisted by lieut. Lewis of the U. S. artillery, who by a forced
march had arrived from Castine with his detachment of 28 men.   Many of the militia were without arms, and most of them without any ammunition, and as our numbers were barely sufficient to man our batteries, I ordered the ship's muskets to be distributed among the militia, and further ordered them to be supplied with ammunition.   Our
sick were sent across a creek with orders for such as were able, to
secure themselves in the woods in case of our defeat.   These arrangements were not concluded until late on the evening of the 2d.   As
the wind was fair for the enemy's approach, and the night dark, rainy,
and favourable for his attempting a surprize, our men were compelled,
notwithstanding previous fatigue, to remain at their batteries.

At day-light on the 3d, I received intelligence from general Blake,
that he had been reinforced by three companies, and that the enemy
were then advancing upon him.   A thick fog concealed their early
movements, and their advance of barges and rocket boats was not discovered until about seven o'clock.   Believing from their movements
that they intended a simultaneous attack by land and water, I placed
the hill battery under the direction of my first lieutenant, Wadsworth,
assisted by lieutenant Madison and Mr. Rogers, the purser, and di-

ter,—it is a feeble tribute of respect to a juvenile acquaintance.

rected lieutenant Watson to place his small detachment of 20 marines in a position to watch the movements of the enemy's main body, assist in covering our flank, and finally to cover our retreat in case that became necessary. I had but just joined the wharf battery under the direction of lieutenants Parker and Beatty, and sailing-master M'Culloch, when the enemy's infantry commenced their attack upon the militia. The launches still held their position beyond the reach of our fire, ready to improve any advantage their troops might obtain. A few minutes only had elapsed when lieutenant Wadsworth informed me that our troops were retreating, and immediately after that they were dispersed and flying in great confusion. We had now no alternative but precipitate retreat or captivity. Our rear and flanks entirely exposed, without other means of defence on that side than our pikes and cutlasses. The only bridge across the creek above us nearer the enemy than ourselves, and the creek only fordable at low water, with the tide then rising, I therefore ordered lieutenant Wadsworth to spike his guns, and retire across the bridge, which was done in perfect order, the marines under lieutenant Watson covering their rear. Orders were given at the same time to fire the ship, spike the guns of the lower battery and join our companions across the creek. Before these orders were fully executed, the enemy appeared on the hill from which our men just retired and were exposed to their fire for a short time while completing them. Retreating in front of them for about five hundred yards, we discovered it impossible to gain the bridge, forded the creek, ascended the opposite bank, and gained our companions without receiving the slightest injury from the ill-directed fire of the enemy. We continued our retreat towards Bangor, when we found and retired upon a road leading to the Kennebec, by a circuitous route of 65 miles. Perceiving it impossible to subsist our men in a body through a country almost destitute of inhabitants, they were ordered to repair to Portland as speedily as they might be able. The entire loss of all personal effects rendered us dependant on the generosity of the inhabitants between the Penobscot and Kennebec for subsistence---who most cheerfully and liberally supplied our wants to the utmost extent of their limited means. Our warmest thanks are also due to the inhabitants of Waterville, Augusta and Hallowell, for their

At the time Com. Preble left the Mediterranean,—that
sea, its islands, and the nations bordering upon it, had be-

liberality and attention. Our loss was but one marine and one seaman made prisoners. That of the enemy was estimated at eight or
ten killed and from forty to fifty wounded, principally by the 18 pounder under charge of lieutenant Lewis of the U. S. Artillery.

As the Constitution was the favorite ship of Com. Preble in the Mediterranean—as Hull and Morris were his favourites in that sea—as
they, in the same ship, achieved the first victory in the Atlantic,
against Britain, the following, amongst the first, and certainly amongst
the best Odes and Songs, during the second war with Britain, is offered to the reader in this place. There is nothing in the author's
" Hubert and Ellen," superior to it.

> Britannia's gallant streamers
> Float proudly o'er the tide ;
> And fairly wave Columbia's stripes,
> In battle, side by side.
> And ne'er did bolder foemen meet,
> Where ocean's surges pour.
> O'er the tide now they ride,
> While the bellowing thunders roar.
> While the cannon's fire is flashing fast,
> And the bellowing thunders roar,
>
> When Yankee meets the Briton,
> Whose blood congenial flows,
> By Heaven created to be friends,
> By fortune rendered foes ;
> Hard then must be the battle fray,
> Ere well the fight is o'er ;
> Now they ride, side by side,
> While the bellowing thunders roar,
> While the cannon's fire is flashing fast.
> And the bellowing thunders roar.
>
> Still, still for noble England,
> Bold DACRES' streamers fly ;
> And, for Columbia, gallant HULL's,
> As proudly and as high ;

come the expanded theatre of his glory.　The " Two Si-
cilies," with their two volcanic mountains, Ætna and Ve-

Now louder rings the battle din,
More thick the volumes pour,
Still they ride, side by side,
While the bellowing thunders roar,
While the cannon's fire is flashing fast,
And the bellowing thunders roar.

Why lulls Brittania's thunder,
That waked the watery war?
Why stays the gallant Gurriere,
Whose streamer waved so fair?
That streamer drinks the ocean wave?
That warrior's fight is o'er!
Still they ride, side by side,
While Columbia's thunders roar,
While her cannon's fire is flashing fast,
And her Yankee thunders roar.

Of BUSH, the gallant spirit,
Starts from the reddening wave;
' For the deck it was' his ' field of fame,'
' And ocean' is his ' grave.'
The waters high their bosoms heave,
For valour now no more;
That in the clouds, glory shrouds,
While contending thunders roar,
And Victory bears from Earth to Heaven.
As the rolling thunders roar.

Hark!　'tis the Briton's lee gun!
Ne'er bolder warrior kneel'd!
And ne'er to gallant mariners
Did braver seamen yield.
Proud be the sires, whose hardy boys
Then fell, to fight no more;
With the brave, mid the wave,
When the cannon's thunders roar,
Their spirits then shall trim the blast,
And swell the thunder's roar.

suvius, which disgorge their adamantine contents, in the midst of columns of fire, and spread desolation around their bases, witnessed the approach of this Christian hero, with a dauntless band of warriors from a distant Christian land. Malta, (the ancient Melita,) where Paul, once the pupil of Gamaliel, and afterwards the apostle of the Gentiles, preached the gospel, and where the renowned Knights of Malta, long enjoyed and practised their mysterious rites —Italy, once the dominion of imperial Rome, which once conquered the world by arms, and then conquered herself by luxury—Corsica, the birth place, and Elba the prison of Napoleon, the modern Charlemagne—Sardinia, Genoa, indeed every country and island in that portion of the globe, which did not acknowledge the supremacy of the Sultan—and even the Pope of Rome, with all his rancour-

> Vain were the cheers of Britons,
> Their hearts did vainly swell,
> Where virtue, skill, and bravery,
> With gallant MORRIS fell.
> That heart, so well in battle tried,
> Along the Moorish shore,
> Again, o'er the main,
> When Columbia's thunders roar,
> Shall prove its Yankee spirit true,
> When Columbia's thunders roar.
>
> Hence be our floating bulwarks,
> Those oaks our mountains yield ;
> 'Tis mighty Heaven's plain decree—
> Then take the watery field !
> To ocean's farthest barrier then,
> Your whitening sails shall pour ;
> Safe they'll ride o'er the tide,
> While Columbia's thunders roar,
> While her cannon's fire is flashing fast.
> And her Yankee thunders roar.

ous bitterness against Protestants, all, all joined their notes
of praise, in one harmonious concord of applause and admiration, for the peerless Hero, from the Republic of the
Western World.

The Pope, the supreme head of the Roman Catholic
regime, forcibly declared that—" All Christendom had not
effected in centuries, what the American Squadron had
accomplished in the space of a single year !"

Even British naval officers, whose tutelary deity upon
the ocean, (Lord Nelson,) declared that " In the germe of
the American Navy, he saw the future rival of Britain upon
the ocean"—suspended, for awhile, their deep-rooted jealousy, and poured forth the effusions of involuntary admiration for Preble.

Grateful as such applause undoubtedly was to such an
aspiring mind as his, no approbation came so " home to
his business and bosom" as the unqualified demonstration
of attachment from his own Comrades—his own Government, and his own Family.

Such approbation from such sources, must have filled
his capacious heart to repletion.   The value of praise is
doubly enhanced, when it proceeds from those whose exalted merit deserves the praise they bestow.   Like " the
quality of mercy"

> " It is twice blessed—it blesseth him,
> " Who gives, and who receives."

The Congress of the United States, the only *legitimate*
government in existence, presiding over the only Republic upon earth, deeply penetrated with the exalted worth,
and vast services of " The Commander in Chief of the
American Squadron in the Mediterranean in 1803 and
1804," bestowed upon Edward Preble, a Vote of Thanks

—a reward more grateful to the feelings of that noble officer, considering the moving cause of it, than would have
been an estate equal to the dukedom bestowed upon Arthur
Wellesley, by the Parliament of Britain.

As a visible token of the regard of that august body, the
Congress voted a splendid gold medal, with devices em-
blematical of his achievements.

This was presented by the same hand that drafted that
unequalled state paper " The Declaration of American
Independence"—by the same statesman who selected Preble, as Commander—then President of the American Republic, now the Philosopher of Monticello—THOMAS JEF-
FERSON. This portable monument of his fame is now, with
the other archives of this ocean-hero, in the hands of his
posterity—an invaluable legacy—a treasure of fame !

His family and his countrymen, when he was " far away
over the billow," cast their anxious thoughts to the sanguinary arena in which he and his comrades were contending
with the thickening hosts of Mahometans.

When the Turkish Crescent bowed to the " Star-spangled banner" of the Republic, and he returned with his
rich harvest of honours, the elder portion of Americans remembered the gallant Lieutenant Preble, in the war of the
Revolution, when in the Protector he assisted in capturing
the Admiral Duff, and *led* in capturing a heavy ship of war
in Penobscot bay, when he sailed in the Winthrop.

The younger Americans, with the writer, enthusiastically recognized in him the redeeming spirit who rescued our
countrymen from Mahometan bondage ; and compelled a
strong power, under the Grand Sultan, to submit to American prowess.

He might well have wished, at this time to retire into the

bosom of his family, at his delightful residence in the capital of Maine ; but he had become identified with the American navy, and its future respectability depended essentially upon the application of the skill and experience of the
Commodore to its future operations.

Although considerable experience, as well as many
splendid victories were gained in the naval warfare with
the French Republic, a few years previous, and many
and much of each under his command in the Mediterranean, yet the complicated system, requisite in the Navy
Department, was by no means thoroughly digested.

The admirable police, which is now systematized on
board 74s, 44s, 36s, sloops of war, brigs, and schooners,
was then in an incipient state—it has ever since been pro-
gressive, and it may now almost be said, that it is perfected.

Com. Preble had, at the seat of government, the collected wisdom of naval officers, and the heads of the different
departments, to aid him in putting the " American Naval
System" into operation.

If it required the wisdom and penetration of OLIVER
ELLSWORTH* to arrange and digest the *Judiciary System*---
if it required the stupendous mind of ALEXANDER HAMIL-
TON, from a chaotic mass, to perfect a *System of Finance*---
it also required the scientific and practical knowledge of
EDWARD PREBLE to arrange a *Naval System*, for the marine
force of the Republic.

* The profound discernment of President WASHINGTON, and the
FIRST CONGRESS under the Constitution, selected this exalted man
and great jurist, to digest the Judiciary System of our vast Republic,
consisting then of thirteen, and now of twenty-four distinct governments. It was a subject full of importance, and abounding in difficulty. To give sufficient energy to a *Federal* court, and yet to secure

His time at the seat of government was not wasted by enjoying the fashionable blandishments of the metropolis, in the " piping time of peace ;" and although he had recently returned from ' attempting the imminent deadly breach,' he was in no danger of being effeminated by "listening to the soft lulling of the lute." He was not one of those courtly retainers who make an accessary of the languishing genius of evanescent amusement, in the murder of time, the most bounteous gift of heaven. With Preble, as with Franklin, ' time was money ;' yea it was more than money —' money is trash,' in comparison to the invaluable results of patient study, sound reflection, and matured wisdom.

The American people employ their civil Rulers, as well as their Naval officers, to act, and to act efficiently. The aggregated wisdom of the Republic is not annually concentrated at the seat of government to convert and pervert the season of legislation into an endless succession of ' holidays,' excursions of pleasure, or intrigues for office.*

the rights of indiviual *State Courts*, was a vast undertaking ; and was accomplished by the vastness of this great man's mind. Oliver Ellsworth succeeded Chief Justice JAY when *he* was appointed ambassador to the Court of St. James; and continued Chief Justice himself until *he* was appointed ambassador to the Court of St. Cloud.

* The following is an extract from a very recent publication ; and is inserted in a note to excuse the presumption of the text.

" Is it for this that the people of the nation send representatives to Washington, and pay each of them $56 a week ? Is it to spend their nights in revelry, and their days in slumber, that they have been sent there ? Is it to enable the higher officers of the government " to feed and plaister," to corrupt and prostitute their representatives, that they have suffered the late great increase of their salaries to pass almost unnoticed ? If this apathy is continued, they will only merit the political degradation and perdition which infallibly awaits them."

The assiduity of the Secretary of the Navy, the Navy Commissioners, and Naval Officers, is a shining light that points out the path of duty to every officer in every station, in every department of the government.

Com. Preble remained at the seat of government until peace was negotiated by Mr. LEAR, which *he* had conquered with the American squadron. Com. Barron returned with the constellation of ocean-warriors who subjugated Tripoli when under PREBLE. Gen. Eaton, with Hamet Caramalli, ex-Bashaw, whom he found an exile in Egypt—whose dying hopes he revived, and whose motley multitude called an army, he conducted through desarts to within a few leagues of Tripoli, also returned to America, to reap the reward of his well-meant. romantic, and daring *endeavours*,* and also to induce the government to *pay* the disheartened Caramalli for the loss of his throne, and the disappointment of his wishes. It is believed that this is the first and only instance of a Mahometan prince begging money of a Christian power—they have, for centuries, obtained it by blood and plunder.

Com. Preble, cool, collected, dignified, and gratified, lived to behold the consummation of the first wishes of his heart---the subjugation of the Barbary powers, and the restoration of the noble Bainbridge,† his gallant officers, and fearless crew, and the rest of the Americans, from dismal bondage, to the fruition of freedom.

He cared little for the scramble for office, promotion, or money. He saw the happy result of his toils for his coun-

* Gen. Eaton, in his letter of Dec. 5, 1805, to the Secretary of the Navy, says—" Mr. O'Bannon and myself united in a *resolution* to pe-

† Amongst the returning heroes, who received the congratulation of Com. PREBLE—the delivered heroes, BAINBRIDGE, JONES, PORTER,

try. He saw his gallant comrades in the Mediterranean, once more in the bosom of the Republic, enjoying the peace they had obtained by valour---the blessings they had rendered secure by their victories, and the applause they so richly deserved for their unparalleled services.

He retired from public life, like WASHINGTON, the father of his country—like ADAMS, the father of the American navy---and like JEFFERSON, his patron and friend, and the patron of the Republic, to enjoy the sweets of retirement in the bosom of his family, in his native town, where every temporal blessing awaited his return.

There, with a consciousness of having faithfully served his country in that tremendous contest, " The War of the Revolution," against Britain, in a subordinate station— having assisted in chastising Frenchmen—having awed the Emperor of Morocco into a peace, and having fought the

rish with him [Caramalli] before the walls of Tripoli, or to triumph with him within those walls." "I have" said a British Peer " resolutions to make resolutions, if I cannot keep them."

BIDDLE, and their gallant crew, once of the unfortunate Philadelphia Frigate, after a dismal bondage of nineteen months, must have poured out the undissembled gratitude of hearts, glowing with feelings, unappreciated by the luxurious, and effeminate sons of indolent security. Their feelings are thus painted by an anonymous poet, who unites, in these lines, two of the fine arts, poetry and painting.

The dawn through my grates the thick darkness dissolves,
And again the huge bolt of my dungeon revolves;
That monster's dread step is a prelude to pains,
When the lash that he bears will drink blood from my veins.

Hark! what notes of sweet music! they thrill through my soul.
Columbia's own strain is that soft melting roll!
Gracious Heav'n! my dear countrymen once more I view,
Hail Liberty's banner! ye base tyrants adieu.

blood-stained Bashaw of Tripoli into subjugation, he enjoyed that repose of body which toils, privations, long service
and sanguinary battles had rendered necessary ; and that
tranquillity of mind which conscious virtue, rectitude and
honour, rendered sweet and felicitous.

But these enjoyments were hardly began before they
were to be ended. Death, which he had so often undauntedly faced in the most appalling forms, removed him from
the scene of his temporal, to that of his eternal glory upon
the 25th day of August, 1807—just three years from the
memorable month of August in which he conquered a powerful nation of Barbary.

Like his beloved comrades in that warfare, STEPHEN DE-
CATUR, and JAMES LAWRENCE, he died in the meridian of
life, being but forty-six years of age.

CHARACTER OF EDWARD PREBLE.

EDWARD PREBLE, possessed peculiar native powers—
those which the heroes of antiquity most craved—a sound
mind, in a sound body. So far as countenance is an index
of mind, his indicated decision of character. It also indicated benignity of heart, and generosity of feelings. His
person was tall and commanding ; his posture erect ; his
movement natural and unaffected. His whole presence
pointed him out as a " mighty man of war."* As to the
qualities of his mind, the prominent traits were a restless

Wy wrongs are all cancelled—your shore is receding—
My country has freed me, my heart has ceas'd bleeding ;
In the arms of affection I soon shall be bless'd,
And my dust with the dust of my fathers shall rest.

* " That form indeed, th' associate of a mind,
Vast in its pow'rs—etherial in its kind,

emulation, and an inquietude for enterprise. For listless
indolence and effeminating inaction, he manifested the most
sovereign contempt and contemptuous pity. Not satisfied
with achieving deeds of common renown, he aspired to
those which would leave previous examples of noble daring
far behind him. Possessing by nature a high-minded sense
of independence, he espoused the cause of his country
when imperious Britain was attempting to subjugate his
countrymen to vassalage. Although then but a youth,

" He gave the world assurance of the man."

Returning to the peaceful pursuit of commerce, he placed
himself and his family in independent circumstances. Ever ready to avenge the injuries of the Republic, from whatever quarter of the world they should proceed, he repaired as Commander in Chief to the renowned Mediterranean.
France, Spain, Italy, Naples, and Genoa, upon the borders
of that sea.—Sardinia, Sicily, Corsica, Minorca, and Malta, islands in its bosom, witnessed with astonishment and
admiration the approach of this Christian hero from the
Christian Republic. To the people of these regions, as
well as to his own countrymen, who were exposed to Turkish capture and bondage, he was a ministering angel of
protection and redemption. But, to the merciless disciples of Mahomet, he was a minister of wrath, armed with
stores of vengeance, to avenge the barbarous cruelties for
centuries inflicted upon unoffending Christians. The vol-
canoes of Vesuvius and Ætna excited but little more con-

That form—the labour of Almighty skill,
Fram'd for the service of a freeborn will,
Asserts precedence, and bespeaks control,
But borrows all its grandeur from the soul."
                                    COWPER.

sternation with exposed Neapolitans and Sicilians, than did
the gleaming messengers of death, " red with uncommon
wrath," hurled by the American Preble, into the capital of
the Tripolitans. Mahometans were subjugated by him and
his dauntless band, and the Turkish Crescent fell beneath
the American Banner. The veteran finished his work in
the Eastern World, and returned to the enjoyment of civil
liberty and religious freedom, amongst his redeemed, protected, and happy countrymen in the Western World. He
died, as a hero would wish to die, before the ravages of
time had debilitated his body or deteriorated his mind.
Never having been humbled by a *mortal* enemy, he yielded all of himself that was *mortal* to the *King of Terrors*, and
gave his *body* to the tomb—

" Till mould'ring worlds and tumbling systems burst,
" Till the last trump shall renovate the dust."

His exalted soul he gave to that GOD who gave it to him,
and he bequeathed his temporal glory to the Republic ;
and if that Republic hath not yet raised a monument* to his

* It would be gratifying to learn how much money has been drawn
from the National Treasury, to erect Mausoleums, Monuments, Sta-
tues, &c. to Revolutionary Heroes. Soon after the death of Gen.
Washington, a resolution was passed in Congress on the subject. In
1813, the following was found in the Congressional Journal :

" The joint resolution for a monument over the remains of General
Washington, and some minor business, was postponed to Monday."

In 1813, the following notice concerning the " Washington Monument Association" was published :

" *Boston, Nov.* 25. We learn that the Trustees of the Washington
Monument Association, through the Agency of our countrymen,
Messrs. West, Allston, and Samuel Williams of London, have engaged
the celebrated sculptor, Chantry, to form a Pedestrian Statue of
GEORGE WASHINGTON, and that some progress has been made in the
execution."

The elegant monument in Portland, to the memory of Capt. Burrows, was erected by the patriotic munificence of Matthew L. Davis,
Esq. of New-York.

memory, he hath a living monument in the heart of every
surviving Naval Officer and Seaman, who knew his virtues,
appreciated his worth, and emulated his valour. But as
the government of the American Republic, in the plenitude
of its gratitude, has seen fit to draw from its treasury the
small sum of *one thousand dollars* to erect a monument to
the memory of Elbridge Gerry ; it may hereafter remember the Father of the Modern Sons of the American Navy ;
and future generations will behold a monument erected to
his glory, and his glory shining in the monument.

REGISTER

*Of American Naval Officers in the Mediterranean, in the
years 1803 and 1804, under*

COMMODORE PREBLE;

In presenting this Catalogue of Officers to the reader it
is impossible to repress the feelings of admiration with
which the mind of every patriotic American must be penetrated. In retrospect, we behold the little infant navy of
our infant Republic, in that renowned sea where the marine
of ancient Carthage, spread dismay and consternation upon
the borders of the three great continents, whose shores are
laved by its waters. In that sea where the Grecians gained their naval renown. In that sea where Cleopatra wafted in her barge, and captivated Antony.

It would be invidious to make a selection from this constellation of ocean heroes, who entered the dangerous path
of glory with the immortalized Preble—some of whom
have followed him from temporal warfare to eternal peace
—from a life of glory on earth to immortal honours in

heaven. Saying nothing of the Commanders, Rodgers, Bainbridge, Stewart, Hull, Smith Somers,* and Decatur,* we find among the Lieutenants,—Gordon, Dent, Jones, Porter, Trippe, Crane, Read, J. B. Decatur,* Lawrence,*, and J. Bainbridge. Amongst Midshipmen, Burrows,* Morris, Nicholson, Gadsden, Wadsworth,* Israel,* Ridgeley, Henley, Patterson, Mead, Macdonough, Gamble, Renshaw, Spence, Pettigrew, Warrington, Ballard, Cassin, Thompson, &c. These then ardent youth were unknown to fame—their names are now inscribed in its temple, and their glory is identified with that of the Republic. Their monuments will hereafter rise in various parts of our vast Republic, and consecrate the places where the naval heroes rest.

It is however, ungenerous, unjust—to bestow all our applause upon the fortunate heroes whose destiny enabled them to signalize themselves by some glorious achievements. Their associates, equally gallant, equally skilful, equally meritorious, are too often obscured by the halo of glory that shines around their companions. Had not Gibbon, perished in the flaming theatre of Richmond, he might have acted as glorious a part on the theatre of naval glory, as his brother midshipmen, Morris, Biddle, Macdonough, Burrows, Warrington, etc. As the meed of praise is the highest reward of a hero, it ought to be bestowed with impartiality.

In page 162 of this volume, a List of Ships and Commanders of Com. Preble's Squadron is inserted. It was all the information the writer had when he *drove through* this imperfect Sketch of Com. Preble's life.

* Dead !

Since it was written, the very obliging and ever attentive Secretary of the Navy, has furnished me with the following " Official List."

Officers attached to the Squadron under Com. Edward Preble in the Mediterranean in 1803, &c.

Constitution frigate, Edward Preble, Commodore.

John Rodgers, Captain.

Lieutenants.

Thomas Robinson, Jun.	Samuel Elbert,
William C. Jenckes,	Charles Gordon.
Joseph Tarbell,	John H. Dent.

Nathaniel Harriden, Sailing Master.

James Wells, Surgeon.

Thomas Marshall, Surgeon's mate.

Patrick Sim,   do.

James S. Deblois, Purser.

Noadiah Morris, chaplain.

Jonathan N. Cannon, Boatswain.

William Sweeny, Gunner.

Isaac Steel, Sail Maker.

Thomas Moore, Carpenter.

Midshipmen.

Hethcote J. Reed,	Ralph Izard, Jun.
David Deacon,	William Burrows,
John Rowe,	Daniel S. Dexter,
Thomas Hunt,	Charles Morris,
John M. Haswell,	John Davis,
Alexander Laus,	Francis C. Hall,
Thomas Baldwin,	Leonard J. Hunewell,
Joseph Nicholson,	Louis Alexis,
Charles Gadsden, Jun.	Henry Wadsworth.
Charles G. Ridgely,	Henry P. Casey,

32

Joseph Israel,   William Lewis,
John Thompson,   Robert Henley.

John Hall, Captain of marines,
Robert Greenleaf, 1st Lieut.

Philadelphia frigate, William Bainbridge, Commander.

Lieutenants.

John S. H. Cox,   Jacob Jones,
Theodore Hunt,   Benjamin Smith,
David Porter.

William Knight, Sailing Master.
John Ridgely, Surgeon.
Jonathan Cowdery, Surgeon's mate.
Nicholas Harwood,   do.
Keith Spence, Purser.
George Hodge, Boatswain.
Richard Stephenson, Gunner.
William Godby, Carpenter.
Joseph Douglass, Sail-maker.

Midshipmen.

James Gibbon,   Daniel T. Patterson,
Benjamin F. Read,   Thomas Macdonough,
James Biddle,   Bernard Henry,
Wallace Wormeley,   William Cutbush,
Simon Smith,   Robert Gamble,
Richard B. Jones,   James Renshaw.

William S. Osborne, 1st Lieut. of Marines.

Brig Syren, Charles Stewart, Captain.

Lieutenants.

James R. Caldwell,   Michael B. Carroll,
Joseph J. Maxwell.

Samuel R. Marshall, Surgeon.
Alexander C. Harrison, Sailing Master.

Nathan Baker, Purser.

John Unsworth, Boatswain.

James Welman, Gunner.

John Felt, Carpenter.

Thomas Crippen, Sail-maker.

Midshipmen.

Thomas O. Anderson,   Robert T. Spence.

John Dorsey,   Cornelius de Krafft,

William R. Nicholson.

John Howard, 1st Lieut. Marines.

Brig Argus, Isaac Hull, Captain.

Lieutenants.

Joshua Blake,   William M. Livingston,

Sybrant Van Schaick.

Humphrey Magrath, acting sailing master.

Nathaniel T. Weems, Surgeon.

John W. Dorsey, Surgeon's mate.

Timothy Winn, Purser.

George Nicholson, Boatswain.

William Huntress, Gunner.

Stephen Hurley, Carpenter.

Charles Smith, Sail-maker.

Midshipmen.

Joseph Bainbridge,   Samuel G. Blodget,

George Mann,   William G. Stewart,

Pascal Paoli Peck,   John Pettigrew.

John Johnson, 1st Lieutenant marines.

Schooner Vixen, John Smith, Commander.

Acting Lieutenants.

John Trippe,   William Crane.

Richard Butler, Sailing-master.

Michael Graham. Surgeon.

Clement S. Hunt, Purser.
John Clarke, Boatswain.
James Bailey, Gunner.
Bartholomew M'Henry, Carpenter.
Joshua Herbert, Sail-maker.

Midshipmen.

John D. Henley,   Lewis Warrington,
William Ballard,   John Nevitt,
John Lyon.

Schooner Nautilus, Richard Somers, Commander.

Lieutenants.

James B. Decatur,   George W. Read.
Edward N. Cox, Acting Sailing-master.
Gershom R. Jacques, Acting Surgeon.
James Tootell, Purser.
Charles Walker, Boatswain.
James Pinkerton, Gunner.
Robert Fell, Carpenter.

Midshipmen.

Octavius A. Page,   Stephen Cassin,
George Marcellin,   William Miller,
Charles C. B. Thompson.

Schooner Enterprize, Stephen Decatur, Jr. Commander.

Acting Lieutenants.

James Lawrence,   Daniel C. Heath,
Jonathan Thorn,   Joseph Bainbridge,
Seth Cartee.

William Rogers, Acting Surgeon,
Alexander M'Williams, Surgeon's mate.
Mr. Bearry, Boatswain.
William Hook, Gunner.

Mr. West, Carpenter.

Patrick Keogh, Sail-maker.

Midshipmen.

Daniel C. Sim,   George Mitchell,

Walter Boyd,   Robert Innes,

Benjamin Turner.

Samuel Slewellyn, 1st Lieutenant of marines.

The very *names* of the vessels composing this little squadron, have become familiar with Americans, for their achievements in the Mediterranean under Com. PREBLE, in the war against Tripoli ; and on the Atlantic, in the second war with Britain.

The Constitution bore the broad pendant of PREBLE in all the victories of the squadron in the Mediterranean. In the Atlantic, commanded by HULL, she astonished British officers in escaping from a British squadron. Commanded by the same officer, she sent the boasting Guerriere to the bottom ; commanded by BAINBRIDGE, she compelled the Java to submit to the same fate, and commanded by STEWART, in one action, added the Cyane and Levant, to the American navy.

The Philadelphia, was conquered only by hidden rocks, and a foe, with hearts harder than rocks, who dared not point a gun at her while wafting. But her loss to America was retrieved by DECATUR, in destroying her under the tremendous batteries of Tripoli, in the midst of her marine.

The Syren, commanded by the ever vigilant and intrepid STEWART, was constantly in the station of duty and of danger. She accompanied the Intrepid to the bay of Tripoli, and witnessed the destruction of the Philadelphia. Her language, unlike the fabled Syren, was more calculated to alarm than to allure.—While commanded by the accomplished NICHOLSON she fell before a "hell of England."

The Argus, commanded by HULL, acted well her part in the Mediterranean ; and, commanded by ALLEN in the war with Britain, spread dismay upon her coast—swept her commerce from her very harbours ; and when she fell before superior force, was deemed a trophy, and her commander who fell gloriously, was

"By strangers honour'd and by strangers mourn'd."

The Vixen, was a terror to Tripolitans, and in the war with Britain, fell a victim to the elements in company with a British Frigate, commanded by the modern pride of Britain, JAMES LUCAS YEO, who publickly thanked the gallant REED and his crew for their gallant courage as enemies, and magnanimity as friends.

The Nautilus, was the favourite of the seas. She menaced Tangier, in Morocco—Tripoli on the Barbary coast —and her nautical skill extorted admiration, from a British Commodore when she fell into his hands, and who returned the gallant CRANE his sword for his masterly exertions to save this ship.

The Enterprise,* ("who can tell her deeds") has become the most renowned schooner upon the ocean. In the hands of STERRETT she battered a Barbarian corsair to pieces—Commanded by DECATUR she captured the wonderful little Intrepid—Commanded by the lamented BUR-

* This fine craft was wrecked and lost in July, 1823 ; so that there is not now, in the American Navy, a single keel of this renowned squadron, but the CONSTITUTION ("Old Iron-Sides.") It is to be hoped that she may never be sent to sea again, lest the *elements* should destroy, what *enemies* never could catch or capture.

rows, she captured the Boxer—and with the frigate Constitution, is still the pride of Americans.

As if the whole of these vessels, possessed an " inanimate ardor," corresponding with the animated heroism of their commanders, they became renowned for conquests, and seemed to extort smiles from the genius of victory in the hour of disaster.

BIOGRAPHICAL SKETCH

OF

ALEXANDER MURRAY,

CAPTAIN IN THE ARMY AND IN THE NAVY

IN THE WAR OF THE REVOLUTION;

POST CAPTAIN IN THE NAVAL WARFARE BETWEEN THE
AMERICAN REPUBLIC AND FRANCE ;

COMMODORE OF AN AMERICAN SQUADRON IN THE WAR WITH
TRIPOLI,

AND

COMMANDANT OF AN AMERICAN NAVY YARD.

Biographical writers, and subjects of Biography....ALEXANDER MUR-
RAY's birth....a lineal descendant of the Highland chief, Murray of
Elginshire, who espoused the cause of the Pretender in the Rebellion of 1715, who was banished to Barbadoes, and his estates confiscated....Houses of Tudor, Stuart, and Brunswick....The grandfather a Scotch Rebel, the grandson an American Revolutionist....Dr.
Murray, Alexander's father....Alexander, the youngest son....His
education....Commencement of his nautical life...His highminded
sentiments....William Murray, Earl of Mansfield....Alexander, appointed a Lieutenant in the Navy, by the Old Congress....for want
of a ship, enters Col. Smallwood's regiment as Lieutenant in the army....As James Monroe did Col. Weedon's....Note....Battles in
which he fought...Sufferings of the American army...Note....Lieut.
Murray seriously affected by explosion of a battery.....Is promoted to
a Captaincy....Becomes an invalid for a short time....Retires to his
father's...Forlorn state of the poor and sick soldier...Extortioners...
Murray recovers, and resumes his station in the Navy as Commander of a Letter of Marque....Fidelity of American officers, but one
exception, Benedict Arnold....Note....Incessant service of Lieut.
Comdt. Murray....He is taken prisoner, paroled and exchanged....
He enters the continental frigate Trumbull, 32 guns....Note....She
encounters a violent gale, and immediately enters into a most desperate engagement with the frigate Iris, 38 guns, and Monk, of 18
guns....Description of the battle....Lieut. Murray is severely wounded....The wreck of the Trumbull is towed into New York by the
enemy ...He again recovers, is exchanged, and enters the frigate
Alliance as 1st Lieutenant....Peace with Britain, 1783....The fame
of Murray, and revolutionary veterans....He resumes the character
of the private citizen....Annihilation of the navy....Meagre resour-

ces of the colonies at the close of the revolution....Caution of American Statesmen.

Spoliations upon American commerce, and indignity to American citizens ...Commencement of a naval force....Lieut. Murray appointed Post Captain....Sails in corvette Montezuma against French....Immense service to commerce...Receives a vote of thanks...Appointed to frigate Insurgente ...Soon after to the Constellation ..Is encountered by the Razee Magnanimique....Returns the fire....Injures his supposed antagonist....Finds him to be friendly....Mutual explanation, and mutual satisfaction....Constellation and Magnanimique, (Murray and Taylor, President and Little Belt, (Rodgers and Bingham) Chesapeake and Leopard, (Barron and Humphrey)....Peace between America and France....Note.

Turkish rapacity against American commerce, and infernal cruelty against American seamen....Commodore Murray appointed to command American Squadron in the Mediterranean, as successor of his revolutionary comrade, Com. Dale....Restricted power....His flag ship, Constellation assailed by Tripolitan corsairs....He disperses them, and drives them under the Bashaw's batteries....He could not act offensively....In the midst of his defensive operations, is superseded by Com. Morris....Secret intrigue and palpable injury. Com. Murray, though not degraded, feels himself injured, and remonstrates....Inexplicable " affairs of state"....Peace with Tripoli, and renown of modern Naval Heroes....Affair of the Chesapeake.... Com. Murray solicits a command....Is detained at home....Secret machinations.

Second war between America and Britain....Com. Murray, senior Commodore and Post Captain in the Navy, again refused a command at sea, and detained at home to discharge duties in the home department....Peace with Britain....Com. Murray is appointed Commandant of an American Navy Yard....Efficiency of Naval defence.... Importance of Naval Architecture....Com. Murray's science, skill and judgment in his new capacity....American and British Naval Architecture....Com. Murray's indefatigable exertions, and unparalleled economy in the service of the Republic....Increase of the Navy and decrease of expenditure...Com. Murray's closing years... His death....His character....Original Ode....Death of Com. Murray's son.

It is the usual course with writers of Biography, to select for the subjects of their researches and lucubrations, those fortunate characters who have signalized themselves by one or more splendid achievements or literary productions, and have become the idols of " the people." The name of the hero is a passport for the volume, whether he is dressed out in the simple, artless, and beautiful attire of

Marmontel, or in the heavy, coarse, and clumsy garb of Boswell.

Our own country, from the landing of the pilgrims to this time, affords as rich a harvest of biography as Rome did for Plutarch—as France has for Marmontel and La Montaigne—and as England, Scotland Ireland, and Wales has, for a countless throng of major and minor biographers. But notwithstanding " the harvest is truly plenteous, the labourers are few."

To the conductors of the Port Folio* and the Analectic Magazine, the American reader is more indebted for the Biography of modern worthies, than to all other American periodical publications. The only regret in the mind of their readers is, that although they have *multum in parvo*, they do not furnish their patrons with half enough.

In the last mentioned publication, is found the following forcible remark—" We have seen works of this kind (" American Biographical Works,") too often made the vehicles of adulation to the living, and extravagant eulogy of the dead, for the sordid purpose of gaining patronage, and swelling subscription lists." And, in speaking of authors, it says that there " is a chance of being dazzled by the glare of fresh blown reputations, or of mistaking transient notoriety for that solid fame which is slowly collected from the sober judgment of the nation."

One fact however is certain, that the " Analectic Magazine itself," has suddenly captivated its readers, with highly coloured and highly finished biographies of " fresh-blown reputations" which were gained in a fortunate hour and not " slowly collected."

* With deference, however, Henry Dearborn's " Account of the Battle of Bunker Hill," must always be excepted.

These biographies were to be found in the offices of men and upon the toilets of ladies. The faces of these favourites of fortune, and heroes of renown were exhibited in galleries of painting, in parlours and in print-shops ; and the lovers of the olfactory cordial could scarcely gratify one of the five senses, without snuffing to the "immortal glory" of some matchless hero, looking from the lid of his pocketbox. The fatigued nymph, while wafting to her relief the refreshing breeze, would suddenly stop—eye the heroe's face upon her fan—give a melting sigh ; and, in tender tones exclaim "May beauty ever be the reward of the brave."

Such has not been the high destiny of the venerable veteran whose life and character, with deep solicitude, I now attempt imperfectly to portray.

AEXANDER MURRAY was born in Chestertown. state of Maryland, in the memorable year 1755—memorable as the year which first involved the infant colonies in a war with a foreign civilized power, for with native savages they had always been at war.

To trace back the parentage of Alexander Murray, would open one of the most capacious fields of biography, and embrace one of the most interesting periods of British history. It would require the polished pen of their own Robertson to detail, with historical fidelity, the various and deeply interesting events, in which his grandfather, the "Highland Chief Murray" was engaged, and the heart-rending scenes through which he, his family and his Clan were doomed to pass.

The Highland chiefs of Scotland have ever been renowned as the most daring, romantic, chivalrous and dauntless race of men upon earth. Their simple. unvarnished histo-

ry will speak their eulogy, far better than the inflated ro-
mances and wizzard fictions which " invade" our country.

When the House of Stuart became extinct, as it regards
regal power, by the abdication of the British throne, by
James II., and the House of Brunswick began, by import-
ing the Guelphs from the continent, real high-minded Scotsmen claimed in the *eighteenth* century, as a matter of right,
what, in the *nineteenth*, has been enforced by the arm of power, that none but a " legitimate sovereign" should set upon
the throne of Britain.

The ardent and chivalrous young Murray, Alexander's
grand-sire, put himself at the head of his Clan, possessed
each of spirits, chivalrous as his own, and espoused the
cause of the Pretender.

Every American reader is, or ought to be, well acquainted with English history at that period, as it is so much connected with the history of our own country. History has
been well denominated " Philosophy teaching by example," and every American, in a certain degree, must be a
historian, philosopher, and politician, to enable him to appreciate the invaluable blessings enjoyed in our Republic,
when compared with the oppression of his fellow-creatures
in other portions of the globe.

The cause that Murray's ancestor espoused was the
cause of the Catholic Religion and the cause of his Prince ;
a religion which may well claim the greatest antiquity of
any system adopted under the Christian dispensation ; and
since the Reformation effected by the immortal Martin Luther, may claim quite as much consistency.

It was a master-stretch of policy in the House of Tudor,
to alarm their subjects about the horrors of the Catholic
religion, and to set at defiance the Papal power, in order

to exercise as corrupt a power themselves over their own
subjects.*

It was well for the House of Brunswick to denounce the
House of Stuart—to adhere to the "Protestant Succession"—to raise the alarm of "gun-powder plots and treason" in order to furnish a pretext for the persecution of
the unoffending Catholics, whom they still persecute ; and,
to secure themselves upon the throne of Britain.

It is unnecessary to ascertain whether the ancient Murrays were advocates of the Pope, of Luther, Calvin, or
Knox—suffice it to say that in the memorable "Scots Rebellion" in seventeen hundred and fifteen, the gallant
Scots Chief, Murray, and his dauntless clan fought as much
in the cause of a legitimate sovereign, as did the Irish general, Arthur Wellesley, in the "Holy Alliance" of eighteen hundred and fifteen.†

* The history of Henry VIII. and his daughter, Queen Elizabeth.

† Attend for a moment to what a high-minded Englishman said upon this subject "to the People"—(in Feb. 1780,) which met the eye
of Geo. III. in an hour after it issued from the press.—

"Let me conjure you to be no longer deceived by the *pious hypoc-
risy* of the present king ; he has done more in the short space of a *few
years*, to subvert your religion and liberties, and to ruin the nation,
than ever *Charles* the *first* did during the whole course of his life, and
yet he was brought to the *block*, by the virtue, firmness, and resolution of our forefathers ; if he had not, we at this day should not have
had either liberty or freedom to have contended for, nor would England have been reduced to its present miserable, disgraceful and ruinous state, by a dasterdly, mulish tyrant, of the house of Brunswick."

"*James the second* at his first coming to the crown of England, pro-
fessed (though not BORN a BRITON) so much tenderness for the
people, and so great a regard for the preservation of their liberties
and their property, that the parliament and people gave him more
money than he asked, and he himself had honour enough to put a stop
to the profusion of their grants and foolish loyalty.   The deluded peo-

A successful rebellion acquires the more courtly name of a revolution ; while a suppressed one is denominated treason. The rebellion of Scotland, in 1715, was crushed by the hand of English power, and her union with the British crown annihilated her ancient greatness forever. Murray's immense estates were confiscated to pay for his valour—he was banished from the land of his nativity, as Napoleon was from Europe, because his presence might endanger the safety of a then new dynasty, but which has now become legitimatized, by the legerdemain of princes and the force of arms.

The British king, little thought that from the loins of this banished Chief, in little more than half a century after the sentence of banishment was promulgated and executed, there would arise a gallant warrior in the New World, who would act a most distinguished part in a drama, the catastrophe of which would be. in wresting from the crown of Britain the finest section of the British empire—and such was ALEXANDER MURRAY, the subject of this sketch. He

ple presently saw their error. for he soon began to put the imperial law of his own WILL in execution, and to exercise an arbitrary and uncontroled power over them."

" *James* being deserted by his priests and chaplains (who had invested him with all his illegal arbitrary power) he was at length obliged to fly from the face of an injured people, and seek refuge in a foreign land, as a proper and just reward for all his villainy. That another base, ungrateful, perjured, hypocritical and blood-thirsty tyrant, may share the same or a worse fate, is the sincere wish of millions."

Thus it would seem from the days of the Charleses and the Jameses of the House of Stuart, and down to the third George of the House of Brunswick, there has been a succession of changes from bad to worse, until no change could render the British monarchy more oppressive to the people. It was the House of Brunswick that the Murrays opposed, and for that they were banished as rebels

was surely a *legitimate*, and he was also a successful *rebel*— a *revolutionist*.

The reader may wish to be informed of the destiny of the Chief, subsequent to his banishment. What would furnish materials for a volume, must be despatched in a few sentences, and this will lead directly to the notice of his descendant, the American Murray.

The banished Highland Chief landed with the wreck of his fortune, and with his family, upon the island of Barbadoes. The attachment of a Scotsman to " Auld Coila" is proverbial ; and although the pensioned Johnson sneered at her barren fields, and oaten cakes, and declared that " The best prospect he saw in Scotland was the high road that led to Old England"—yet a more high-minded—a more profound literati—a more virtuous peasantry, were never known than she has always produced.

Although on the beautiful island of Barbadoes, it must, for a season, have seemed to him like a waste, and he to himself but an exile and a wonder.*   But his innate greatness could not be diminished by being driven from a once powerful kingdom to an island in the West Indies.

It was here the father of our hero was born, as was also a sister of his father, the grand-mother of Benjamin Chew. Esq. of Philadelphia.

His father and his aunt, in early life, directed their views to America, which was then, is now, and heaven

* The situation of this banished chief, reminds the historian of that of the Doge of Genoa, at Paris, who had been ordered to leave his dominions, and appear before his Most *Christian Majesty*. A French courtier asked the Doge " What was the greatest wonder he there saw ?" He indignantly answered, " The Doge of Genoa in the city of Paris."

grant it ever may be, the most capacious field for manly enterprise, and the safest ' asylum for oppressed humanity.'

He selected Chestertown, in Maryland, as the place of his residence, and soon became distinguished as a physician. His dignified manners, his scientific acquirements, and his manly virtues, attracted the attention of people of the first rank, and secured the affection of a Miss Smith, the daughter of a distinguished citizen, whom he married. They were blessed with a numerous progeny, who have all sustained the high standing of their exalted progenitors.

ALEXANDER MURRAY, (the late Commodore) was the youngest child of this numerous family. Had he been born in the dominions of Britain, where the hereditary principle exalts the first-born, and leaves younger sons to press forward to fortune and to fame, by their own efforts, this circumstance alone would have served as a sort of impetus to urge him forward. But in our beloved Republic, primogeniture is known only in family records, or the parish register. All sons are here ' born equal,' and like Paul, are ' born free.'

Young Murray received as good an education as the seminaries of learning in that portion of the country, at that time, could afford. The literary and scientific acquirements of his father led him to appreciate duly the inestimable value of knowledge, in any and in every situation in life ; and he spared no pains to qualify his numerous children to act well their parts, as they entered, one after the other, upon the stage of life.

It will not comport with the limits or design of this imperfect Sketch, to notice further any branch of this interesting family, except the one who is the subject of it. A

Biography of the *Family of Murray* would make a capacious and deeply interesting volume.

Born and educated in a state, which bounds upon the
largest bay in the world, and has for its capital one of the
most important commercial cities in the Republic, the animating scenes upon the bosom of the Chesapeake, and the
ceaseless activity in the city of Baltimore, led young Murray to select the nautical profession as his pursuit for life.

It was a circumstance peculiarly favourable to the then
future renown of the American navy, that those who afterwards became commanders in it, first made themselves
masters of the theory and practice of navigation.   As it
would be but repeating what the writer hastily expressed
in a recent publication upon this subject, he hopes to be
excused for referring the reader to that volume.*

In the organization of the British navy a vast many
young men, who can scarcely distinguish the main from
the quarter-deck—the starboard bow from the larboard
quarter—the mainsail from the jib, being " younger sons
of younger brothers," " the cankers of a calm world," and
yet having the clumsy blood of a degenerated nobility
sluggishly coursing through their nerveless bodies, are appointed officers to command the weather-beaten sons of
Neptune in their floating dungeons, who were forced into
them by a press-gang.   Such men there, have to obey
such boys there.

Not so was it in the little marine force of the Thirteen
Colonies in the War of the Revolution, which sprang up,
as if by magic, and as if by magic conquered the floating
bulwarks of the " Queen of the Ocean."

* " Life and Character of Com. Decatur."   2d Edition.

The little Continental Ships were then commanded by such men as *Nicholas Biddle, George Little, John Manley, James Nicholson, Edward Preble, John Paul Jones, Thomas Traxton*, the *Subject of this Sketch*, and a list of men too numerous to mention here, and too valiant and patriotic ever to be forgotten.

They learned to serve themselves, before they ordered others to service—they learned the necessity of obedience, before they aspired to the rank of commanders.

So indefatigable was young Murray as a navigator—so skilful, so trust-worthy, that at the early age of *eighteen*, he became master of a valuable ship in the European trade.

The early education of this high-minded descendant, of a high-minded race, made him well acquainted with the history of the country of his ancestors, and more minutely with the tragical history of his ancestors themselves.

His classical parents infused into his naturally ardent mind, a high sense of independence—detailed to him the scenes of sufferings through which his grandsire passed—gave him an account of the confiscation of his ample estates in Scotland, to satiate the almost insatiable cupidity of the reigning House of Brunswick, wielding the sceptre of power over the land of Wallace, Bruce, Lovatt, and "Murray of Elginshire."

As the same dynasty began to stretch her powerful arm across the Atlantic, and to wield the rod of oppression over his adopted, as she had for a century over the native land of his ancestors, he rekindled in the bosom of his son the noble flame which three quarters* of a century before glowed in the bosom of his grandfather, a Chief of the Clan of Elginshire.

* The Rebellion in Scotland began in 1715, in America in 1775.

It was not so with all the Murrays who sprang from
Scotland. The classical William Murray crossed the River Forth,—became a subservient courtier to George III,—
left the muses which he had courted in the land of Ossian,
Campbell, and Burns, and became a peer of Old England.
This defection made Pope, the Bard of Twickenham, exclaim,

"How great an *Ovid* was in *Murray* lost."

This Prince of British poets, had he not been somewhat
captivated with the princes of Hanover, might better have
sung,

"How great a *Murray** was in *Mansfield* lost."

* William Murray, by his subserviency to the house of Brunswick,
was created "Earl of Mansfield." Well may the American Murrays despise the memory of a Scots Murray, springing from the same
country, and from the same stock, when they reflect, that he, in the
court of Britain, advised his master George III. to exterminate them
in their adopted country.

In " The Scourge" No. IV. published in London, Feb. 19, 1780,
his lordship is thus addressed.

To the Right Hon. (subtle Scotsman) William Murray, Earl of
Mansfield.

My Lord,

The wicked, mischievous, and hellish conspiracy your Lordship
had formed (in conjunction with others,) under the auspices of a das_
tardly tyrant, against the common rights of mankind, and envied constitution of the British empire, was laid deep, and it spread wide, you
urged it on with a steady zeal, and an unwearied application, but as
soon as your infernal scheme of destroying charters, and arbitrarily
imposing taxes, on a people whom you never saw, in America, contrary
even to any pretence or legal claim of right failed; you watched all
opportunities to begin the bloody execution and slaughter of mankind,
that you might satiate your Scots revenge with human gore ; the first
opposition to despotic power you declared in the privy council, to be
an act of rebellion, and in consequence of that diabolical advice which

But the Earl of Mansfield, once the companion of Pope,
and once the idol of the House of Brunswick, and still the

you knew would please the temper of your master, whose aim is to be
the imperial tyrant and butcher of the human race ; many thousand
distressed orphans, and unhappy widows are now bewailing the loss
of their murdered fathers and husbands, and daily call to Heaven for
vengeance on your head, as the author of their miseries ; for they
well know, my Lord, that you have been the artful friend who planned
and advised their total extirpation by the sword, if they would not
submit to be slaves. This, my Lord, the whole kingdom must be convinced of, and believe, for none but a monster in human shape, or
some malignant devil could have said what you uttered in the House
of Peers against the people of America more than four years since,
" If we don't kill them, they will kill us ;" yes, my Lord, it was your
advice and your design to kill them, and you, together with your humane master, gloried in the slaughter : Heaven be praised, your success has not been so great as you expected, they have gloriously and
manfully resisted your tyranny, and frustrated all your schemes of
despotism and arbitrary power over them.

As you found, my Lord, the Americans were too wise, too brave,
and too virtuous to be cheated out of their birth-rights as Englishmen,
by your chicanery, sophistry, and Scotch cunning, or by force ; you
and your master the tool of a desperate faction, are now determined to
try the same experiment upon the deluded people of this country."

It is well known to the legal profession what broad strides towards
despotic power " Lord Chief Justice Mansfield," made in the trial of
Woodfall, for publishing the " Letters of Junius"—Letters which
now rank with the very first of the " British Classics,"—Letters which
William Murray might have considered as cheaply suppressed at the
price of his " Earldom in Scotland,"—Letters which must make the
present hereditary Earl of Mansfield blush at the " bad eminence" of
his ancestor, and which may well make the American Murrays exult
that their ancestor became a victim instead of a favourite to the
House of Brunswick. The following language was used by another
patriotic Englishman.

" Freedom of speech and public writing, is the birthright of every
man, a sacred and most invaluable privilege, so essential and necessary to the happiness of a free people, that the security of property, and

oracle with the legal profession, will never be forgotten, for the Letters of Junius will forever be read ; and William Murray, will " Be dam'd to everlasting fame."

Alexander Murray, when the olive branch of peace ceased to wave over his native land, and the clarion of war echoed along its extended shores, and over its lofty mountains, left the peaceable and profitable pursuits of commerce, to face the enemies of his country arm to arm.

From eighteen to twenty-one, he had been in command of merchant vessels, and had become acquainted with every part of the Atlantic ocean, where it was most probable, that the British marine, would bring its force to operate, and where British commerce would be most exposed to capture.

the preservation of liberty, must stand or fall with it. Whoever, like the present king and his ministers, would undermine an equal, limited and free government, and destroy the natural rights of mankind, must begin by subduing freedom of speech and public writing (this was attempted in the second year of this blessed reign, against the authors, printers and publishers of the Monitor, North Briton, &c.) which that hoary traitor Mansfield (who has more than once on his knees drank damnation to the present family on the throne) calls the licentiousness of the press, because he and his master wish to do public mischief without hearing of it, conscious that it has been a terror to tyrants, traitors, and oppressors."

That great and able statesman, the Lord Treasurer Burleigh, used frequently to say that England would never be ruined, unless it was by a Parliament ; he consequently foresaw, that other oppressions wrought by violence, would be at once resisted and by violence shaken off again. This maxim those notorious enemies to the peace and freedom of mankind, Lords Bute and Mansfield, instilled into the mind of the king, and he with a narrowness of soul, peculiar to himself, and to every tyrant upon earth, sucked in the poison ; and Lord North, the contemptible puppet of the court faction, was singled out as a proper tool to carry into execution the grand design of public mischief and public ruin.

In 1776, he was appointed a Lieutenant in the Continental Navy, although there was then no navy but " in embryo."

Although privateering was then, as it still continues to be, a legalized mode of warfare, yet it was a pursuit not congenial with the lofty sentiments of the lieutenant.

Although the ocean was his adopted and favourite element, he solicited a command in the first Maryland regiment, then about to be organized under the command of Col. William Smallwood,* who afterwards highly distinguished himself.

* Fully persuaded that the reader will be gratified with a conclusive testimony of the high reputation of Com. Murray's first commander upon land, I present him with that from the lips of the dying and gallant Baron De Kalb, communicated by his gallant aid-de-camp, Chevalier Dubuyson, who, when his general had received eleven wounds, flung his own body between him and the enemy's bayonets, and received them himself.

Charlotte, August 26, 1780.

" Dear General,

" Having received several wounds in the action of the 16th instant, I was made a prisoner with the Honourable Major General the Baron de Kalb, with whom I served as aid-de-camp and friend, and had an opportunity of attending that great and good officer during the short time he languished with eleven wounds, which proved mortal on the third day.

" It is with pleasure I obey the Baron's last commands, in presenting his most affectionate compliments to all the officers and men of his division : expressed the greatest satisfaction in the testimony given by the British army of the bravery of his troops : and he was charmed with the firm opposition they made to superior force, when abandoned by the rest of the army. The gallant behaviour of the Delaware regiment, and the companies of artillery attached to the brigades, afforded him infinite pleasure, and the exemplary conduct of the whole division, gave him an endearing sense of the merit of the troops he had the honor to command. I am, dear General,

With regard and respect, your most obedient, humble servant,

La Chevalier Dubuyson

To Brigadier General Smallwood.

He was immediately appointed a Lieutenant in this regiment, and, with his gallant company of Marylanders.

In less than thirty days after this battle, (at Camden, S. C.) in
which Brig. Gen. Smallwood bore a distinguished part (and in which
the Maryland regiment in which Alexander Murray was once a Captain, " covered itself with glory,") he was appointed Major General
of the division then lately commanded by the heroic De Kalb.

Confident that the reader will be pleased with the following letter
in my possession, I insert it ; and would add, that Gen. MORGAN mentioned in the letter was the Hero of the battle of the Cowpens, and
afterwards commander of the Virginia forces in suppressing the
·' Whiskey Rebellion," in the western counties of Pennsylvania.
Col. WASHINGTON was a captain at the victory of Trentou ; and, with
Lieut. James MONROE, (the President) took from the British artiller-
ists two cannon in the act of firing, and were both there severely
wounded.   The pine log stratagem was admirably calculated to intim-
idate the detested tories of the south, who infested that country as
much as they did New York, when Capt. Murray was in the army.

(Copy)   Camp, Dec, 6, 1780.
    Dear Sir,

Receiving intelligence, on the first of this instant, that parties of
the tories were advancing from the outposts of the British, up to Cane
and Lynche's creeks, with a view to intercept our waggons, and avail
themselves of the supplies in those settlements, from whence the principal support of the troops under my command has been drawn for
some time past.

I detached General Morgan, with 500 infantry, and Lieut. Colonel
Washington with 100 cavalry, to cover a number of waggons which
were ordered down in that quarter after corn and pork, and if possible
to intercept the tories.

The enemy, gaining intelligence of the advance of our troops, retreated, and whilst the covering party remained on that duty, Lieut.
Col. Washington, with the continental and some militia horse, reduced
Col. Rugely, Maj. Cook and 112 tory officers and soldiers, (in a log-
ged barn, on Rugely's plantation, strongly secured by abatis) to surrender at discretion, without firing a shot.

The Colonel's address and stratagem, on the occasion, deserve ap-

followed Colonel Smallwood to the "tented field," as
Lieutenant Monroe (now the admired President of the
American Republic) did, with his company of gallant Vir-
ginians, follow Col. Weedon.

Both of these regiments joined the main army near New
York. Both of these ardent Lieutenants fought in the
battle of White-plains. Both of them were promoted to
a captaincy for their steady conduct and cool courage.
Each contracted a friendship for the other, which lasted
and which strengthened until the day of Alexander Murray's death.

Lieut. Murray was also in the sanguinary battle of Flatbush, where he displayed his usual gallantry. In this battle Maj. Gen. Israel Putnam was senior officer, as he was
the preceding year, at the battle of Bunker Hill. Lieut.
Murray was in the masterly retreat from Long Island with
Gen. Putnam's division of the army, and again joined the
main army in the city of New York.

Capt. Murray had hitherto escaped unhurt, although in
the midst of danger. But he was soon to receive an injury
which was to end only with his life.

Gen. Washington's whole force in New York was less
than 20,000, while Sir William Howe's army, as estimated

plause ; having no artillery, he mounted a pine log, and holding out
the appearance of an attack with field pieces, carried his point, by
sending in a flag, and demanding an immediate surrender.

With very sincere regard,

I remain, your most obedient,

Humble servant,

Wm. Smallwood.

Hon. Gen. Greene.

Published by order of Congress,

Charles Thomson, Sec'ry

by the British minister, consisting of British and Hessian troops, amounted to more than 30,000.

The city was invested by a strong naval force—Hudson and East rivers were commanded by British men of war, and the whole American army seemed to be in the same state as a " forlorn hope."

That consummate general, Washington, like the Roman Fabius, and the French Moreau, knew that the salvation of an army by a skilful and military retreat,* was far more glorious than to expose it to almost inevitable destruction,

*In relation to this retreat, which might be said to have been the salvation of the American cause, I find the following fact in relation to the imminent danger of about one fifth of the whole force, in "Thatcher's Journal."

" When retreating from New York, (in 1776) Major General Putnam at the head of 3500 continental troops, was in the rear, and the last that left the city. In order to avoid any of the enemy that might be advancing in the direct road to the city, he made choice of a road parallel with, and contiguous to, the North River, till he could arrive at a certain angle whence another road would conduct him in such a direction as that he might form a junction with our army. It so happened that a body of about 8000 British and Hessians were at the same moment advancing on the road which would have brought them in immediate contact with Gen. Putnam, before he could have reached the turn in the other road.—Most fortunately, the British generals, seeing no prospect of engaging our troops, halted their own, and repaired to the house of a Mr. Robert Murray, a Quaker and a friend of our cause. Mrs. Murray treated them with cake and wine, and they were induced to tarry two hours or more. Governor Tryon frequently joking her about her American friends. By this happy incident, Gen. Putnam, by continuing his march, escaped a rencontre with a greatly superior force, which must have proved fatal to his whole party.—One half hour, it is said, would have been sufficient for the enemy to secure the road at the turn; and entirely cut off Gen. Putnam's retreat. It has since become almost a common saying among our officers, that Mrs. Murray saved this part of the American army."

35

a rushing precipitately upon an overwhelming superiority of force.

Capt. Murray at about the time of the evacuation of the city of New York, was stationed at the battery, and there, by the bursting and explosion of numerous pieces of cannon was severely deafened.

The loss of one eye and one arm to Nelson, was scarcely a greater calamity than the partial loss of hearing was to Capt. Murray. Nelson had one eye remaining to descry the enemy, and one arm left to wield his sword ; but Murray could not distinctly hear the deserved applauses of his friends, or the mysterious whispering of his enemies—for such a man will always have them.

The approbation of Washington, the Commander in Chief,—of Putnam, his chief Commander at Flatbush, and of Smallwood, his immediate commander, all evidenced by promoting him to a Captaincy, was a volume of commendation.

Had Capt. Murray retired from the army with such a rank—obtained for such services,—from such exalted men, it would have been announced at his death that he was an HERO IN THE WAR OF THE REVOLUTION.

But Murray knew that his countrymen had " passed the Rubicon ;" and although but a youth of twenty-one, he was resolved to face the enemy, until the last glimmering of hope from resistance was extinguished—then sullenly to retire before them, fighting as he retired ; and, when he had reached the utmost verge of the land of liberty, that place should be his sepulchre.

He continued in the service of the American army, until the close of the campaign of 1777, embracing, from the time he entered it, to that period, the most gloomy, des-

pairing, and desperate period, of the unequal contest between the infant colonies of America, and the kingdom of
Great Britain, probably when he entered into it,—during
the progress of it, and to the close of it, the most powerful
kingdom in Europe.

During the two campaigns of '76 and '77, Captain Murray was always at the post of duty and of danger, as a *soldier ;* but he impatiently awaited the time when he could
resume his station of Lieutenant, as an *ocean-*combatant.

The service he had to perform when in the army, as was
that of all the officers and soldiers in those two desponding
years, was more arduous and dangerous, than during any
other period of the revolutionary struggle.

They not only had to contend against the best disciplined
troops which Europe could produce, but they suffered all
the wants. privations, sicknesses, and despair which an ill
appointed camp invariably occasions.

There was scarce any arrangement that would make an
American officer of 1823 think of a Quarter-master, Commissary, or Hospital Department.

In addition to these disheartening circumstances, that effeminate, nerveless, heartless race of beings called then by
a name, which is now almost synonimous with traitor,—the
American tories, were an annoyance to the American
troops, worse, if worse could be, than the arms of a foreign
enemy in the field of battle, or the ravages of want and disease in the camp.   But, as the clemency of the American
government then spared them, let them now be remembered only with indignant and contemptuous pity.

Of the many thousand patriotic Americans who aided in
the holy cause of freedom, in the city of New York and
its vicinity : more became victims in British prison ships

—by the predatory incursions of tories and cow-boys, (not meaning the stern unyielding patriots, Williams, Van Wert, and Paulding, who captured Andre,) and also by unwholesome food and want of medical aid, than ever fell by the arms of the enemy in open contest.*

Capt. Murray, besides the serious injury sustained by the explosion at the battery in New-York, was so much

* The writer, not having been born until the close of the War of the Revolution, hopes to be indulged with a brief note, to allude to circumstances relating to his immediate connections, detailed to him by the surviving veterans of that awful contest.

In 1777, Gen Putnam, from incessant anxiety and exertions as Commander of the most important post between the armies of Sir Henry Clinton and General Burgoyne, was seized with sickness, as a prelude to the paralytic shock, which afterwards suddenly prostrated one half of his powerful frame. His Head Quarters were near West Point, where the Military Academy, and Fort Putnam are now situated. Major (now Col) Daniel Putnam, his son, his constant aid, and unlimited confidant, endured the excessive fatigue attached to his office, and the anxiety of a son for a sick father. Doctor Albigence Waldo,—the intimate of Gen. Putnam—the principal surgeon of his division—and afterwards his eulogist at his grave, by perpetual professional labour, in attending upon his sick, and dying comrades, was reduced almost to the grave himself. Mr. Samuel Waldo, (son in law to Gen. Putnam,) and a non-commissioned officer in his division, beheld more than one half of the company to which he was attached, carried corpses from their beds of straw to the grave, expecting every hour to follow his departed companions to the common grave of the soldier.

Such tales of distress. made an impression upon the mind of the writer, in very early years which become more deepened as he advances in life. How must the hearts of the present race of Americans, glow with admiration, when they know, that amidst this army of calamities, as well as amidst an army of foreign and domestic foes, not a murmur was heard but against the common enemy—not an execration was uttered but against the barbarous banditti of Tories and Cow-boys.

affected in his health, as to render it indispensably necessary for him to retire for a season to the hospitable mansion of Dr. Murray, his father, in Chestertown.

Happy for him was it that he had such a refuge from the
" peltings of the pitiless storms" which he had for twenty-
four tedious months, endured.

But " pitiful, wondrous pitiful" like the sufferings of
Othello, was the destiny of many war-worn and veteran
officers and soldiers, whose frames had been mutilated by
wounds,—emaciated by want of food,—uncovered for want
of clothing—and debilitated by hard service and wasting
sickness, when wandering towards their distant homes
through a country swarming with tories, more merciless
than the king of terrors, or with avaricious tavern keepers,
whose pendant signs, perhaps with the face of Washington,
Putnam, Warren, Montgomery, or Greene, upon them, to
induce the war-worn veteran to enter for refreshment and
repose—for which these harpies extorted from them, perhaps the whole avails of a campaign, for twenty-four hours
rest, and a small pittance of food.

Many overgrown estates in the country were begun in
this way ; and the present holders of them roll in wealth
and splendour upon the hard-earned gains of the veterans
of the revolution ; and who would now spurn from their
doors these few surviving heroes, unless their pockets were
lined with the pension money from government, obtained
for them by one of the wounded Heroes of Trenton, JAMES
MONROE.

Capt. Murray, as soon as his health would permit, resumed his station in the navy : and although there was no government vessel of suitable force for him as first lieutenant:
and as the grade of Master Commandant was not then established : he urgently solicited some *immediate* command.

He had become well acquainted with the enemy by two years' constant service in the army. He had seen them divest themselves of the noble sentiment of the ancient Saxons from whom they derive their origin, and assume the ferocious character of Goths.

His whole soul was enthusiastically alive in the sacred cause of his country, of liberty, and of man. Inaction to him, was next to despair.

The Marine Committee, for there was then no Navy Department organized as it now is, selected Lieutenant Murray to command a Letter of Marque.

The Old Congress confirmed the appointment; for the congress, then as a body, discharged nearly all the various duties which are now discharged in the various departments of the Treasury, War, and Navy, and as to the "Department of State," that consisted ostensibly of CHARLES THOMSON,* whose counter-signature to that of "President

---

* It may not be uninteresting to some readers to learn, that the venerable Secretary of the Old Congress still survives; and that at his retired mansion in the vicinity of Philadelphia, he has occupied much of his time in latter years, in translating the whole of the *Old* and *New Testament*, and, with the utmost care and scrupulous accuracy, revising the proof sheets as they issued from the press, when his translation was printed in four volumes. A perusal of that translation would be interesting in this age of *Biblical* criticism. It is however to be regretted that this "Octogenarian" did not occupy the same time in giving outlines of the proceedings of the *Old Congress*. We have, to be sure, his official signature to the most important Acts, Resolutions, Recommendations, &c. &c. of the 18th century—But we want *detail, minutæ, incidents, characters,* in the *Army, Navy,* &c. from such a source. The exalted Secretary, in his exalted employ of translating the Bible, *may be* in danger of being remembered with such sacrilegious translators as Hone, &c. in Great Britain, who by Mr. Gifford is called "*The mocker of his God, the rude scorner of his Saviour, the buffoon parodist of Holy Writ—the cold blooded, heartless,*

of Congress" operated upon American officers much more forcibly than does the amulet and charm upon Mahometans.

To see the names of PEYTON RANDOLPH, JOHN HANCOCK, HENRY LAURENS, JONATHAN TRUMBULL, &c. with Secretary Thomson's upon the same parchment, was a pledge that those who carried this evidence, were true to their country; and what must forever excite wonder, but *one* officer of any considerable grade, ever proved to be false, and he was the once gallant, but afterwards the disappointed, revengeful, diabolical, and traitorous Benedict Arnold.

While I feel a pride as a native citizen of Connecticut, whose ancestors were true to their country, and evidenced their fidelity by leading and joining the embattled ranks of the Republic—when I remember that that little beloved and patriotic state furnished double her proportion of soldiers, and treble her quota of officers in the army—when it is not forgotten that she furnished Major Gen. Israel Putnam—Major Gen. Parsons,—Major Gen. Huntington— Brig. Gen. Wooster, Col. Trumbull, Col. Allen, Col. Humphreys, Col. Knowlton, Col. Grosvenor, Col. Chester, Maj. Daniel Putnam, Maj. Pierce and others of inferior grade, but probably of equal valour ;—and that in the Navy she furnished Capt. Harden, Capt. Tryon, &c. as engaged in the same cause with Alexander Murray,* all of whom distinguished themselves—while this gallant catalogue is looked upon with a laudable pride, with the very extremity of mortification is it remembered that Arnold

malicious infidel, who labours day and night to rob the sick of their consolations of religion, and the dying of their hopes of immortality."

* In the war of '98 with France, of 1803 and 4 with Tripoli, and in 1812 with Britain, Connecticut also produced Isaac Hull, Isaac Chauncey and Charles Morris

also was a native of Connecticut.* His gallantry at Que
bec and Saratoga was tarnished, yea, obliterated by his
treason at West-Point, and his barbarity in Virginia and at
Groton and New-London in Connnecticut. The mental
happiness he once derived from integrity and patriotism,
was converted to anguish of heart for his treason.†

* Since the above was in type, the Author has been informed, by
good authority, that Arnold was a native of New Jersey.

† While the detested Arnold was plotting " treason, stratagems,
and spoils" at West Point, the most important inland post in America, the Father of the Republic, the now sainted WASHINGTON, was in
council at Hartford, Con. at the residence of the patriotic JEREMIAH
WADSWORTH, devising measures of defence and offence against the
enemy, with Gen. KNOX, and other American officers, together with
Count ROCHAMBEAU, Admiral TERNAY, and Marquis DE LA FAYETTE.
The treason was announced by that consummate general, NATHAN-
IEL GREENE, in General Orders.

Orange Town, Sept. 26, 1780.

Treason, of the blackest die, was yesterday discovered. General
Arnold, who commanded at West Point, lost to every sentiment of honour, of private and public obligation, was about to deliver up that
important post into the hands of the enemy. Such an event must have
given the American cause a deadly wound, if not a fatal stab ; happily, the treason has been timely discovered to prevent the fatal misfortune. The providential train of circumstances which leads to it, affords the most convincing proof the liberties of America are the
object of Divine Protection. At the same time the treason is to be
regretted, the General cannot help congratulating the army on the
happy discovery.

Our enemies, despairing of carrying their point by force, are prac-
tising every base act to effect by bribery and corruption, what they
cannot accomplish in a manly way.

Great honour is due to the American army, that this is the *first* instance of treason of this kind, where many were to be expected from
the nature of the dispute, and nothing is so bright an ornament in the
character of the American soldiers, as their having been proof against
all the arts and seductions of an insidious enemy.

The reader is now respectfully invited to leave the gallant Murray as a Captain in the army, and follow the writer in attempting to portray his no less, and, if possible, his more brilliant career, from a lieutenant, to the senior Post Captain and Commodore in the American navy.

In the narrative thus far, it was totally impossible to avoid noticing events in which he was an actor, and individuals with whom he acted. Indeed, history and biography are like twin brothers, and as they were produced together by nature, so history and biography must travel hand in hand ; and, to make a quotation from ' The word,' which never should be quoted with levity—" Can two walk together unless they are agreed ?"

In his Letter of Marque, Capt. Murray made his passage into the Atlantic ocean ; and, in the midst of an implacable, boastful, and imperious enemy, fought " various battles with various success."

To give a particular detail of all his services---of all his rencontres—of all his dangers, and all his escapes, would

Gen. Washington, who by the direction of Congress, reprimanded Arnold, even *before* his treason, says, *after* he had committed it—" 1 am mistaken, if at this time, Arnold is not undergoing the torments of a mental hell."

When upon his expedition against Virginia, he had a Virginian captain as prisoner, whom he asked—"What would the Americans do with *me* if they should take me ?" The noble Virginian, worthy of the state that produced Washington, answered—" They would first cut off that lame leg, which was wounded in the cause of freedom and virtue [at Quebec] and bury it with the honours of war ; and afterwards hang the remainder of your body in gibbets." But let us dismiss the disgusting subject, and of *all traitors* say, with the Prince of the drama---

Why let the *stricken deer go weep,*
The *hart ungalled play.*

36

be so similar with those previously attempted in this volume, that it would be, to readers, like "tales twice told to the ears of a drowsy man."

Suffice it to say, that as long as he sailed under the 'Continental Flag,' he acted worthy of the glorious cause in which he patriotically engaged ; and advanced in reputation, as his country advanced towards the conclusion of the glorious struggle for independence.

After a long, laborious, and incessant course of service, the persevering Lieutenant, near Newfoundland, encountered an enemy's armed ship, of about equal force to his own.

After a determined contest for victory, the proud Briton struck to the undaunted American.

Murray's ship was encumbered by prisoners equal in number to his own crew, and manifested strong indications of attempting a re-capture.   But the Lieutenant bore away for a port in France, with his prize in company, until his hopes of landing with it were blasted, and his solicitude for *his* prisoners was relieved by being himself, together with his officers and crew, his ship and his prize, captured by a British fleet, and all were carried into New-York, then in possession of Sir William Howe's army,

This was the theatre of the once gallant Capt. Murray's military career.   He now found himself, by pursuing his naval profession, a prisoner to an overwhelming naval force.

But the time had come when imperious Britain began to treat her rebel children in her possession as prisoners of war ; and to extend to them the rights belonging to civilized nations.

Lieut. Murray was not incarcerated in the Jersey prison-ship, once "a floating," but here a stationary, "hell of Old England," in which thousands of his gallant country-men had perished as the victims in the cause of freedom.

If the reader has condescended to peruse the preceding sketch of Com. Biddle, he will recollect the measures pur-sued by that noble hero of the revolution—by the Old Congress, and by Gen. Washington, to insure proper treat-ment to one of his lieutenants by the name of Josiah.*

Powerful as Britain was, and feeble as she imagined the "rebel colonies" to be, she began to be deterred—yes, *de-terred*, from treating American prisoners with barbarity. lest *their* government should resort to the *lex talionis*.

Capt. Murray was paroled—visited his admiring friends in Philadelphia, and was soon after exchanged for a British prisoner of equal rank with himself.

Although he had been commandant of a number of well appointed letters of marque, yet he expressed the deepest anxiety to enter as a subordinate officer, on board of a con-tinental frigate.

That heroic and consummate officer, and gallant warrior in the cause of his country, Capt. JAMES NICHOLSON, had been for some time the victorious commander of the Fri-gate Trumbull.

Believing that the reader will be gratified with a brief account of an engagement between this frigate and a supe-rior ship of war, before Murray entered her, I present it as published in a Boston Gazette, of June 15, 1780.

" Yesterday arrived here the Continental frigate Trum-bull from a cruise, James Nicholson, Esq. commander, who on Friday the 2d inst. in lat. 45, lon. 64 10, had an engage-

* See sketch of Biddle, where the particulars relating to lieutenant Josiah, and Capt. Cunningham, are detailed.

ment with a British ship of 36 twelve and six pounders. The action was close and severe, and supported with great gallantry by the Captain, officers and company of the Trumbull, against the superior force of the enemy, for five glasses, when both ships were equally disposed to part, the Trumbull having all her masts wounded in such a manner as to render it impossible for her to continue the engagement, and the British ship in a situation equally unfit for it. In ten minutes after the action ceased, the Trumbull lost her main and mizen topmasts within musket shot of the enemy, which they took no notice of, and soon lost her main and mizen masts. The masts of the British ship were left in a tottering condition, and it is supposed, must be gone. She was hulled in many places, all her pumps going, hove over many dead ; and, it is presumed, she suffered more than the Trumbull, and must have struck to her, if the Trumbull had not unfortunately sustained the loss of her masts. The Trumbull had 8 men killed, and 31 wounded, six of whom have since died of their wounds ; among the latter was Daniel Starr, the third Lieutenant. The British ship appeared to be bound to Charlestown ; but, as no questions were asked, and the action commenced without ceremony, her name or destination are unknown."

As much as the American reader has been astonished at the almost miraculous effect of American naval gunnery in the splendid triumphs of our navy in the second war with Britain, yet if the combats in the first, were as well known as those in the last, they might well excite equal wonder. Witness the Richard and Seraphis—the Randolph and Yarmouth—the Protector and Admiral Duff, the one just detailed, and to which another will now be added.

Such a commander as Nicholson, and such a ship as the

Trumbull,* were well fitted for such an officer as Murray, and he entered her as first lieutenant.

As soon as the Trumbull was fitted for sea, a most gallant band of officers and seamen were ready, and anxious to catch the first favouring breeze that would waft her along side of any hostile sail of equal force, that would presume to point her guns at this " rebel Frigate" named after the " Rebel Governor of Connecticut."

Capt. Murray, as lieutenant on board the Trumbull, al-

---

* This frigate was named after JONATHAN TRUMBULL, of Connec-ticut, president of Congress, and the first of that name, governor of Connecticut. His son, the renowned historical painter, who is now, (1823) in the employ of Congress, delineating, and painting, historical views of the most interesting events of the Revolution, was imprisoned in London during that war, in consequence of the following " word to the wise," from a " loyal American," *alias*, an American tory. He did not perish in the " conflagration," as appears from a note announc-ing his arrival in America. He returned to London after the peace, and there finished his " Battle of Bunker Hill," and the " conflagra-tion of Charleston."

From the London Morning Post, August 17.

" As a loyal American, and a friend to the best of kings, I think it my duty through the channel of your paper, to inform administration, that there are arrived in this city, two Americans (via Holland) and the one is son to the rebel Governor† of Connecticut; the latter an in-habitant of Boston, New England, and a Major in a rebel regiment, by the name of Massachusetts.‡ If such persons are suffered to be at liberty in England, another conflagration may soon happen.—A word to the wise is sufficient.

Your humble servant,

J—— T—PLE.

† Mr. John Trumbull.
‡ John-Steel Tyler.

" I have the pleasure to acquaint you, that Governor Trumbull's son, who was a prisoner in England, is arrived at Falmouth, Casco-Bay, and a number of vessels from Holland."

though not first in command, yet, being next to the first, a very important duty devolved upon him. The reputation. of his commander, as well as the fame of the ship, from previous achievements, inspired him with a restless emulation to identify his name with both.

The Trumbull sailed about the middle of August, 1781, to convoy a fleet of merchantmen to the Havanna.

It was the last cruise she ever made under American colours ; and probably the last she made under any colours.

Flushed far more with hopes of victory over some of the boasted " wooden walls of Old England" than over rich transports or merchantmen, which would swell their coffers with prize money, the gallant and daring Nicholson, with officers and sailors, daring and gallant as himself, bore away for the Capes of Delaware with his convoy.

Lieut. Murray was as familiar with these waters as the village swain is with the rivulets and fish-ponds of his district, and as fearlessly wafted towards the station of the powerful foe, as he angles for the finny tribe. But,

" A storm was nigh—an unsuspected storm."

Scarcely had the Trumbull cleared the dangerous Capes before she was struck with a most violent gale of wind. To this, in rapid succession followed the most tremendous peals of thunder, and momently succeeded by gleaming chains of lightning, which increased the horrors of the surrounding darkness.

The ship was severely injured in her spars, and rigging ; and needed a port to refit. But, such is the fate of naval warfare, the war of the elements which was rending the tackle of the Trumbull asunder, was also precipitating her

into a host of foes, though less powerful, more malignant
than the elements themselves.

The darkness was so intense, that no sail could be descried, until the gale had somewhat abated.   Capt. Nicholson then discovered that his ship was close along side
H. B. Majesty's Frigate the Iris of 33 guns, and Sloop of
War Monk, of 18 guns ! !

The phlegmatic calculator of chances would perhaps
gravely declare that Capt. Nicholson ought immediately
to have lowered his flag.   But amongst his officers were
Lieut. Murray, and Lieut. Dale,* who, like their commander, took no counsel from fear, were ready to enter
into the contest.

Instantly all hands were beat to quarters, and with fearless promptitude repaired to them.   The sea was still in
terrible commotion from the gale, and the rival ships went
furiously into action.   The combat was long and doubtful,
and the first signal of a cessation of it, was the extinguish-
ment of the battle-lanterns of the Iris, which enveloped her
again in darkness.

The exulting victors were about to board the Iris, as a
prize, when the Monk which had before taken but little
part in the action, gained a raking position—run directly
under the stern of the Trumbull, which was almost battered to pieces, and poured into her a succession of raking
broadsides.

In this dreadful situation—the ship unmanageable—
Lieuts. Murray and Dale severely wounded, and more than
one third of the crew killed or bleeding upon the deck, or
in the cockpit, Capt. Nicholson, cool and collected, lowered the flag of the gallant little Trumbull.

* Afterwards the justly respected and valiant Com. Dale,

She was towed into New-York, a useless wreck,—and object of curiosity—a hard earned trophy of the prowess of Britain !

As her name does not appear in the "List of the Royal Navy" of the "Queen of the Ocean," she is probably in the same state (allowing for the decay of a third of a century) as the Chesapeake, Essex, and President frigates, which like the "Continental frigate" Trumbull, were so gallantly defended against superior force as to render them better fitted for the situation of the once British frigates, the Guerriere, and Java, and the British Sloops of War, Peacock, and Penguin !

Capt. Murray might have said, in regard to this action, as he did, as President of the Court Martial, in 1815, which tried the lamented Decatur, for surrendering the frigate President to a squadron, after conquering the Endymion, " The enemy gained a ship—the Victory was ours."

After languishing with his wounds—fortunately (for his country) surviving them, and obtaining an exchange, Lieut. Murray, was appointed by the government of The Colonies, (for so the British continued to call Congress to that time, 1781,) to be First Lieutenant, of the Continental frigate, Alliance.*

This ship was for some time upon the coast of Britain, and belonged to Com. Jones' squadron, when the memorable engagement between the Good Man Richard, and the Seraphis occurred.

When Lieut. Murray entered her, she was commanded by Capt. Barry, one of the earliest " Naval Heroes of the

* This frigate was so named from the Treaty of Amity and "Alliance," between America and Louis XVI. and belonged to the squadron of Com. Jones. See "Sketch of Jones."

Revolution," and who, through a great variety of grades, and a long succession of important services, became the senior Commodore of the American navy.

The revolutionary services of Capt. Barry, and Capt. Murray, (acting as lieutenant,) were now drawing towards a close ; and it would be useless to tell what these gallant officers " might have done" had not the proud, and hitherto unconquered " King of England," sued for peace with his " Rebel Colonies."

George III. was happy to give a quit claim deed to his tenants in America, in 1783, and to suffer them to be " Lords of the Manor ;" and, by the Treaty of Ghent, in 1815, he very nearly promised to " warrant and defend the premises."

His son, then " Prince Regent," now George IV. may rest assured that if Americans surrender the Rupublic, the surrendry will be made to a power " more powerful" than the United Kingdoms of Great Britain and her dependencies.

Peace, " with healing in her wings" now shed her benign influence over the " Free, Sovereign, and Independent American Republic." The clarion of war, which for seven years of sanguinary contest, had echoed from the embattled hosts of Republican soldiers, and from the floating bulwarks of Republican seamen, was now succeeded by the harmonious " concords of sweet sounds-" The Olive Branch waved tranquilly over the swelling hills and fertile vallies, where late the unfurled banners of hostile foes challenged to combat.

A grateful, a protected, an emancipated people, rapturously embraced the peerless champions of their national salvation.

37

Conspicuous in the midst of this band of matchless warriors, stood the grandson of a Highland Chief, Alexander Murray.

If the immortalized spirits of the illustrious dead are permitted to blend with their ceiestial joys a participation in the scenes of terrestrial felicity, the ancient Murray, who was banished from the land of his fathers, by the implacable vengeance of the house of Brunswick, must have looked down with complacent delight upon his heroic descendant, who had avenged the injuries *of his own house*—the house of Murray.

Capt. Murray of the Navy, and Capt. Murray of the Army, uniting in himself the gallant soldier, and the ocean-hero ; and divesting himself of the double wreath of laurels acquired in both, assumed the character of the plain and dignified citizen ; proving *then*, by his amiable and unassuming deportment, that, with the scars of honour as a warrior, he could return to the gentle pursuits of peace as a citizen; and proving afterwards that he could re-assume the character of the determined warrior, and conduct the victorious arms of his country to any ocean or sea where the enemies of his country were to be found. It might be amusing to trace the life of this early veteran through the season of uninterrupted peace, (excepting the occasional skirmishing with native savages and native insurgents*) which intervened between the conclusion of the war of the revolution, in 178.5, and the commencement of the naval warfare with France in 1798. But his life is so exceedingly fertile in incidents of a public nature, that a description of his private virtues, however exalted, would be like

* Shays' Insurrection in Massachasetts, and the Whisky Rebellion n Pennsylvania.

the transition from an animating breeze that swells the canvas of the ship upon her course, down to the lifeless calm, when sleep, the image of death, holds dominion.

Upon the conclusion of the war, every single vestige of the little gallant wonder-working navy of America, was annihilated; or, what is the same as to warlike power, was converted into merchantmen.

The same keels, that for years had carried the thunder of freemen to the very shores of tyrants, were now transporting the productions of every quarter of the globe into the bosom of the Republic.

The civil fathers of the country knew well that although America was at the *Zenith* of national glory, she was at the *Nadir* of national bankruptcy—that she was *plus* in fame, that she was *minus* in wealth.

It would have been the very extremity of madness to continue the expense of a naval establishment, when the wounds of the revolutionary heroes were scarcely healed ; and the treasury had scarcely coin enough to defray the expense of medicine for healing them.

The gigantic statesmen of that portentous period knew it was as difficult to secure, by constitutional, legislative, judicial, and financial regulations, the rights and liberties of the Republic, as it had been to obtain them by some of the best blood that flowed in the eighteenth century.

They acted upon the great and exalted principle, that national glory would be more permanently established by national justice, than by standing armies and powerful fleets in time of peace, requiring a never-ending succession of taxes and burthens to support them.

The reader will again excuse the writer for referring him

to a previous publication, and for adopting some hasty remarks therefrom into this volume.*

The profound sagacity, and wary policy of American
Statesmen, who set the intricate machine of government in
operation under our Republican Constitution, well understood the overwhelming bankruptcy in which the British
empire was sinking, or rather sunk, by her immense naval
force.

They sought to bestow upon their Republic richer blessings than the blessing of national debt. No human sagacity, however, could, at that time foresee that American
commerce would soon become the direct road to sudden
national wealth; although they must have known that an
extended commerce could not long be protected without a
naval force, nor a naval force be supported without commerce.

England, the imperious, and then almost undisputed mistress of the ocean, wielding the trident of Neptune over
every sea, beheld American canvas in every latitude.

Her jealousy was roused; her armed ships searched our
vessels for " contraband goods," and impressed our seamen,
and immured them in their " floating dungeons."

Other petty naval powers, whose power on the ocean is
now merged with that of Britain, the real dictator of, because the most powerful nation in, Europe, followed the
example of aggression, as feeble whappets follow in the
train of a ferocious mastiff.

The pride of American seamen arising from the national
glory of America, acquired in the glorious revolution, was
compelled to succumb to the mandate of every puny whip-

* Vide Life of Decatur, 2d edition, chap. VI. " National glory and
national taxes."

ster who could show a gun upon his deck.   It was not voluntary submission, but submission "*ex necessitate rei,*"—
the necessity of the case,—a most painful necessity.

The national resources had been almost exclusively derived from individual wealth, and that wealth had for years
been committed to the ocean as the road to immediate opulence.

Other nations, which were contending for dominion upon
land and upon water, for a considerable period, lost sight
of the advancing wealth, and, as a consequence, national
power of the American Republic.

Contending for crowns which sat loosely upon the fearful heads that sustained their ponderous weight, and dreading to see them fall, these nations, although contending
with each other, seemed to unite in trying to blast the
growing commercial importance of America.

The Barbary powers, whose corsairs hovered over that
portion of the ocean where some part of our enterprising
merchantmen were pursuing their lucrative business, plundered their vessels, and made slaves of their crews.   The
greater commercial nations, with more power, and also
with more humanity, endeavoured to extirpate American
commerce, and check the rapid progress of American
wealth.   They possessed naval power ; of which our Republic was then destitute.

Our patriotic rulers, as soon as they found our country in
possession of the means adequate to the hard task of supporting our natural rights upon the ocean, began to devise
"ways and means" to do it.

It would require more pages than the limits of this sketch
will admit, to epitomize the diversified arguments resort-

ed to by the most eminent of American statesmen, in favour of, and against, an efficient naval power.*

Some of them looked upon the " thousand armed ships" of England, and despaired. They saw also the Russian, French, Spanish and Danish fleets, and dismissed all hopes of ever coping with any naval power.

But Washington was still alive ; and guiding the high destinies of our Republic in peace, as he had done in the war of the Revolution. His prescience readily suggested to his great and expanded mind, the indispensable necessity of a naval force to protect our extensive and extending commerce.

Negotiation, to be sure, had obtained some indemnification for spoliations upon it ; but the most successful negotiations have always been made at the mouth of the cannon.

Our rulers could no longer endure the thought that our citizens, who had sought a " home upon the deep," should become victims to every prince who could send out a few cruisers, with a rapacious crew. They were determined that American citizens, pursuing a lawful commerce upon the ocean should, as they ought, be protected there as well as those pursuing lawful business on land.

This was not the gasconading threat of a nurse, who only brandishes the rod before the eyes of a truant child, without daring to strike ; it was the decisive language of a parent, having a right to command, and power sufficient to enforce his decrees.

The year 1794, the auspicious period which laid the foundation of our present naval power, ought to be remembered with equal enthusiasm as that of 1776, which made

* See Journal of Congress, 1797, 98.

the declaration, and laid the foundation, for American Independence.

The first keel of a frigate that was laid by our government, was the key-stone to the triumphant arch of American glory.

If fancy might be indulged upon a subject which needs not its felicitous aid, we might see Neptune approaching our shores, and surrendering his trident to the banners of Columbia, when the first American frigate was launched into the bosom of the deep.

The writer, then a boy, may hope to be indulged for expressing now, the enthusiasm he felt when he beheld the frigate Constitution launched from a Boston ship-yard. This untutored enthusiasm was occasioned, not by knowing then, the immeasurable power of a navy, but from the immense assemblage of animated citizens who witnessed the animating scene. They might have exclaimed :—" There is one of our protectors upon the ocean ; while she swims, she will not only protect our individual wealth, but she will manfully sustain our national rights upon the waves." What might have then been prophecy is now history.

Proceeding with that caution and judgment which must mark the course of our rulers, they authorised the building of only four frigates of forty-four guns, and two of thirty-six.

Although this diminutive force was hardly sufficient to defend a single port in our own country, or to blockade a single island of any belligerent power, yet the amount of the force was of a secondary consideration to the adoption of the principle that a NAVAL FORCE was necessary for the defence of the vast extent of the seaboard of the American Republic, and for the convoy and protection of her immensely extended commerce.

For fifteen years, the naval ardour of Americans, which, during the revolutionary struggle elicited such brilliant sparks of ocean-valour, had been extinguished by the lucrative pursuits of commerce—the sordid love of wealth, and the luxury and effeminacy which wealth invariably produces.

Towards the close of the administration of the political father and saviour of the Republic, WASHINGTON, the younger and middle-aged class of Americans seemed to have degenerated alarmingly from the exalted spirit of their ancestors ; who, from the conclusion of the " French war," to the commencement of the " War of the Revolution," were inspired with the " Amor Patriæ," far more than they were with the gaudy charms of wealth.

The historian will never forget, that the victorious army of Hannibal was conquered upon the plains of Capua where there was no enemy but luxury ; and that Rome herself, having conquered Greece by arms, was herself conquered by the effeminate refinements of Greece ; and the Grecians themselves, after the lapse of many centuries of abject slavery, seem again to be returning to the heroism of the days of Achilles ; and may the God of armies fire their souls and strengthen their arms, till the Crescent shall bow to the banner of Greece.

John Adams, who with John Hancock, Samuel Adams, and others, first began to rock the " Cradle of Independence"—who manfully sustained the majesty of the warring colonies in foreign courts, when alone and unassisted, and which defied the gigantic power of Britain, was advanced, by the suffrages of his countrymen, in 1797, to the chair which the exalted, the august, the almost adored WASHINGTON, had left.

No prince of the House of Brunswick—of Bourbon—of Braganza, or of any other house, or of any other realm, ever ascended a throne so really exalted, as the Chair of the Chief Magistrate of the American Republic.

And here, let every surviving American Murray feel a glow of patriotic rapture, that, amongst the first acts of the second President, was giving his signature to the commission of ALEXANDER MURRAY as a POST CAPTAIN* in the American navy, and designating him to assist in organizing it.

This early notice of the new President, must have been doubly gratifying to Capt. Murray, as it was an unsolicited appointment—unknown to his nearest friends, and wholly unknown and unexpected to himself till the moment it was announced to him.

Notwithstanding the long and arduous course of service in the army and navy, and the numerous battles in which he had valiantly fought, upon land and water, Capt. Murray when called again into service, was but little over forty years of age.

As soon as the French marauders in the West Indies laid aside all disguise, and began to prey upon American commerce, as wolves prowl and prey amongst unprotected flocks, Capt. Murray was ordered to leave the further organization of the navy to other hands, and to conduct a small Corvette into the midst of picaroons (another name for buccaneers and pirates) and neither of them deserving even the humble name of privateersmen.

Capt. Murray, in the Corvette Montezuma, with officers and a crew of real Americans, dashed fearlessly amongst these despoilers of merchant ships; spread dismay and

* The writer is not positive that this commmission was signed by Adams. If it were by Washington, it was equally flattering.

38

consternation amongst them,—rescued thousands, and perhaps millions of dollars from their grasp, and diffused joy
amongst hundreds, and perhaps thousands of American
merchants, who might otherwise have been reduced from
independence to bankruptcy.

While he was thus securing the wealth of individuals, he
was pouring treasures into the national coffers.

So sensible was the government of his invaluable services, that Congress passed a vote of thanks* to him, and
promoted him to the frigate Insurgente, which had been
captured by Com. Truxton.

Before he had an opportunity to turn the guns of this ship
against the nation that built her, he was removed to the
ship that took her.

Capt. Murray was then appointed to the command of
the frigate Constellation of 32 guns. This little ship had
before become a favourite with sailors from her splendid
victory over the Le Insurgente, one of the finest frigates
in the marine of France. While her gallant commander was
walking upon her quarter deck, where the veteran Truxton
had walked and conquered before him, his naturally ardent
mind must have experienced a sort of extra stimulus. He
felt, if he did not *express*, these sentiments. " This little
ship is one representative of the power and energy of the
American Republic. The French Republic, once the
friend of America, when the murdered Louis XVI, and his
matchless queen, Maria Antoinette of the house of Theresa,
wielded the gentle sceptre of power over that most charming portion of our world, is now the deadly enemy of my

* It is believed that this was the first and only vote of thanks by
Congress for similar service. Thanks for single victories have become (perhaps) too common.

beloved country. Washington, who went on majestically conquering and to conquer, with Fayette, Rochambeau, and Ternay, in the War of the Revolution, resolved that my country, which he, and his compatriots, of which I was one, and whose commission I then bore, rescued from the despotic power of the House of Brunswick, should not be overwhelmed in the tremendous vortex of the French Revolution. His prescience enabled him to fathom the very dedth of that destruction which would accompany the modern Gauls, when they tore asunder the ligament of despotism with which they had been bound from the time of Clovis, her first monarch, to Louis XVI., her last and her best. He declared America a neutral power. Adams, his successor, now presides over the destiny of the Republic, and will support, by an armed neutrality, what Washington published as an edict."

Capt. Murray was as indefatigable in this ship, as he was in the corvette Montezuma, in extending protection and affording convoy to merchantmen. It can hardly be conceived how an American Frigate can be more profitably, or indeed, more honourably engaged, than by preserving the wealthy commerce of their countrymen from the rapacity of marauders and picaroons, and their persons from, imprisonment, indignity and insult. It is a fact communicated directly to the writer from some of the present distinguished officers of the American navy, who were then midshipmen upon the West India station, that the French, and even the Spanish officers and seamen, treated Americans in their possession with a barbarism which would assimilate the naturally humane Frenchman to the morose and sullen Spaniard, and both of them to the malignant and implacable disciples of Mahomet. This treatment arous-

ed all the latent sparks of American indignation in the bosom of Capt. Murray, and his manly and determined ship's
crew. They panted for an opportunity to let the little
Constellation once more exhibit her *corruscations* to the
boasting Monsieurs and sulky Dons. They knew that the
gallant Little, in the Boston frigate, had all but sent the La
Burceau to the bottom. They most impatiently waited
and sought for an opportunity to achieve deeds and gather
laurels of equal renown.

It would be a hopeless undertaking to endeavour to con-
trovert the prevalent sentiments of the sons of glory who
make a profession of arms; and it would be deemed arro-
gance to doubt the correctness of their opinions. Far be it
from Americans to entertain even a thought in opposition
to that high sense of honour and fame, which inspires the
bosoms of our noble countrymen in the navy and army.
It is that, that has pressed them forward to give to Americans a pre-eminent rank, and to America the title of THE
ONLY REPUBLIC. But it may well be asked, if in the be-
stowment of applause, of medals, of swords, and rewards,
the favourites of fortune are not always the favourites of
the nation? In the naval warfare with France, the names
of Truxton and Little, echoed from the Atlantic to the
Mississippi—from the lakes to the Mexican Gulph, while
those of Com. Decatur the elder, Capt. Murray, Capt.
Tryon, and others whose unceasing assiduity and sleepless
vigilance had swept the ocean of picaroons, and filled our
harbours with richly laden merchantmen, are remembered
only as " good men and true," who instead of encountering and conquering an equal or superior armed ship, have
only saved the citizens and the commerce of the country
from the rapacious grasp of ocean robbers.

Allusion might be made to the war of 1803 and 4, with Tripoli and of 1812, with Britain; but as we are drawing the sketch of the venerable veteran, Alexander Murray, towards those periods, in which many of his cotemporaries acquired a deathless fame ; and as many of them, thank heaven, still survive, as the honour and the hopes of the Republic, a deep solicitude is felt lest the labours, even of the " honest chronicler," should be converted into a " vehicle of adulation to the living or extravagant eulogy of the dead."

But, *living*, Alexander Murray never courted the ephemeral adulation of the day.   He possessed a native energy of mind which could not be enervated by fulsome praise, or disheartened by censure or neglect.   And, *dead*, his memory needs not " extravagant eulogy" to transmit his name down to latest posterity amongst the high worthies of his species, and the benefactors of the Republic.

During the most sanguinary period of the naval contest between America and France, the British had a considerable naval force on the West India station.

The *natural* hostility of Britons against Frenchmen, was heightened by the tremendous strides that mighty power was making through the falling kingdoms of Europe.

The *unnatural* hostility of Britons against Americans, was in some measure lowered by the splendid victories they had recently gained over their deadly foe.

The naval commanders of " the Queen of the Ocean" were compelled to manifest at least an involuntary respect towards the American flag.

The *Magnanimique*, once a French ship of the line of 64 guns, was captured and razeed down to a British frigate of 48 guns.   She was able to sink the Constellation at a single well-directed broadside.

Capt. Murray was cruising in the leeward islands in the Constellation, (then of 32 guns) Capt. Taylor, in the Magnanimique, in the dead of night gave the Constellation a gun.

This was done, without exhibiting any signal, or in any way discovering the character of his ship.

Whether this was an intentional insult to Capt. Murray— a design to disgrace the ship, as the Little Belt attempted to disgrace the President frigate, and as the Leopard actually did disgrace the frigate Chesapeake, years after, the reader will judge from the sequel.

Capt. Murray, in the Constellation, set the first example to his brother officers of repelling *any* indignity to the American flag, proceeding from any cause whatever.

His gallant cotemporary, Com. Rodgers, followed his example ; but the commander of the Chesapeake, in 1807, did not follow it.

That ill-fated ship, manned from the fine bay where she first embraced her destined element, and on the borders of which still was visible *insignia* of the Gothic devastations, perpetrated by a Gothic British Admiral in the second war between America and Britain, seemed to have something ominous in her very name.

A field for digression is here opened ; but *here*—" Beshrew the sombre pencil ;" and return, with delight, to the gallant Capt. Murray, who, upon this singular occasion, discovered that cool discretion which constitutes the character of a great warrior, quite as much as dauntless bravery.

Upon receiving the shot, he immediately ordered his ship cleared for action. The result I have the pleasure of giving in the language of a Philadelphia correspondent :

" In that doubtful moment of conflict, in the bosom of

his officers, he ordered the reefs out of his topsails, to gain time in preparing the ship for battle.   As soon as that object was attained, the ship was put in stays—all hands beat to their quarters—she passed close under the lee, on opposite tacks, bringing all the guns to bear and poured into the strange sail a most destructive broadside.   As the sail did not return the fire, the Constellation was immediately put about ; and it was resolved to hail before a second fire was made.   This was instantly done, and it was soon discovered that the ship had fired into a friendly sail.   Her boat was then despatched to the Constellation, and satisfactory explanations were made.

" The British officer, from the Magnanimique, assured Capt. Murray that nothing but the uncommon prudence of Capt. Taylor, her commander, and the course pursued by Capt. Murray, checked a dreadful combat, which would have ensued.   Every officer and seaman on board each ship, could scarcely be controled from keeping up the fire, as *each* supposed that it was a *French frigate* that each had encountered, *both* which ships were on the look-out for.

" Capt. Taylor cast not the least censure upon the conduct of Capt. Murray ; but observed, that he had been severely injured in his spars, sails and rigging, that he should be obliged to go into port to repair damages."

Capt. Taylor probably discovered his error from the fire of an American frigate, as suddenly as Capt. Murray did his, from the display of a British ensign.   British officers had become sufficiently familiarized with French and Spanish manœvering and gunnery to know that a single broadside, even from a French or Spanish ship of the line could not have produced such disastrous effect as the fire of an American frigate of the smallest class.

It was the *first* broadside which a ship of war, bearing St. George's cross, had received from one, carrying the American stars and stripes, since the war of the Revolution ; and fortunate would it have been for the boasted superiority of British naval prowess, had it been the last.

From this brief detail of an interesting incident in Capt. Murray's " meridian life," a useful lesson may be deduced by those who traverse the highway of all nations, in public ships ; which, when afloat, are as sacred as the territory of the nation, whose power they in part represent.

Had the " affair of the Chesapeake and Leopard," been adjusted on the spot, as was that of the Constellation and the Magnanimique, the leading cause of the second war between America and Britain might not have widened and widened the breach between the two countries, until it could be healed only by an appeal to arms, which cost some of the best blood which the American Republic and the British Empire have, in modern days, produced.

When hostilities ended between America and France, by negotiation, in 1802, the gallant little American navy was rendered still smaller by an act of Congress for the reduction of it.

A great number of accomplished officers, either left the service entirely—retired upon half-pay, or held themselves in readiness once more to unfurl the banners of their country.

Capt. Murray, having passed through the whole revolutionary struggle, either in the army or navy—having also been in constant and active service during the whole naval warfare with France, might well have wished to retire.

THOMAS JEFFERSON, who, like his immediate predecessor, was assiduously engaged in the cabinet and council of

the nation, and of Virginia, in the revolution---who drew
the Declaration of American Independence, and who is
now one of the three survivors who signed it--was Secretary
of State, and Ambassador, by the appointment of Washington, was elevated to the chair of Chief Magistrate of the
Republic, when the war-worn Murray was once more relieved from incessant and toilsome duty.

The French Republic, as the great and powerful, and
humiliated French Empire was then called, notwithstanding she had, with resistless strides, prostrated surrounding
kingdoms, and out of their wrecks carved kingdoms for
herself, was ready and willing, and even anxious to avail
herself of the pacific disposition of the American administration, to negotiate a peace with the American Republic.
She had a specimen of such kind of negotiation as Truxton,
Little, Murray, Barry, Decatur the elder, Tryon, &c.
displayed upon their *tapis*.

Charles Maurice Talleyrand, once the traveller in America, afterwards bishop of Autun, and then the " primum
mobile" of the vast designs of Napoleon, the modern Charlemagne, perfectly understood the American character and
country,* and, in OLIVER ELLSWORTH, C. COTESWORTH
PINCKNEY, and GOUVERNEUR DAVIE, recognized dignified
and decided American diplomatists.

* The writer enjoyed the high honour of hearing from the tongue
of the great Oliver Ellsworth, many deeply interesting anecdotes of
that unsurpassed minister, Talleyrand. Said Judge Ellsworth, " My
official duty, as Chief Justice, led me to explore the most interesting
portions of the United States. I thought myself tolerably acquainted
with the relative situation of the different states,--the different pursuits of the people, in different portions of the country. I thought I
had a considerable acquaintance with the American character ; judge
then of my surprise, in occasional interviews with Talleyrand, when I

An honourable peace was made, and the American character, which had begun to decline, was restored to its
pristine vigour. It somewhat declined again, and was again
restored by the second war with Britain.

During the naval warfare with France, the detested and
vengeful barbarian Turks, and the graceless and ruthless
disciples of the arch impostor of Mecca, were preying in
the Mediterranean upon American merchantmen, and
American citizens, with that diabolical ferocity which forever is stamped upon the conduct of cowards, when they
conclude they can rob, ravish and murder, with impunity.

Having, in the imperfect sketch of the veteran Edward
Preble, a successor of the veteran Alexander Murray,
briefly alluded to the merciless treatment of the Mahometan Turks towards American Christians, I will barely refer
the reader to that sketch, as it is almost impossible, in our
copious language, to find terms of abhorrence and execration sufficient to pour out against the ireful, detested, implacable, blood thirsty, God defying, infernal Turks, who
are now preying upon the noble Grecians, as they then
were upon our noble countrymen in bondage. Although
we may well exclaim with the bard,

> "Let not this weak and erring hand,
> Presume thy bolts to throw,
> Nor deal damnation round the land,
> On each I judge a foe."—

heard from this arch Frenchman, more minute descriptions of the
country, and more penetrating observations upon the comparative
wealth, and power, and future prospects of the various states, than I
have often heard from an American; and I must confess I was astonished at obtaining ideas of my native country, at a hotel in Paris,
which were entirely novel to me." These, according to recollection,
and a common-place book, are very near the remarks of Judge Ellsworth.

yet, when reflecting upon the unvarying ferocity of Mahometans towards Christians, it is hardly possible to express
our sentiments in Christian language ; and to make us hope
that the spirit of crusading may revive—that a war of subjugation, if not of extermination, be waged by the Christian
against the Mahometan world.*

Capt. Murray had hardly come out of the smoke and
thunder of the West Indies, in chastising Frenchmen and
Spaniards, before he was designated as Commodore of a
small squadron designed to pour out a portion of American
wrath against the Tripolitans, at the head of whom the
blood-glutted Jussuff had placed himself, after embruing
his hellish hands in the blood of his father and elder brother ; and driving another brother, the miserable Hamet
Caramalli into exile ; either of whom, with equal power,
would have been equally merciless as Jussuff himself.

Com. Murray hoisted his broad pendant upon that matchless little frigate, the Constellation.

He seemed to be as partial to that ship, as Nelson, in his
earlier life, was to the Agamemnon, a heavy British ship
of the line, which, to use the language of one of his nume-

---

* The following forcible description of the Mahometan Turks, in
the 19th century, is from the production of an anonymous writer, published since this Sketch was written. Another late author says :—
" The bitter draught prepared for Christians by Mahometans, is drug-
ged by the hand of death, and brewed in hell."

" The character of the Turks is too well known to require comment. Ignorant, fanatical, brutal, and ferocious, destitute of almost
every virtue, and tainted with every vice, the sworn foes of every
thing bearing the name of Christian, whom no treaties can bind, and
whose faith with all but Mahometans is given but to be violated, they
ought to be treated as enemies to mankind ; and all civilized nations
ought to combine, either in exterminating them from the earth they
have polluted, or in depriving them of power for future mischief."

rous biographers—" Nelson wore out the Agamemnon, and the Agamemnon almost wore out Nelson."

Com. Dale, his gallant associate in the war of the Revolution, and his brother officer in the Trumbull, when she beat the Iris, and then struck to the Iris and the Monk, and in which both were severely wounded, had preceded him in the command of an American squadron in the Mediterranean.

It would be extraneous to the object of this sketch to dwell upon the services rendered to his country by Com. Dale.

It is sincerely hoped, that some hand far abler than the one that is now attempting a faint outline of his energetic, persevering, and valiant comrade, will present to the American reader, a full biography of this hero in three wars— in the most important ocean, and in the most extensive sea in our world.

It may, however, be remarked, that Com. DALE led the American *van* in the Mediterranean—first exhibited a small specimen of that increasing naval power, which, in the hands of one of his successors, Com. PREBLE, produced such astonishing dismay amongst Turks.

One of Com. Dale's officers, Lieut. Sterrett, in the little schooner Enterprise, (which has become the most celebrated schooner in the world) gained the first American victory over Turks, as Capt. Hull in the second war did over Britons, in the most celebrated frigate, the Constitution.

Com. Dale's squadron was so small, he was not, by his government, permitted to act *offensively* on any occasion. Lieut. Sterrett acted only defensively, when he battered a Tripolitan corsair of much superior force, almost to pieces, and sent home the wreck of her and her surviving crew, to be bastinadoed, and to be ridden on asses, (like Christians) as an indelible disgrace, for striking his flag to a "kellup en saurha" (Christian dog.)

Com. Dale thus restrained by instructions from his government—thus inhibited from striking, until he was struck, and perhaps from the blow, unable to strike at all, was in the worst possible situation a naval commander could be placed.

If he had been unable to blockade his enemy, and they should have escaped from port, and assailed him with treble his force, he must either have escaped, if possible, or have patiently waited for a general attack from the whole marine of Tripoli before he could fire a gun, or board a corsair!!

Com. Murray relieved Com. Dale from his arduous duty, and embarrassing situation, and had a duty equally arduous, and a station equally embarrassing to fill himself.

This contracted sketch might be swelled to a volume by dilating upon the peculiar relations subsisting in 1802, between the American government and the Barbary states, as they had a peculiar effect upon Com. Murray.

Although this skilful and consummate commander could exercise the coolest judgment, and the soundest discretion, yet he never could be brought to think with the gasconading knight in Shakspeare, that "the better part of valour is discretion," or to act like him in "counterfeiting death, thereby to save life."

However much the philanthropist, the moralist, and the Christian may applaud that pacific disposition in governments which endeavour to bring about "Peace on earth, good will to men," yet, when civilized and christianized nations, who scrupulously regard the faith of treaties—the dictates of reason, and the injunctions of humanity, are compelled to enter into collision with the modern Saracens, and the disciples of Mahomet, who habitually violate them all, it would be feminine pusillanimity to exclaim Peace! peace!

Missionary societies may send missionaries to convert them to Christianity—governments may send ambassadors to negotiate with them—the wealth of nations may be exhausted in paying them tribute—they detest the very sound of christianity—they hold it a canon of Mahometan faith to violate compacts with christians, and the tribute they extort, increases their means of waging war with the whole Christian world.

They are restrained by nothing but fear; and fear can be excited in them by nothing but the display of power, and the roaring of hostile cannon.

From 1803 to 1823 the American Republic have wisely acted upon this principle; and a Turk would now as soon rattle his beads in the face of an emir of the Sublime Porte, as to offer injury or indignity to an American.

Com. Murray, with the frigate Constellation, displayed the American banner, the insignia of which the Tripolitans had learned from his predecessor. He had but little other force; but so vigilant was he and all his officers and seamen, that these lawless robbers were kept in continual check.

Their marine force was sheltered in the bay of Tripoli, under the protection of the powerful batteries of the Bashaw. He still felt the most sovereign contempt for Americans, and yet the extremest mortification at beholding his inactive navy moored under his immediate view for safety.

He however derived a sort of devilish satisfaction in

feasting his infernal eyes, by gazing into his dungeons. where many Americans were in pinions and in chains.

Although the American commander could not relieve them, the hapless captives felt the cheering balm of hope. even in their dungeon. It was a consoling consideration that they were held in remembrance by their gallant countrymen ; and that the government of their country was beginning the work of their redemption.

The name of Alexander Murray was familiar with them, as was that of Dale and Sterrett; and they felt assured that there was a redeeming spirit in the American Republic, that would sever their chains asunder—rescue them from Mahometan bondage, and emancipate them by the arm of power, rather than by exorbitant ransom.

But their hope was to be " long deferred;" and hundreds of their countrymen, who afterwards came to redeem them, were to linger away many—many tedious months in the same gloomy cell with themselves.

Com. Murray so distributed his small force, as not to suffer a single Tripolitan keel to escape, to prey upon American merchantmen.

By this arrangement, he was, at one time, entirely alone with his ship before the bay of Tripoli. He was for some time totally becalmed, but a little distance from the same fatal rock upon which one of his gallant successors, Com. Bainbridge immoveably struck ; and who with his unrivaled officers and crew, became prisoners to the detested Jussuff, the reigning bashaw of Tripoli.

In this perilous situation, an overwhelming superiority of force came out in small vessels which would be managed in a calm, by sweeps, and gave battle to Com. Murray.

He sustained the attack for a long time, by wearing ship and keeping the enemy at a respectful distance, who still felt secure of victory.

A favourable breeze at length sprang up—he made immediate sail into the midst of the Bashaw's fleet—poured out starboard and larboard broadsides, and shots from his forecastle guns and stern-chasers with such astonishing rapidity, and destructive effect, that the Tripolitan vessels, shattered, battered, and scattered, made their escape into their harbour, and under protection of their own batteries.

The nature of the warfare was such, that had Com. Murray been able, as he unquestionably was, to have captured a part at least, of *this* squadron, it would not have corresponded with his *instructions*. He could only defend himself.

Com. Dale, after the gallant Sterrett had silenced and completely beaten a heavy corsair, could not make a prize of her, but sent her home to the bashaw.

It was as impossible for the bashaw to conceal his severe chagrin at the result of this rencontre, as it was for the American prisoners to conceal their high exultation at the success of it, on the part of the gallant commodore.

During his continuance upon this station, he had no other opportunity to display his skill and valour in defending his force against the enemy. He had " scotched the snake, but not killed him ;" and the bashaw was permitted to eject his venom at a harmless distance ; or, like the castigated ape, to bruise himself by the threshings of his own arms. The American Commodore, by his instructions, could do nothing but brandish his rod—he could not strike offensively.

Com. Murray continued to stand off, and to stand on,—

blockading and defying the mortified Tripolitans. It was a sluggish pursuit for an active warrior, who had conquered Britons upon land and upon water ; and who had administered effectual chastisement to boasting Frenchmen and insolent Spaniards.

But, devoted, from innate and acquired principle, to his country, he would serve it in any station, so be it he could support its rights, and advance its interests.

He little knew what secret influence was operating in his own country, to displace him, even from the station he then held. He was soon to receive a blow from the other side of the Atlantic ; but the hand that was to inflict it, was concealed from his view. President Jefferson had ever manifested the utmost respect for Com. Murray, and continued to manifest it till the day of his death. Without attempting to deduce the reasons, *a priori*, for the measure, we know the *ultimatum* was, that Com. Murray was superseded by Capt. Morris, and returned to America in the Constellation.

This was the third war from which Alexander Murray had returned to the bosom of his country, and to the circle of his friends, with unfading laurels acquired in each, and without a blot to tarnish his escutcheon. It is often the fate of rash and impetuous valour, heedless of fixed principle, to commit some untoward act that dims the lustre of brilliant achievements. The applause that is justly bestowed upon " deeds of noble daring," is immediately followed by expressions of regret that some indelible stain is impressed upon the actor, that can never be obliterated. It was not so, most fortunately for his imperishable reputation, with Com. Murray. Although he was superseded, in his command in the Mediterranean by Com. Morris, as one

40

of his immortal successors, Com. Preble was, by Com.
Barron, Murray could not be degraded. As a finished statue upon a lofty pedestal is diminished to the view only by
its superior elevation, so the fame of this warrior cannot
be lessened, only by surpassing the comprehension of those
who contemplate it.

Although at this period, Com. Murray had not reached
fifty years in the calender of his life, he had spent nearly
one third of that time in sanguinary warfare in fighting for
the cause of the Republic. Yes! he had fought, and
fought valiantly in THIRTEEN battles! Many of his gallant
countrymen have acquired their fame and their fortune too,
in one victory, and in one hour; and the great mass of
their countrymen who never faced an enemy, or exposed
their lives in the perils and dangers of war, now participate
in the glory which they have attached to the name of
American.

As to the course pursued by the immediate successor of
Com. Murray in the command of the American squadron in
the Mediterranean, it belongs not to this brief sketch of
his immediate predecessor. At this period of American history, the writer was too young, and ought to have been en-
grossed too much by other pursuits, to take any interest in
the political commotions that then agitated the councils of
this country. They did not then interest him : but, anxious
to acquire at least a superficial view of measures then adopted, he has recently recurred to the publications of that
day. It was like groping one's way through a wilderness
of "thorns and thistles," and as the traveller made his
egress, ingress, and regress, he would be most sensibly convinced, at every step, that the curse denounced against this
world in consequence of " Adam's first transgression," had

not ceased to operate ;—that the sentence against the serpent, " on thy belly shalt thou go," was then in full force.

Com. Murray had then the proud satisfaction of recording in the catalogue of his friends and patrons, the exalted names of George Washington, John Adams, and Thomas Jefferson ; and at the day of his death might add those of James Madison, and James Monroe.

At the time Com. Morris was appointed to succeed Com. Murray, the Navy Department had become so organized, that the President did not deem it his duty to interpose his authority in regard to the arrangements therein digested. That department acted to a certain degree as a nominating body, and the President as the approving power of the nominations therein made. When he approved of the nomination of Com. Morris, he could not foresee what would be the course of that officer as commander of the Mediterranean squadron. But the American people now know what took place at the seat of government, after that officer was succeeded by the veteran Preble.

Here that subject will be dismissed. The man of research needs not to be reminded of it ; and those who catch their opinions second handed, from those who adopted them without reason, and cannot be reasoned out of them, will be dismissed with perfect indifference, whether they approve or disapprove of the treatment towards Com. Murray.

To a sluggish and neutralized mind, which is neither elevated by pleasure, or depressed by pain—which knows not how to appreciate the acute sensibility of a highminded man, when honoured, or the extremity of his mortification when neglected, it would seem that Com. Murray

ought to have been satisfied, and even thankful for being
removed from active service !

The prince of the drama makes the injured Leonato thus
address the consoling Antonio—

> " It is *all men's* office to preach *patience*
> " To those who *wring* under a *load of injury.*"

The phlegmatic beings, whose hearts are as cold as an
anchorite, and whose affections can no more be warmed
than polar ice, most generally place themselves uncalled
into the monitory chair, and deal out a string of thread-bare
proverbs, which their nurses taught them upon the stool
at the same time they cudgelled into their brains the or-
thodox catechism.

Such neutral creatures will have the presumption to offer advice and consolation to such a man as was ALEXAN-
MURRAY ! " Fillip me with a three-man betle," (as Falstaff said) " before I would condescend to receive either
advice, consolation, or cash from such miserable comfort-
ers."

It is a man's own soul that measures the injury that is
done him ; and it is aggravated or softened as his mind is
more elevated, or more stupified.

Com. Murray was too exalted to descend to the low level of the swarms of insects who were warmed into life by
the resuscitating rays of Presidential favour. He would
neither smile upon them for their officious intermeddling
in his favour, or frown upon them for their machinations to
effect his degradation.

He brushed these *ephemera* away from him, as a lion
would shake dew-drops from his mane, and remonstrated
against his removal to the Executive. He had one privi-

lege left him : the privilege of complaining, and he did it at " Head-Quarters."

It was ever the course of the sainted WASHINGTON, so far as executive favours could constitutionally extend, to bestow the rewards of honour and emolument upon those who had devoted themselves to the service of the Republic.

If any sort of proportion could be maintained between services rendered, and rewards to be bestowed, what would have been the reward of Com. Murray ?

It is unhesitatingly averred, that at the time he returned to America from the Mediterranean in 1802, there was not a single American living who had passed through more arduous duty ; faced more dangers—fought in more battles ; or achieved more victories.

His locks were blanched by the elements ; his body was wounded by hostile arms ; his sense of hearing was affected, by the concussions of roaring cannon, and a premature old age had insidiously stolen upon him by his prodigality of his own blood.

This is no coloured fiction, unless the plain story of the unsurpassed services of Murray, may be ranked amongst the varnished tales of romance.

When speaking of rewards due to this veteran of the Republic, money is as far from the conceptions of the writer, as it was from him.   It was *rank*—it was *station*—it was *command*, he sought for, and which he so meritoriously deserved.

Was age an objection to him ? let it be remembered that the then President, at just about this time, when answering an objection to an officer in Connecticut on account of age, said, " at eighty, Franklin was the ornament of human nature," and at eighty-five he is now, himself.

Com Murray to be sure had reached the meridian of life; and, by regular gradation, had ascended to the meridian of glory; and had the American government permitted him to go forward in the path to the temple of fame, in which he had so successfully travelled all his life, Com. Morris, his first successor, might have escaped from the adimadversions of his government, and country—Com. Preble, his second successor, might have died without some of the laurels which he won, and carried to his grave—and Com. Barron, his third successor, might have returned to Ameriica without the honour of blockading the Tripolitan navy, until Mr. Lear had *negotiated* a peace which Preble had *conquered.*

One of the profoundest, and altogether the most interesting of Roman historians, remarks (to put it in plain English) " A wise government will avail itself of the successful example of its enemy." The British government, when *Nelson* had continued to conquer, continued him in service, until he prostrated the combined navy of France and Spain at Trafalgar; and it is no extravagant conjecture to presume, from the uniform judgment and courage of Com. Murray, that if he had been continued in the command of the Mediterranean squadron, with its subsequent augmentation, he would have triumphantly returned to America in 1805 ; and that he would now be remembered as the first Christian hero who made the followers of Mahomet humbly submit to Christian prowess.

To use a term of the legal profession, the " *quo animo*" with which he was treated, cannot, at this remove of time, be fathomed ; and, to resort to another axiom of lawyers, " *suggestio falsi, et suppressio veri,*" are stamped in a moral sense, with eqnal turpitude.

Whether it was the suggestion of falsehood, or the suppression of truth, that removed him, the surviving officers of the Navy Department at that period, may possibly determine.

These remarks are not made to harrow up the acrimony of party feelings. The writer rejoices, most sincerely, that the " era of good feelings" now most happily prevails in our beloved Republic. But, notwithstanding Alexander Murray is removed from his temporal to his eternal glory—notwithstanding his sublimated spirit is now equally regardless of the deserved applause of his earthly friends and the insidious machinations of his ungenerous competitors, it is the solemn duty of his surviving countrymen, to enter a solemn protest against any injury committed against this sleeping hero, when in life.

Com. Murray, after having expressed his dignified indignation at the course pursued in regard to the command in the Mediterranean, retired with the consciousness of having served his country, and in that way, served his Creator faithfully.

He was not one of those querulous, petulant men, who utter forth their quotidian ditties of effeminate and useless lamentation.   But, with the heart and with the ken of a patriot, he watched the progress of the American navy. He gloried in the fame of Preble, who finished what his compatriot and friend Com. Dale began.   He welcomed the returning Bainbridge, Porter, Jones and Biddle from bondage ; and Decatur (the younger) Stewart, Hull, Lawrence, Morris, (the younger) Macdonough, Trippe, &c. from victory.   He might then have said to his Maker—" Now let thy servant depart in peace, for mine eyes have seen thy salvation."

But, scarcely had two years more rolled over his honoured head, before the most flagrant outrage was committed against the American Republic and her little navy.

An imperious British officer, in H. B. Majesty's ship the Leopard assailed the American frigate Chesapeake!

It was the tocsin of war to all true Americans; and the leading cause of the second war between America and Britain.

Notwithstanding more than half a century had been added to years gone by since his birth; like a sleeping Sampson, he was again aroused to the highest possible pitch of patriotic indignation.

He saw Britons, with a course unvarying as the march of time, still determined to treat Americans as rebels, as she continued to treat Scotsmen, till Scotsmen bowed to her prowess.

A monitory voice from his grandsire, the Highland Chief, seemed to arise from his cerement, " My grandson, never submit to Britons. Her grasp is the grasp of death; and if Americans bow to her, the tranquillity that will afterwards remain to them, will be like the tranquillity of my surviving countrymen in Scotland—the tranquillity of trembling slaves."

Com. Murray again urgently solicited a command in the navy, and was again repulsed. He had exhausted his all, but his life for his country, and his magnanimous spirit could but illy brook this mysterious neglect.

Romans sometimes made voluntary sacrifices of themselves, if they could not sacrifice their lives for their country. Englishmen have improved upon the example; and Americans, for this cause, have capped the climax, by sacrificing each other.

But Com. Murray was too courageous to turn those arms which he had so successfully wielded against the enemies of the Republic, against himself; and above all deeds of desperation, he shuddered at the thought of imbruing his hand in the blood of his countrymen, however regardless his country were of his merits.

He remembered that Aristides was banished his country because he was " too just ;" and that his grandfather was banished Scotland because he was too unyielding to bow to foreign or domestic foes.

The young, and ardent, and ambitious candidates for fame were impetuously rushing forward to the Executive, and to the Navy Department, for office and for promotion ; and however much a junior officer might respect his seniors, they were willing to see them removed to make a place for themselves.

The admirable nautical song of the British " Post Captain" is familiar with seamen. He had grown bald in the service of his king and country ; and, when asked why his locks had left him, coolly answered :

" Because so many have travelled o'er my head."

The executive was not only thronged with those who wanted and who deserved promotion, but was surrounded by hordes of caterers for their companions.

Without any pretensions for themselves, they fell, like hyænas and jackalls, upon those who stood between them and their friends.

Richard of England and Jussuff of Tripoli, forgot consanguinity, and waded through the blood of fathers and brothers to their thrones. Bloody as were their deeds, there was something in them more noble than in the conduct of the sycophantic grovellers---secret underminers---

41

assassins of reputation, who tried to rob from veterans the hard-earned fame they had acquired by their toils, their valour, and their blood.

The character of Murray, with all who knew him, (and the whole of the five Presidents of the Republic knew him well) all dignified men at the American court knew him personally, and all intelligent Americans knew him by reputation, carried with it an antidote against the vile, villainous, venomous vermin, whose clandestine machinations endeavoured to effect his degradation ; knowing that miners, by a concealed train, may demolish a fortress which might defy the attacks of open assailants.

The excitement produced by the disgrrceful affair of the Chesapeake, was in some measure allayed by the disavowal of young Mr. Erskine, then British minister at the American court; but a wound inflicted upon national honour, is always slow in healing; and although Mr. Rose was sent to America on a special mission to effect an accommodation, the masterly diplomatic correspondence of Mr. Monroe, then Secretary of State, presented the subject to his countrymen, in such determined and dignified language, that althongh all the atonement and reparation which Britain could make, was made, yet, like a secret malady in a robust system, it preyed upon the feelings of all true Americans, and especially upon those attached to the nautical profession ; and upon no one more than upon Com. Murray.

Although he had now arrived at the head of the profession, and was senior to all the Post-captains and Commodores in the American Naval Register, yet the Navy Department chose to detain him at home.

Certainly he was of vast importance, from his unequalled experience, in the "home department;" yet like British admirals and able American naval officers, he was tenacious of rank; not only from seniority, but from ability to command.

Because Admiral John Jervis, afterwards Earl of St. Vincent, and now first Lord of Admiralty, designated Horatio Nelsion to command a squadron, detached against the French fleet menacing Egypt, John Orde, *senior* to Nelson, challenged the Earl, when they both met at home; and had not the civil power interfered, John Orde might have acquired as much honour (with men " highly honourable,") by conquering John Jervis at Hyde Park, (the Bladensburgh of England) as Horatio Nelson did at Oboukir.

Com. Murray, with " honours thick upon him" still displayed the great man; for a great man cannot be rendered small by being placed by his government in a small place. But I must retract. It is not a *small place* to be director of naval stations, and ship yards, as will hereafter be shown.

From 1807, when the noble, the heroic, the chivalrous Decatur succeeded Barron in the command of the Chesapeake, a systematic course of aggressions was pursued against American commerce, by the two great belligerant powers of Europe—France and Britain; and a "restrictive system," by way of temporary retaliation, was resorted to by the government of the American Republic.

The widely extended commerce of America, was subjected to the insatiable grasp of the Orders in Council of Britain, and the Berlin and Milan decrees of France, when abroad; and detained in port when at home.

Each was almost equally destructive of national and individual prosperity. The whole system of American business was diverted from its established channel.

American seamen, amounting to as many as an eighth of a million, were driven from their wonted employ, and compelled, for subsistence, to become followers of the plough, handlers of the scythe, sickle and hoe, or spinners of cotton.

Having from change to change been reduced from independence to a bare competency—from active pursuits, to the irksome business of gathering in out-standing debts, from debtors deprived almost of the means of payment, by loss of prosperous business, Americans demanded of their government a decisive course.

In 1812 America " *was herself again.*" In the war of 1755, she had driven Frenchmen from their American colonies. In the war of 1775 she compelled Britain to surrender all their American colonies excepting those *they* had conquered from France for *her*, when Americans were subjected to British power.

In the war of 1798, she had, by her infant navy, compelled France to respect—yea, to *fear* the American flag.

In the war of 1802, with the Turks, she had completely humbled that portion of the dominions of the " Sublime Porte," bordering upon the shores of the Mediterranean.

Com. Murray was born the year the first of these wars broke out. The second of these wars, of nearly eight years continuance, he went completely through. The third he also passed through as serviceably and as victoriously as the second. In the fourth war, he succeeded the first commander, and just begun to conquer, when he was checked in his progress, and called home.

When the fifth war in which his countrymen were en-

gaged with a foreign foe commenced, he once more step-
ped forth as the champion of his country.

Having been neglected by preceding Secretaries of the
Navy, from 1802, the Secretary in 1812 found a sort of excuse for detaining him still at home!!

It is said that defective hearing was again urged as a reason why this faithful and victorious veteran should still be
consigned to some domestic station.

It was no objection to Nelson that he had lost one eye,
and the fact that his last despatches to the admiralty were
signed by his left hand, for the want of a right one (and
Com. Barclay at Lake Erie had but one arm) shows that
our bitter enemy, when carrying their arms against almost
the whole of the world, never *degrade* their own heroes by
neglecting them.

If, at a time of such high excitement in our government,
from the unceasing aggressions of Britain, and the deep and
hostile machinations of a secret domestic junto, made pel-
lucid as glass, during the progress of the war—If political
considerations had any influence upon the Navy Department in designating officers, they surely ought to have pre-
ponderated in favour of Com. Murray; for not an American who inhaled American air, was a more sincere, devoted, and patriotic friend to the Republic, or more determined enemy to Britain.

As Andrew Jackson's Irish ancestors had been almost
annihilated by British vengeance, so had Alexander Murray's Scots ancestors been banished by the same power;
and both were born Americans. A parallel of services rendered by, and rewards bestowed upon, each, will not be
attempted.

Com. Murray's attachment to his country was never

evidenced by inflated protestations of patriotism ; nor his decided opposition to Britain by noisy and frothy declamation.   He surely had no predilection for France, for he had fought that power nearly half as long as he had Britain.   He was not merely *eo nomine*, American, but he was in heart and soul an American ; and his body carried honourable wounds, received in the cause of his country ; and his archives, now in the hands of his surviving friends, show that he carried arms and carried them victoriously against Britons, Frenchmen and Turks, for one eighth of a century.

In 1812, this ardent veteran fervently wished for an opportunity to afford his active aid in *securing* the independence by that war, which was *acquired* in the arduous conflict, the War of the Revolution.

In the campaigns of 1812 and 13, he saw many officers of the highest grade taking the field, many years older than himself; and he panted to resort to the ocean as the theatre of his exertions.

He longed to meet the inveterate foe of America, which assailed his country in 1775, comparatively an infant upon the ocean, to what she had become, (small as her marine was) in 1812.

His application for a command, correspondent with his rank, was received with the utmost respect, at the Navy Department ; for Com. Murray had too much weight of character—too much dignity, to meet with a disdainful repulse.

In the Executive at that period, indeed, in all the preceding Presidents, he had found friends who evinced their high estimation of his character, by their courteous deportment, and marked attention to him.   But owing either to

exterior influence around the Navy Department, more
potent than the Department itself, or some other unfath-
omable cause, with which " strangers intermeddle not,"
Com. Murray's *senior* claim to command, was granted to
his *juniors ;* for every Post-Captain in the American Navy was junior to him at the commencement of the second
war between the American Republic and the Kingdom of
Great-Britain.

It is readily admitted that Com. Murray retained his
rank in the Navy—that he was paid—that every man in
America who could read, and boys who could not read, but
who could be taught the Naval Register, as boys sometimes
learn the alphabet and catechism by recitation, pronounced the name of ALEXANDER MURRAY, *first.*

As a first-rate ship, with timbers as sound as they were
when they studded the mountain's side, is sometimes laid
up " in ordinary" until the " powers that be" put them in
commission, so this veteran warrior was detained in port,
while many aspiring and gallant young officers, who were
Midshipmen when he was Commander of a squadron, were
sent forth to encounter an enemy which he had conquered
when still younger than they were.

While Com. Murray was at home, presiding in Courts-
martial for the trial of his juniors, who lost their ships by
the war of the elements, or by the overwhelming superiority
of force of the enemy.—While, with his countrymen, he was
exulting in the splendid victories of that navy in which he
served in the whole naval warfare with France, until the
peace in 1802, and of which he was Commander in Chief
in the Mediterranean in 1802 and 3 ; he was deprived of
an opportuniy of adding to the number of battles in which
he had fought, and to the victories he had won.

Although his advice and counsel, from his superior judgment and practical knowledge, were of incalculable service during the last war, yet he would have much preferred to have died in the arms of victory, yea, in the hour of defeat; or, as many of his younger brethren did, to have returned the Conquering Hero.

The achievements of the war of 1812, were heightened with exploits in the little American navy of equal splendour with those of any period since the power of nations was exemplified in floating batteries.

To mention names in the order in which they stand according to seniority, and not regarding the time when victories were obtained over H. B. Majesty's ships of war of equal, and often of superior force—and what was of as great, or greater detriment to the enemy, and benefit to the Republic, the capture and destruction of the immense amount of British merchandise, and protection of our own —the names of Rodgers, Bainbridge, Decatur,* Stewart, Hull, Chauncey, Porter, Jones, Morris, Perry,* Macdonough, Warrington, *Blakeley, &c. were familiar with every reader of the journals of the day. But the name of *Murray*, senior to them all, *was not*—excepting with those who knew and who duly appreciated the vast services he had previously rendered to the Republic.

The unqualified respect and admiration of the surviving veterans of the revolution—of the statesmen who guided the helm of state, when American naval officers made imperious Frenchmen bow, and merciless Turks tremble, was a full measure of consolation to this dignified warrior, conscious as he was of his own services, and his own high deserts.

This time-honoured and war-worn hero, knew that he
* Dead.

had been prodigal of his blood in the cause of his country from his boyhood ; and that he should reap a rich harvest of reward in the plaudits of a grateful people.

He lived to rejoice in the peace of 1815, and to exult in the augmented glory of the American navy. The navy had become the theme of all Americans, of all parties ; and from that day to the time when these hasty sketches are writing, (1823) every American naval officer, from a Post-Captain to a midshipman, finds a ready passport to the presence of the great—the circles of the refined, and even to the admiration of the fair.

When the gust of joy, at the conclusion of an honourable peace, had subsided into tranquillized pleasure, and the high honours and rewards to the officers of the army, as well as the navy, had been apportioned, the sound judgment and deep penetration of the American cabinet, directed its attention to those who could best advance the growing importance and future greatness of the American navy in the " home department," as America was at peace with all the world.

Alexander Murray was appointed Commandant of the Navy Yard at Philadelphia ; and, as will be shown in the conclusion, he soon evinced that he still possessed a sound mind, in a sound body.

As to his mental faculties, the result of his exertions will elucidate their original and augmented vigour. As to his bodily powers it will be shown that he could *see*—that he could *feel*—that he could even " *hear*."

To adopt a fashionable expression, the small American navy had " conquered a peace" with France in 1802—with Tripoli in 1805—had essentially hastened a peace with Britain in 1815 ; and one of the greatest conquests it had

42

made, it had " conquered the principle" that a navy was
the most safe, most efficient, most immediate, and least
expensive mode of defending the coast of our vast Republic, and if necessary, carrying on offensive operations
against her enemies.

Most safe, because it is the crowning glory of American
seamen, never to desert from their country, or to turn
their arms against her. In their floating garrisons, they
never annoy their countrymen, or depredate upon their
earnings.

Most efficient, because a ship of war, has her crew, her
munitions, her stores, her implements of movement, and
all the " pomp and circumstance of war," always in complete preparation.

Most immediate, because, at a " moment's warning,"
they move with the celerity of the wind, and, with the
power and celerity of lightning, strike the approaching foe.

Least expensive, because, 74s, 44s, 36s, 18s, &c. can
face a foreign enemy destined against any port from Ma-
chias to New-Orleans ; and, when necessary, can concen-
trate their dispersed power at any given point, (if the expression is allowable) like so many portable fortifications.
Therefore, as a *guarda costa*, naval power is almost incal-
culably less expensive than the immense number of stationary fortifications necessary to defend a sea-board extending from the 30th to the 45th degree of north latitude.

For centuries, the " Wooden Walls of Old England"
have been her impregnable defence. They have defended
that " fast anchored isle" from the Armada of Philip of
Spain, to the Flotilla of Napoleon of France.

But while orators are exhausting their eloquence, and
poets are draining their store-houses of imagination in eu-

logizing " Naval Heroes ;" and painters are delineating in
vivid colours, naval achievements, it ought not to be forgotten, that while expatiating upon the astonishing *effect* of
naval power, the *cause* of it should come in for a share of
consideration. That cause originates in NAVAL ARCHI-
TECTURE, and NAVAL ARMAMENT at home.

The following documentary evidence of the efficiency
of naval defence, is from a Secretary of the navy who
" knew what he said, and said what he knew."

" The importance of a permanent naval establishment
appears to be sanctioned by the voice of the nation ; and
I have a satisfaction in stating, that the means of its gradual increase are completely within the reach of our national
resources, independently of any foreign country. The
materials for building and equipping ships of war are all
at command. Steps have been taken to ascertain the best
growth and quantities of timber for naval construction,
preparatory to contracts and purchases. The want of a
mould loft for the naval constructor to lay out the moulds
by which the timber is to be cut and shaped previous to
transportation, has delayed the completion of arrangements
for an adequate supply. A building has been erected at
the navy yard in this city for that purpose, and will soon
be finished, when the business will progress.

Cannon founderies, manufactories of sheet copper, cor-
dage, canvas, and the mechanical branches, are in a state
to furnish the several supplies mhich may be required.

The commerce of the United States increasing with the
resources and population of the country, will require a
commensurate protection, which a navy alone can afford ;
and the experience derived from the active and vigorous
employment of a limited navy, during the period of the late
war, has demonstrated its efficient utility.

I do, therefore, with confidence recommend an annual increase of our navy, of one ship of the rate of seventy-four guns, two frigates of the first class, rates at forty-four guns, and two sloops of war, which can be built with the surplussage of smaller timber, and with a great saving in that material.

The act to increase the navy, passed January 2d 1813, authorized the building of " four ships to rate not less than seventy-four guns, and six frigates to rate forty-four guns each." This act has partly been carried into effect, by building three ships of the rate of seventy-four guns, and three frigates of forty-four guns, in the Atlantic ports.— The residue of the appropriation under that act, was applied to the building of large ships and frigates upon Lake Ontario.

The concentration of our navy in one or two of the principal ports of the United States, where the depth of water is sufficient for the convenient ingress and egress of the larger vessels, will necessarily lead to the enlargement of the navy yards at such places, with docks for repairs, and the collection of all important materials for the armament and equipments of the different classes of vessels, in order to bring them into active service, upon any emergency, with the advantage of combined force.

A general system for the gradual and permanent increase of the navy, combining all the various objects connected with an enlarged naval establishment, such as building docks, and extending the accommodation of navy yards and arsenals of general deposit, will form the subjects of a more extensive report to be laid before congress during the present session."

To such energetic, and scientific minds as ALEXANDER

Murray's ; and such theoretical and practical geniuses as Humphreys, and Ecford, are our unequalled captains in the navy indebted for much of the renown justly attached to their deathless names.

But the aspiring sons of fame, when pressing forward, are too prone to forget the unostentatious aids who facilitate their progress to its lofty temple.

When Com. Murray assumed the command of the Navy-Yard at Philadelphia, he brought into operation the extensive and minute knowledge he had acquired from long and continued experience.

In Mr. Humphreys, he found a coadjutor exactly corresponding with his own views ; and they went forward, hand in hand, supporting and supported, in their highly important pursuit.

To shew the inquisitive reader the progress of Naval Architecture, I present him with a copy of the following document in the Navy Department, prepared nearly twenty-five years since, by one of the architects just mentioned.

It is a precious document, as it goes to show, that, as the ship-builders, in the employ of government, have been advancing with rapid strides towards perfection in the construction of ships from the highest to the lowest rates, they have, in about the same degree, diminished the expenses of building and fitting them.—

" Estimate of the expense of building and equipping a 74 gun ship of 1620 tons, prepared some years since by Joshua Humphreys, Esq. of Philadelphia, a shipwright of great respectability and professional talents :

Live oak timber,	$40,000
White oak and pine ditto,	30,000
Labour,	85,100

Cables, rigging, &c.	32,400
Smith's work,	30,400
Anchors, marling,	8,700
Sailmaker's bills, two suits, including canvass,	16,200
Joiner's bill, including stuff,	7,800
Carver's bill,	1,620
Tanner's ditto,	700
Rigger's do.	2,240
Painter's do.	3,240
Cooper's do.	4,860
Blockmaker's do.	3,210
Boatbuilder's do.	1,620
Plumber's do.	2,430
Ship Chandlery,	9,720
Turner's bill,	1,215
Copper bolts,	10,960
Sheathing copper, nails, &c.	17,440
Woollens for sheathing,	1,215
	311,100
Contingencies,	31,600
Total,	$ 342,700

The frigate President, of 1444 tons cost the sum of
$220,910. The frigates Constitution, United States, and
Philadelphia, probably the same sum each. These frigates
and some others, were built twenty-five years since; before the naval warfare with France commenced.

Americans have, by some piquant foreigners, been denominated a " cyphering race"—by others "shop-keepers,
pedlars and jockies"—and by others " penny-wise and

pound-foolish." If, twenty-five years ago, (1798) although in the midst of the "golden days of commercial prosperity" our cyphering countrymen could calculate far enough to ascertain that twelve 74's and twenty-four frigates of 44 guns, at the above rate would amount to $9,414,240—and that the *annual* expense of a 74, *in commission* was $202,110, and a frigate of 44 guns, about $135,000, they might well have asked, when "counting the cost" what will this *come* to?

The profound statesmen, and the profound leaders of statesmen in the American Republic, when they commenced the establishment of our present Navy, aimed at nothing but *defence* against foreign aggression.

No mad or diabolical schemes of foreign conquest entered into their views. The safety of the Republic was committed to their care; and they little thought of draining its wealth to gratify the wicked projects of unhallowed ambition. This steady and magnanimous course has been pursued to near the close of the first quarter of the nineteenth century; and ten millions of happy and independent freemen now reap the fruits of their wisdom.

Our respectable navy has progressed gradually from infancy towards manhood. It has afforded protection to our commerce—it has chastised our foes abroad; and even *now* can afford protection to our immense coast—and. Americans feel not the burden of it.

Turn now to the vaunting "Queen of the Ocean" and behold her, to be sure at the height of Naval glory, and in the lowest depth of national distress, national bankruptcy and (remember India) national guilt!!

I feel both pleasure and pain in presenting to the reader the following picture, drawn by the hand of a master.

Pleasure, that we find no resemblance to it in our Republic—Pain, that the land of our ancestors presents, in per-
spective, the following figure :

" We have before us the warning fate of the British nation, where the avails of the hard earnings and the life-labor
of thousands and tens of thousands are screwed from them
to glut the rapacity of an individual, who regards them less
than he does his dogs.   Time was, when the people of the
British Isles would not have borne with this ; but, with the
people's money, the devouring government buys men and
arms to enable it to wrest the means of defence from the
oppressed, build prisons to incarcerate, and gallowses to
hang those on, who dare to murmur or complain."

To the departed Alexander Murray is our Republic vastly
indebted for that system of economy, which for the last years
of his laborious life, he introduced into our navy-yards.

He had one of those rare minds which enabled him to
reach the most comprehensive views ; and, at the same
time, to investigate the minutest concerns, relative to his
important station.   It is related of Nelson, that after he
fell mortally wounded upon his deck, and as his officers
were carrying him below, he exclaimed, in the agony of
death, " don't you see the tiller is not right ?"   A great
mind is never too exalted to descend to things that are
small, and never so little as not to embrace things that are
great.

Com. Murray, with the constant aid of Mr. Humphreys,
the chief shipwright, spared no labour nor pains in the very
important business of superintending the erection of public
ships.

Public property, to an immense amount, was at his disposal ; and waste and improvidence, unless palpably enor-

mous, would pass unheeded. From the immense variety
of articles necessary in the construction and equipment of
a public ship, and from the great variety of artists engaged
in working them, losses, too trifling to mention in detail,
but too serious to be overlooked in the aggregate, may be
incurred by public agents, who are more anxious to amass
a fortune for themselves, and to aggrandize their posterity,
than to advance the essential and permanent interest of the
Republic.

There is often a pompous affectation discernible in
public officers and public agents, which seems to render it
inconsistent with their official dignity to descend to the mi-
nutiæ of debit and credit—day-book and ledger—income
and expenditure.

The channels through which wealth flows into the national treasury are few—the outlets are as numerous as
their calls for supply are insatiable ; and like the many
mouths of the Nile, or those of our own majestic Mississippi, disgorge the contents as fast as they are accumulated.

That portion of public expenditure which is bestowed
upon Executive, Legislative, Judiciary, Army and Navy
officers, in specific compensations, for services rendered
the Republic is not here meaned—the moderate amount of
salaries and pay to such men, who are fit for the stations
they fill, is acquiesced in by Americans with pleasure, and
looked upon by foreigners with astonishment.

But that expenditure is meaned, which consists of annual
grants of " round numbers," to be expended, and accoun-
ted for, not only with mathematical accuracy, but with
sound judgment, and rigid economy. Instance the grants
for the Commissary, Quartermaster, and Hospital depart
ments.

But of all annual grants, that for the " gradual increase
of the Navy," according to its amount, is of the greatest
importance to the American Republic ; and it requires
the most sound heads, honest hearts, and skilful hands, to
make an advantageous application of it.

Entering such a " protestation," as Coke calls the " ex-
clusion of a conclusion," against the supposition that this
sketch is designed as an eulogy, it is averred that Alexander Murray possessed such a head—such a heart—such a
hand.

He availed himself of the knowledge and wisdom of his
predecessors so far as it was tested by the sanction of
" successful experiment ;" but he never said to experiment,
" thus far shalt thou go and no farther."

Essential improvement in the mechanic arts, oftentimes
equals and sometimes surpasses original invention.   Com.
Murray had an original strength of mind, which, while it
enabled him to comprehend the principles upon which human inventions were founded, enabled him also to extend
them.

Architecture is justly ranked amongst the sciences ; and
it is certainly amongst the first and most useful arts.   But,
it will readily be admitted, that there is scarcely an analogy
between land-architecture, and naval architecture.   *The
ancient orders of architecture, in erecting temples, palaces
and mansions upon earth ; and the little improvement, and
great injuries they have sustained by modern architects,
are easily learned by the commonest ability, and reduced
to practice by mere mechanical ingenuity.

So plain is the correct road in this art, that he who reads
may run in it ; and if, by ignorance or wilfulness, he strays

* See " Life of Decatur."

from it, he gets involved in an inextricable labyrinth of blunders, from which he can only be relieved by retracing his wandering steps.

But in the erection of Ships, there can hardly be said to be an established principle ; for where there is, there may be uniformity.   Why is it often said, that such and such a ship is the best sailer in the American or British navy ? Why did Com. Decatur say so of the Macedonian ? and why was his noble father, in the Philadelphia, beaten by Capt. Tryon in the Connecticut in a sailing match ? Why did the naval architects of Britain take models from the wretched Chesapeake, when broken up, when she was deemed altogether the most ill-constructed ship in the American navy ? It was owing even to her superiority over their own.   If the President and the Essex frigates were not too much battered and riddled by the squadrons of Commodores Hays and Hillyar, to have reached British ports, perhaps the ship carpenters of his majesty Geo. IV. may derive a still greater benefit from scrutinizing the wrecks of them.   They are the only American models they will ever have in their ports, unless they are gained by the same overwhelming superiority of force.   As to the Chesapeake, Britain is welcome to her—she was disgraced by British outrage in 1807, and captured by British stratagem in 1813.

Although our navy cannot number the years contained in a quarter of a century ; in point of elegance, strength, power, and celerity, our ships, most decidedly surpass any that have floated upon the ocean, from the days of Carthage to this age.   Witness the *escapes* of the Constitution, Argus, Hornet, Peacock, &c. and the *victories* of every one of them in fair and equal combat—and, to mention the

most signal instance of rapidity in movement, witness the
Guerriere, and Com. Decatur's second* squadron, of nine
sail in 1815.

It is to the skill, genius, and inventive faculties of our
Navy-Commissioners, Superintendents of Navy-yards, and
naval architects, that we owe this American superiority,
in the construction of our ships. But their armament also
is of prime consideration.

The reader may be gratified by a very brief sketch; made
from voluminous documents of the comparative force of
ships of different rate.

In the British navy there are four denominations of ships,
1. Ships of the line, from the largest, down to Sixty-fours.
2. Fifty-fours, to fifties, a distinct class, but rated with line
of battle ships. 3. Forties, to Twenties, unexceptionably
rated as Frigates. All the foregoing are commanded by
Post-Captains. 4. Eighteens to Sixteens, are Sloops of
War. All are pierced for, and mount more guns than they
are registered at. Besides these, there are Schooners, Fireships, Bombards, Gun-boats, Tenders, Cutters, &c. &c.

In the American navy are Seventy-fours, Forty-fours,
Thirty-sixes, Eighteens, Brigs, Schooners, Gun-boats, &c.

The comparative force of Seventy-fours, and Forty-
fours, (although at first it may excite surprise) is as one to
three. It is demonstrated thus, a 74, at one round, discharges 3224 lbs. of shot, a 44 discharges 1360 lbs. As the
class of ships is increased, the force is increased, in proportion of one to three.

Seventy-fours are stronger in scantling; thicker in sides
and bottom; less penetrable to shot, and less liable to be

* Decatur's first squadron, in 1815 was the President, Hornet, and
Peacock.

battered. A Seventy-four is a fair match for three 44's
in action. To give the frigates the most favourable position ; two at the quarter and stern, and one abreast of the
74. From the superior weight of metal in the destructive
battery of the 74, the frigate abreast would be dismasted
or sunk with two broadsides. In the mean time, the quarter and stern of the 74, might not be essentially injured ;
and when a broadside could be brought to bear upon the
other two frigates, they must share the fate of the first.—
Still, three frigates *might* take a 74, and what is quite as
probable, a 74 *might* capture or sink three frigates.

The relative efficiency, of Frigates and Sloops of War,
is at least as one to two ; and nearly the same reasoning
will apply to them as to 74's and 44's. The Cyane was
frigate built, and mounted 34 guns, the Levant 21, and yet
the galiant and accomplished Capt. Charles Stewart (from
whose communications the preceding statement was collected) captured them both in 40 minutes.

From the preceding concise sketch, the reader may have
a faint conception of the importance of the duties devolved upon Com. Murray, as Superintendant of the Navy-
Yard at Philadelphia, as it regards Naval Architecture and
Naval Armament.

The Commodore must have been gratified with the unqualified and undivided approbation of his intelligent fellow
citizens at home—of inquisitive and investigating visitors
from every portion of the Republic, and with the admiration of distinguished foreigners, at the rapid progress of
naval science, in this NEW WORLD.

But how much would the satisfaction of this veteran officer, and practical financier have been abated, if, in the
midst of this concord of approbation, many sullen and dis-

cordant notes—many " *curses, not only loud, but deep,*"
were heard from a people, groaning under a weight of taxes
excise, and impositions upon every thing they ate, drank,
and wore—the ground upon which they walked—the horses
upon which they rode, and the bridles that guided them—
upon the chaises in which they rolled along, and upon the
harness that glittered upon their horses—upon the light of
heaven that enlivened their habitation by day, upon the
candle that enabled them to labour, or study at night, and
upon the taper that lighted them to bed—upon the bed upon
which they reposed, and upon the curtains that concealed
them from intruders.

Such taxes had been avoided and such murmurs had always been prevented by the provident economical government of the Republic ; and Com. Murray, with his co-
adjutors, the Naval Commissioners, and the skilful Humphreys carried retrenchment and economy in the navy
department to the minutest objects under their direction
and superintendance.

Twenty-five years ago the expense of a 74 was $342,700
and of a 44 gun frigate, $220,910 ; and the expense of
smaller rates, in the same proportion.

It would fatigue the writer, without amusing the reader
to point out the specific objects in which savings to the
government have been effected in the erection of our unequalled ships of war of every rate.   Suffice it to say, that
under the superintendance of ALEXANDER MURRAY, at the
navy yard in Philadelphia, ships of war, of superiour model,
beauty, and strength, have been erected at only a fraction
more than TWO THIRDS OF THE SUMS JUST MENTIONED.

The following observations upon that all-important arti-
ticle *ship timber,* are well worthy of the consideration of

Superintendants of Navy Yards. To use a popular adage " an ounce of experience is worth a ton of conjecture."

" A piece from the National Intelligencer, signed " EXPERIENCE," has induced me to offer some further observations upon this subject. I had touched upon it but slightly before, and am always pleased to hear of *Experience,* if it be really founded upon just *experiments.* The subject may be useful, but is not interesting to many readers. As an amusement, I have attended to the growth, durability, and decay of vegetable substances ; but of ship-building I have no practical knowledge, therefore I extend my observations no further than the two last qualities in timber which appear to render it fit, or unfit for that purpose. Fermentation, in vegetable substances, is equivalent to putrefaction, in animal ones. The three great agents in their decomposition or decay, are heat, air, and water; the same which support them when alive.* In timbers, water is the primitive agent, as it brings the other two into operation. Acting upon the saccharine matter it produces spiritous fermentation, and upon acidity, the acid fermentation. In its progress, fermentation excites heat and air. A more minute and technical explanation would be foreign to my purpose ; it may be found in essays expressly upon the subject.

I have seldom found the saccharine or acid principle to abound in any tree, which was durable as a timber. For instance, the *black walnut* and *hickory* belong to the same genus of plants, the walnut to the taste is destitute of saccharine matter, and the hickory abounds with it—the consequence is, that the walnut is as remarkable for its dura-

* *Oxygen,* which gives much life and spirit to animals and vegetables, is the greatest decomposer.

bility, as the hickory for premature decay—when I speak of acidity in timber trees, I shall confine myself to the gallic acid, as the other acids are seldom found in large trees. The gallic acid is a second great cause of decay. The live-oak has very little, in proportion to the black-oak (quercus tinctoria) or the black jack (quercus nigra) yet the first will last for half a century, and the two last not a tenth of that time. The loblolly-bay (gordonia) abounds with the gallic acid, so much so, that the bark is thought better than that of oak for tanning—but the wood, when exposed to wet, will scarcely last a year. Upon this subject I could multiply instances. Both these *secondary causes of decay* are brought into operation by a *partial* wetting, and yet may be removed by *total* immersion. Instance, the furs dug out of the bogs in Ireland, and the oak piles found in the harbour of the ancient Brundusium, which were driven down there by Julius Cæsar; both of them in a sound state. The reason is, a partial wetting excites only a slight motion of the particles, and produces fermentation; where-as, immersion excludes the air, and on account of the affinity of water for the acid and saccharine, it will, in time, attract and diffuse them throughout the surrounding fluid. Thus, it is, that timber may be seasoned and preserved by total immersion.

It is much to be regretted that there is so little of the live oak in the southern states; and to make way for cotton, the little we have are constantly falling under the axe. It inhabits only the sea islands, and a slip of about twenty miles along the coast. Ten miles from the sea it generally becomes scarce; but the turkey-oak, which " *Experience*" says is the second best timber, abounds in our uncultivated swamps. Many trees also attain a great size there, which are seldom used for any purpose. The water-oak (quercus palustris) and the cotton tree (populous nigra) are of this description, and in fence-rails appear to be durable. " Experience" says " the Chesapeake frigate had a number of her top timbers of black cypress, and when that ship was stripped down at this navy-yard, the cypress was found to be totally rotten, so that no further experiment is necessary on cypress."—How ominous is the name of the Chesapeake! Those timbers could not have been black cypress, but an inferior and sappy species found near the sea. The region of the best cypress commences where the flowing of the tides ceases ; but one experiment contrary to the mass of *experience* upon this subject, is not sufficient. I know two houses built of cypress, which men of the last century informed me were built about seventy years ago ; about five years since one of them had never had but one coat of shingles ; it was tight, and both of them appear as though they would last seventy years or more. An indigo planter having a set of indigo vats to build, chooses black cypress for this purpose ; he calculates that his vats, although alternately exposed to wet and heat, will last thirty years before they begin to decay at the grooves—after that, he or his sons, if he be dead, cut away the ends of the boards, and either reduce the size of the vats, or convert them into pannel-worked window-sashes. Rice planters universally prefer black cypress* for their rice field-trunks, which are exposed to the alternation of the tides. Yellow-

* To the botanists, there is a curious *lusus naturæ* allied to the cypress, called cypress knees. It is an imperfect tree, wanting leaves and branches. They are said to be excrescences from the roots of the tree, but all I have examined have perfect roots of their own.

44

pine is thought quite inferior for this purpose. Finally, cypress boards and shingles command the highest price in market, and cypress boats are preferred both in fresh and salt water. Yet upon the spot where these things occur every day of our lives, we are told *from Washington*, that cypress is worth one slight experiment. It is ceded, that it is " well calculated for boats." Now, I ask, if in point of durability it be calculated for boats, why is it not for ships, supposing both to be exposed to sea air and water? But lest it should be thought that I am interested in the matter, I can assure all who think it worth while to read my observations, that I own no cypress but the shingles of my house. I wish only to contribute my mite of experience where it might be of service to my country."

While this astonishing reduction of expense in the erection and armament of ships has been effected in at least, one navy yard, the annual expense of ships of war in commission, have also been surprizingly reduced.

In this respect, as well as in the erection of ships, it is unnecessary to point out the specific objects in which retrenchments have been made. Suffice it again to say, our country is year after year gradually increasing the most efficient defence of the Republic, and annually decreasing the National Debt. Yet Americans scarcely feel a moment's gratitude towards the indefatigable Officers attached to the Navy Department, while Europeans contemplate this miracle in the Science and Art of Republican Government, with that wonder which is the effect of novelty upon ignorance.

While the writer of this imperfect sketch of the life of the patriotic, the gallant, the faithful, the venerable Murray, claims for his memory the unqualified respect of his surviving countrymen, he would presume to claim for the present Secretary of the Navy,* and the Navy Commissioners, their full share of respect, as constituting the centre of the American Naval System, around which all the primary and secondary agents revolve in the spheres designed for them.

These claims however, are wholly unnecessary. The citizens of the Republic, from the hoary headed statesmen down to the school-boy with his satchel, voluntarily pour forth the notes of applause in harmonious concord to the scientific and practical powers of the officers of the Navy Department, and to the gallantry and glory of the officers and seamen of our justly renowned navy.

The duties devolved upon Com. Murray from the time he was superseded in the command of the American squadron in the Mediterranean, to the day of his death, had but little of that imposing glare which draws forth the gust of applause from an admiring and an enraptured populace. He led the "noiseless tenor of his way" in discharging the more retiring, but yet no less important duties imposed upon him by his government in presiding at courts of en-

* The Hon. Smith Thompson, formerly Chief Justice of the State of New York. I cannot forbear to extract into this note a part of a Letter from a Philadelphia Correspondent, as it goes to corroborate what I have ventured to incorporate in the preceding Sketch. "He (Com. Murray) was slighted and disregarded by every succeeding Secretary of the Navy, until the appointment of Mr. Smith Thompson to that office, from whom he received the kindest attention and civility; but he has notwithstanding (this slight and disregard,) been treated with the most polite and courteous attention by all our Presidents, whom I presume did not think proper to interfere with the arrangements and appointments of the Navy Department."

quiry, courts martial, and in council with the officers of the Navy Department and of the navy. In the multifarious duties of the Senior Officer of the American Navy, he constantly called forth from the capacious storehouse of experience, the maxims of matured judgment, sound science, and practical knowledge.

But it was as Commandant of the Navy Yard, that the mild rays of his setting sun shone with a splendour, surpassed only by its meridian glory. He lived to enjoy the most satisfactory reward of an exalted mind—" The approbation of his country" at the closing scenes of his life.

To a mere sordid heart, a Vote of Thanks, without a golden reward as an accompaniment, is looked upon as nothing superiour to a " sounding brass and a tinkling cymbal." It was not so considered by the veteran Murray, when he received such a vote, but a few months before he closed his temporal career, couched in terms of unqualified approbation.

Although less expressive, yet no less flattering were the numerous letters, of the most distinguished officers of the Republic, received from time to time by the Commodore in his declining years.

Such cheering notes of commendation, emanating from those whose high deserts impart an inestimable value to praise, must have produced an exhilaration, in a heart which had beat near three score years and ten, and must have made it re-beat the animated throbs of meridian life.

In a recent communication from the very obliging Secretary of the Navy, in answer to one soliciting information from him on various subjects connected with this publication, he says—

" The vote of thanks to the late Com. Murray, to which

you allude, did not emanate from this Department; though his character as an officer and gentleman, was held in the highest estimation ; and his uniform discretion, fidelity and zeal for the public service, were always duly appreciated by the government."

"*Fortunatus Senex*," may we well say of this departed patriot and hero ; fortunate, almost beyond conception, when his declining years are contrasted with many of his compatriots in the war of Independence.

Says Gen. Washington, in his last letter to Gen. Putnam —" Ingratitude has been experienced in all ages, and Republics, in particular, have ever been famed for the exercise of that unnatural and sordid vice."

What a catalogue of names which might be ranked with the best Grecians in the best days of ancient renowned, and modern struggling Greece, whose declining years were embittered by the relentless grasp of indigence ; and with whom the meagre genius of poverty " Froze the genial current of the soul ;" and of whom might well be asked the torturing question put by the anonymous insurgent to the matchless officers of the Revolutionary army before they were disbanded :

" Can you consent to be the only sufferers of this revolution, and, retiring from the field, grow old in poverty and wretchedness, and contempt ? Can you consent to wade through the vile mire of dependancy, and owe the miserable remnant of that life to charity which has hitherto been spent in honour ?"*

Maj. Gen. Arthur St. Clair was not the only Hero of the Revolution who lived to witness the fulfilment of the mutinous prophecy.

* See Revolutionary Pamphlets.

Admitting the Pension Law has recently, in a small degree, wiped off the stain of " avarice, that unnatural and
sordid vice," the very terms upon which the small boon is
obtained, are excessively humiliating to the high-minded
soldier.

With a just claim upon the government for a right, they
are compelled in "*forma pauperis*" to call God to witness
that they are in the depths of bankruptcy, before they can
obtain now what was the most meritorious due forty years
ago.

Whether Com. Murray inherited a fortune from his scientific father, is unknown to the writer.   But it is known,
that from his exalted grandfather, the Chief of Elginshire,
his descendants inherited nothing but his fame—a most invaluable legacy.   His estates were confiscated for his fidelity to the House of Stuart, by the rapacious Guelphs, to
erect gibbets for the ancient heroes of Scotland, the descendants of Wallace and Bruce.

Com. Murray had a fortune sufficiently independent to
save him from dependance upon the treasures of the Republic.   God knows they are hardly sufficient to satisfy the
retainers of government, who, like birds of prey, harpies,
and devouring locusts, are perpetually preying upon a fund
which is constantly diminishing, and augmenting the civil
list of the Republic faster than did ever the same list increase in the profligate government of Britain.*

* Lest this " bold assertion" should be deemed presumptuous, I will
just state, that in 1790 the civil list was $141,492 72.   In 1821, more
than $1,500,000.   In 1790, the Departments of State, the Treasury,
the Navy, and the Department of War, cost the Republic $16,750.
In 1821, the expenditures of the same Departments were $51,500.
" Mark now, how a plain tale shall put you down."

While such sterling men as Alexander Murray were enriching the nation by economy and retrenchment, thousands of officers, little better than sinecures, who would no sooner than the grave exclaim " it is enough," were draining the treasury of its very dregs ; and wresting from the " mouth of labour" its merited reward.

The command, " Thou shalt not muzzle the mouth of the ox that treadeth out the corn," seemed to be revoked, that drones might wallow in insolent wealth, and luxuriate in effeminate indulgence.

The perpetual succession of these hungry swarms of office-hunters, would remind one of Esop's fable of the fox and the flies, and of Pope's ideas of resuscitation.

" All forms that perish, other forms supply,
By turns they catch the vital breath and die,
Like bubbles on the sea of matter borne,'
They rise, they break—and to that sea return."

Com. Murray, in the full possession of his mental and material faculties—in the active and vigilant discharge of his high trust upon earth, was summoned to his final audit in heaven, upon the 6th day of October 1821.

Like a " shock of corn fully ripe in its season," he appeared before the GREAT COMMANDER and SUPREME ARCHITECT of the Universe to render an account of his services in that world, where man was destined to discharge his duty to man, and to prepare to meet a GOD in heaven.

His life evinced that " man was created little lower than the angels"—his death impressively taught, that " all flesh is as grass."

As his life filled a capacious space, his death occasioned a vacancy, which may be filled, but cannot be filled better.

The deepened marks of sorrow that were depicted upon

the countenances of the great and good men who viewed
his sheeted manes, were a speechless eulogy from fixed
eyes, and dumb mouths; far more impressive than the
sonorous exclamations of funereal eloquence.

It would be useless to insert the order of the funeral
procession at his interment. As he lived without ostentation, he would, (could he have wished) have desired to be
carried to his cemetery without imposing ceremony.

CHARACTER OF ALEXANDER MURRAY.

Alexander Murray possessed the qualities of a vigorous, decided and energetic mind. He seemed to be designed by Heaven as a blessing to his country.

Born at an era pregnant with the most important events
of the *eighteenth* century, his life embraced near one half
of it. It also embraced near one quarter of the *nineteenth*
century, a period still more astonishing.

Although he did not move in the highest sphere, he was
ever in the midst of the ardent beings who approximated
it. If he did not *design* vast operations, he was amongst
the first active agents who insured their *execution*.

He was born with an innate detestation of tyranny, and
his arm was constantly nerved and raised against oppressors. He inherited from his progenitors, a high sense of
Independence, and an invincible hostility against the ancient enemy of the land of his ancestors in Europe, and
the inveterate foes of that of his own birth in America.
Hence when the potent arm of imperious Britain was lift-
ed in wrath against her high-minded children in the New
World, Murray, then in ardent youth, manfully espoused
the cause of Freemen against tyrants.

He commenced his career of glory in the Army of Washington, and followed the destiny of the Father of the Republic, through the most desponding period of the Revolution.

Without any respite, he repaired to his favourite element, to face in arms the vaunting " Queen of the Ocean." In numerous battles, and with various success, he co-operated with the peerless " Naval Heroes of the American Revolution ;" and desperate wounds received in furious contests furnished demonstrative evidence that he was at the post of duty and of danger.

When Peace, crowned with Independence and glory, blessed the new-born, and first-born Republic, in the Western Hemisphere, the war-worn Murray became the unassuming citizen.

His native energy and decision of character, was exemplified in the mild arts of peace, as signally as was his courage in the midst of war, carnage, bloodshed and death.

When the house of Bourbon fell, and the French Republic rose upon its ruins, like a Phœnix from embers—when, in her ravishing strides, she laid her rapacious hands upon American Commerce, Murray, with the high approbation of Washington and Adams, repaired again to the floating bulwarks of his country, and with the unrivalled ocean combatants in ocean warfare, afforded protection to Americans, and spread dismay amongst lawless French marauders.

The objects of his government effected, and the naval ardor of his countrymen revived, the Post-Captain Murray again retired to the bosom of his admiring friends and applauding countrymen.

He was retained in the naval service of the Republic, and was one of the thirteen original Captains in the American

Navy designed to keep alive the naval flame, and to avenge the injuries sustained by Americans upon every ocean and in every sea.

When the detested disciples of the arch impostor Mahomet, raised the blood-stained Crescent over the Star-spangled Banner of America—robbed her commerce, and enslaved her citizens, the sagacious and profound JEFFERSON selected the cool, experienced, and veteran MURRAY as the Commander in Chief of a little American squadron in the renowned Mediterranean.

His character scarcely began to develope itself, as a Commander in Chief, before he was required to yield his command to a successor. In this capacity, he shewed that he possessed the courage of the champion, but he was *permitted* only to menace his foe at a distance, and defend himself when assailed.

For the third time, he retired from the warring ocean as a distinguished ocean warrior. In three different wars, with three different powers, he had fought and fought valiantly in thirteen battles, and the crimsoned current that copiously flowed from his mortal body, evinced the heroism of his immortal soul.

When imperious Britain, a second time by her unhallowed aggressions, caused the second war between the American Republic and that haughty power, Murray's name stood at the head of the American Naval Register, and his fame, without a blot, in the register of American glory.

The cautious and wary Madison, then, and the no less penetrating Monroe, afterwards, detained this experienced veteran in the home department, to digest and mature the system which has given imperishable glory to the American navy, and almost absolute perfection to American naval architecture.

In fine : this honoured Naval Hero and American Patriot, went forth, from grade to grade, spending his life and exhausting his bodily vigour, in the cause of our beloved Republic, which he loved better than he loved himself.

He lived well known, highly honoured, and invariably respected by Washington, Adams, Jefferson, Madison and Monroe, the five renowned Presidents of the only pure Republic on earth ; and of how many departed worthies can higher honours be told ?

But, with all his justly merited honours, he shewed no ostentation. He was a dignified, genuine, Republican ; who, although honoured by the great, was courteous to the small ; and " those who knew him best, loved him most.

[ORIGINAL.]

THE SENIOR COMMODORE AND POST-CAPTAIN IN THE AMERICAN NAVY.

Tune—" The sea was calm," &c.

I. Young MURRAY, brave, of noble mein
    Gave " strong assurance of the man,"
With Neptune's sons, was often seen,
    The ocean's vast expanse to scan.
        When eighteen years had mann'd his brow.
        A master on the deck he stood,
        Of merchant's ship, with lofty bow,
        A youth esteem'd both great and good.

II. When first Americans arose,
    Against the hostile British foe :

Did valiant MURRAY, firm, espouse
　　The purest cause of Man below,·
　　　With young MONROE,* placed in command
　　　　By WASHINGTON—both straight repair'd
　　　To join the fearless patriot band,
　　　　Who, (dauntless,) haughty Britons dar'd.

III. Next MURRAY on the deck was view'd,
　　　There pouring Freemen's thunders forth;
　　There spill'd his blood—but quick renew'd
　　　His vengeance 'gainst the fiends of wrath.
　　　　From waves return'd with wounds and scars,
　　　　　He found the lov'd REPUBLIC Free;
　　　　He stood 'mongst men, like son of *Mars*,
　　　　　And *Neptune's* fav'rite from the sea.

IV. Next, dauntless MURRAY wafted off,
　　　To meet the boasting Frenchmen's frown;
　　He gave broadsides, for Gallic scoff,
　　　And gain'd Columbia's tars renown.
　　　　Once more return'd, he saw, with joy,
　　　　　His country rising high in Fame;
　　　　He found his name, by high employ,
　　　　　Inscrib'd upon the rolls of Fame.

V. Again, in high and chief command,
　　　Murray, the Commodore, repair'd
　　To that fam'd sea " midst famed land"
　　　Where Greece and Rome in glory shar'd.
　　　　'Twas there the Crescent, quiv'ring, fled,
　　　　　When his proud banner waved high

---

* Lieut. Monroe, (the President) fought with Lieut. Murray in the sanguinary battle at White Plains, before he took command at sea.

On that proud Ship,* which cloth'd in dread
    Made Frenchmen—Britons, frightened, fly.

VI. Once more the "Conq'ring Hero" came—
    Murray, with deathless honours crown'd;
Was welcom'd home, with loud acclaim,
    A "Naval Hero"—high renown'd.
    There, by the great and good rever'd,
        He liv'd admir'd, and died in Fame;
    A monument's already rear'd,
        In Patriots' hearts to MURRAY's name.

———

While the preceding sketch was in preparation for the press, the disastrous intelligence was announced, that a favourite son of commodore Murray fell a victim to the malady which proved fatal to so many gallant spirits on board the well known Macedonian Frigate.

She was well known to the gallant Carden, as a British ship, in which he lost more than eighty of a gallant crew when the matchless Decatur captured her. She was well known to the chivalrous hero, Jones, when he challenged the Statira, and when commanding her in the renowned squadron of Decatur in the Mediterranean, in 1815. She was well known, alas! too well known, by the heroic, the accomplished Biddle, the younger, in the cruise which was terminated in 1822; and which terminated the lives of so many promising American officers and seamen.

ALEXANDER M. MURRAY was the son of the late Com. Alexander Murray. His excellent father educated him

———

* The Constellation frigate; in which Truxton captured the Le Insurgente, French frigate, and in which then Capt. Alexander Murray beat off by *mistake*, the Magnanimique, British line of battle ship in the naval warfare with the French Republic.

with the view of making him an accomplished young officer in the navy, of which he might himself be called a venerable father.

His studies were principally directed to this primary object, although he became an early proficient in the liberal
sciences.

It would be superfluous to descant upon the inestimable
value of early literary and scientific attainments to gentlemen of the Navy, from the lowest grade to the highest.

Their duty often leads them to oral discussions, and
written correspondence—to make official communications
to their own government, and sometimes to the enemies of
the Republic.*

* The following very recent specimen of a communication from the
American " Senior Naval Officer of the U. States, in the West Indies" once one of Com. Murray's midshipmen, shows that Capt. R.
TREAT SPENCE, although a warrior, can maintain the dignity of the
Republic by his pen, as well as sustain its rights by his cannon.   The
" decree of Francis Thomas Morales," the gasconading representative
of the puerile, weak, and vascillating Ferdinand VII. is known to
the reader.   Captain SPENCE's note to the " general in chief" does
honor to him and his government.

                              " CURACOA, 10th November, 1822.
From the commander of the U. S. ship Cyane, and Senior Naval Offi-
cer in the West Indies, to his excellency FRANCIS THOMAS MO-
RALES, General in Chief of the Spanish Royal Forces on the Main.

SIR—I have been presented with your Excellency's public decree of the 15th of September last—a declaration of the most despotic
and sanguinary nature, against all foreigners, whose love of glory,
commercial pursuits and lawful occupations, may enlist in the service,
or detain them in the territories possessed by the enemies of Spain,
recognized by the U. States as independent governments.

A manifesto so extraordinary, so hostile to the rights of nations, so
disparaging and prejudicial to the character of the era in which we
live, cannot fail to excite astonishment, and to attract the attention of

To the high honour and reputation of American Naval officers, their official accounts of engagements, and other

all who wish to preserve civilization from the encroachments of barbarism, or have rights to protect from military misrule and invasion.

As commander in chief of the royal forces ineffectually employed in Venezuela, you are accountable to your king only for your proceedings against his subjects. But for acts of rapacity, cruelty and oppression, exercised against foreigners—for their illegal imprisonment —for their seizure and confiscation of their property—for their degradation under the aforesaid proclamation, you are answerable to the world, because by such acts of hostility you wage an indiscriminate war against all governments, and by trampling on the sacred rights of men, place at defiance nations, who hold the laws and humane usages of civilized society as rules of action.

War, under the mildest aspect, is a calamity to be deplored; but when to its inseparable horrors are superadded cruelties perpetrated without necessity, and men pursuing peaceable avocations are included in the most sanguinary proscriptions, without reference or respect to the nation which owes them protection, it becomes a demoniac scourge, a hydra curse, which policy and humanity are equally interested in arresting.

Against such a course of violence as you have proclaimed to the world, in behalf of my countrymen I protest, and do hereby premonish your excellency not to enforce the penalty, punishment and ignominy, threatened in your manifesto against the citizens of the United States, who are at present, or may hereafter be found by your excellency, in the independent territories to which you refer, prosecuting their commercial concerns under the guarantee of laws and usages, which no Christian soldier, fighting either for glory, his monarch, or his country, can violate with impunity. The soldier, whose sword is stained with the blood of unoffending men, superfluously shed, wins not the wreath of the warrior, but the reputation of the recreant.

The blockade declared by Gen. Morillo, to which your excellency alludes, exists not, neither has it, at any anterior period been enforced in conformity to rules prescribed by the accepted decisions of the highest authorities rendered valid by time and acquiscence. It therefore has hitherto been a pretext for the interception of our lawful trade—for the seizure and detention of our property, for the abuse and

events in the Second War with Britain, acquired for them
unqualified approbation from the enemy, and undissembled
admiration from Americans.

maltreatment of our mariners---for purposes of plunder and outrage---
all of which evils it has produced.

For spoliations committed on the commerce of the United States,
under the sanction of that paper interdiction, restitution will be re-
quired---and to the dignity which characterizes the govenment of the
republic is Spain indebted for that magnanimous forbearance from
reprisal, justifiable on every principle of self preservation and defence·

The citizens of the United States, from the peaceful and neutral
course prescribed by their government, are justly entitled to the respect of the belligerent parties, and if their enterprize induces them to
reap the advantages of a lawful trade within territories alternately in
the occupancy of either, they are there as citizens of a truly neutral
power---a power that has at no time afforded aid, or exercised influence of any kind in the present unhappy contest.

Between the United States and the Sovereign of Spain there exists
a treaty recently made, and consecrated by the most formal observ-
ances, the acknowledged basis of which is good will, and a cordial
spirit of conciliation. How then, in the face of this pledge and concord, do you sir, undertake to threaten with forfeitures and ignomini-
ous penalties---with slavery and death---the citizens of a Republic who·
have a right to expect, under this token of friendship, safety and ex-
emption from molestation.

Wrongs and injuries that may accrue to citizens of the Union from
your unlawful decrees, whether visited on their persons or property,
will be numbered with the catalogue of outrages already sustained,
and for which Spain must be answerable. Against all such wrongs
and injuries I protest, and do hereby solemnly call upon your Excellency to abstain from the adoption of measures fraught with most evil
consequences---measures coercing a spirit of retaliation and reaction,
the end and issue of which may be conceived, foreseen and prevented
by your Excellency. And I invite your Excellency, as a lover of the
character and honor of Spain, of the amity and good faith so happily
preserved between her and the Republic, to annul all such restrictions
as lead to a violation of the laws of nations---as infringe the just rights
of citizens of the United States---as deprives them of the benefits of

Their modest perspicuity in describing, was equal to their cool courage in achieving victories. They evince, that our naval heroes can wield the pens of scholars, as well as the swords of champions.

The rapidly increasing reputation of young midshipman A. M. Murray, was amongst the most cheering hopes of his venerable father in his declining years.

He looked upon his son Alexander, as the great friend of America, Edmund Burke, once looked upon his admired son Richard ; but, like Burke, he did not live to witness the death of a son, who the former hoped, would transmit *his* name to posterity

Had young Murray died upon the deck of the Macedonian, as the lamented Allen lately fell, in chastising unhallowed pirates, in the region where the beloved midshipman languished, and died of a raging fever, it would have been no greater loss to the Republic ; but, such is the caprice of men, it might have been a theme of more glory to the memory of the accomplished young Murray.

The following very recent extemporaneous effusion of Com. Porter, who was a warm friend of the late venerable Com. Murray—a patron of his lamented son, and who is the designed avenger of Lieut. Allen's murder, by Pirates, shows that he has a mind to express his indignation against the infernal enemies of man ; and that his arm is raised to avenge their audacious and sanguinary murders.

" The cause we are engaged in is the most just and right-

peace, tend to augment to an alarming amount the account which hereafter must inevitably be *balanced* between the two nations.

I have the honor to be, &c.

ROBERT TREAT SPENCE,

Senior Naval officer of the U. States in the West Indies.,,

46

eous, as we war against the enemies of mankind—monsters who disgrace human nature—we carry with us the best wishes, not only of our own country, but of the civilized world. And it is only necessary to pronounce *one name* to awaken our resentments, and inspire us with vengeance —a name distinguished in the annals of our country—a name synonymous with patriotism, courage and self devotion—*The name of* ALLEN.

"Let then, " *Remember Allen*," be our watchword. If it is honorable in our country to be the first to take measures to exterminate those enemies of the human race, it is no less so in us to be the instruments of its will—A martyr was *necessary* to rouse its sleeping energies. The blood of Allen has sealed the pirates' doom—and humanity will shudder less at their punishment than at their crimes. Justice demands it—and the world will approve it."

Amongst the first acts of Com. Porter, after conducting his squadron to the West Indies, was the following impressive general order, to demonstrate the grief felt at the outrageous murder of Lieut. Cooke. It shows that in the depth of sorrow he can,

"Think as a sage, and feel like a man."

GENERAL ORDER.

The afflicting intelligence which has this day been received, relative to the death of that most excellent officer and man Lieut. William H. Cooke, by a shot fired from the castle at St. Johns, has filled us with the most lively sorrow and regret. Had he fallen in battle—had he died by the hands of declared enemies, our sorrow would be assuaged by the knowledge of his having died in the defence of the rights of his country, and while doing his duty as an officer. But to be thus cruelly torn from his family, his friends, and from his country, by the conduct of a dastard, (whose aim was rendered more sure by his perfect safety, and by the helpless condition of the vessel of our lamented friend,) is heart-rending in the extreme.

But while we deprecate the act of the individual who committed it, we must not involve in it the conduct of the whole people. The Captain General of the Island has given the most unequivocal proofs of the most sincere regret that the event has taken place. Every thing has been done by him that I could reasonably expect of him to do at present, to satisfy me of his friendly disposition towards us, and as no act of ours can recall to life the estimable man who has been taken from us, we must leave what remains yet to be done to our country, whose demands will no doubt be prompt and effectual. All that remains for us to do is to grieve ; and as a slight token of what we feel, it is proposed to wear crape on our left arms, and on our swords for one month.

Signed   D. PORTER.
U. S. ship Peacock,
          March 10, 1823.
          A true copy from the General Order Book
                         J. M. MAURA,
                              Captain to Squadron.

The following is an extract from the Letter of Com. Porter, to the Governor of the island of Porto Rico, in regard to the murder of Lieut. Cooke. It contains "thoughts that breathe and words that burn."

"Your excellency in conversation with the officer you wish to implicate, adverted to the affair of the Panchita as one of palliation for the offence, and there is too much reason to apprehend that the officer who gave the order to prevent the entrance of my squadron, as well as those who executed it, thought this a fair opportunity to retaliate. Otherwise why heat shot in the furnaces to destroy my squadron? Why open two batteries on the schooner, and why fire round shot and langrage, while the lamented victim was hailing the fort, and why the remark of the man who pointed the gun, that the shot was intended to avenge the Panchita?

" Your excellency will recollect that in the case of the Panchita, there was an equality of force. Such an occurrence would not have taken place had there been as great a disparity as in the present instance. The cases are not therefore parallel, and if the satisfaction of retaliation was sought for, the offenders have failed in their object; it is yet to be obtained.

" I shall leave the Island to-morrow morning with a heavy heart, and shall without delay communicate to my government the melancholy result of my visit here, which was intended for the benefit of the civilized world in general."

Within eighteen years, the patriotic and ancient city of Philadelphia, has been called to deplore the loss of six brilliant ornaments of the ancient and modern navy of the Republic—TRUXTON, MURRAY the elder, DECATUR the elder, his two noble sons, (" the property of our country") STEPHEN DECATUR, and JAMES B. DECATUR, and ALEXANDER M. MURRAY.

Amidst the tears of grief for this " wide waste of greatness," the smiles of joy may be seen that this city still claims, as living citizens, Bainbridge and Biddle, and many other juniors of these exalted heroes; the two first of whom, if possible, may add to their already gathered laurels ; and the others, yet unknown to fame, may hereafter be enrolled in its temple.

From an obituary notice, is taken the following elegant encomium upon the deceased father and son. Speaking of the accomplished, deceased, and lamented midshipman, it is said—" He was a son of the late Com. Alexander Murray, and, from the high opinions entertained of his rising merit by his commanding officers ; by his enterprising disposition, his gallant and generous feelings, and above all, by his humane and affectionate heart, he gave fair promise to prove to his country and kindred a worthy representative of that venerable and highly valued officer."

The author of the following pathetic and solemn effusion, occasioned by the death of midshipman A. M. Murray, will excuse the writer for adding it to the Sketch of his exalted father's eventful life.

No, he will not return—in a distant land,
  Far from home and from kindred they laid him ;
And lonely and sad was the hour, when the hand
  Of his messmate, the last duties paid him.
The wild burst of grief it is over, and now
  Fancy flies where the white surf is roaring ;
And then, on the shore, 'neath the orange tree bough,
  Or, where the broad bananas are waving,
They picture the spot where the brother and son
  Has entered his last narrow dwelling,
His course it was finished ; his race it was run ;
  And sighs, murmuring sighs, they are swelling.
For he will not return—and in this vale of woe,
  Why ! why ! should'st thou e'er wish to greet him ?
No, haste on thy journey—to Him thou shalt go,
  And where joy reigns forever shall meet him.

But he will not return ! Cans't thou wish his return
   To this region of darkness and sorrow ?
No ! haste on thy journey ; thou shalt pass from this
   bourne
   And rise on that glorious morrow,
Where friends meet him again—never, never to part ;
   Where hope is all lost in enjoyment;
And to praise the *Redeemer*, of each grateful heart
   Is the soul's everlasting employment.

While Americans may justly feel proud of their naval
glory, from the revolution to near the close of the first
quarter of the nineteenth century—while as freemen
they exult in our unsurpassed achievements, and as moral-
ists rejoice that our navy has never been stained by unhallowed aggressions against feeble powers, but has saved
Christians of many different nations from the accumulated
horrors and hopeless misery of Turkish bondage, as well
as the citizens of the American Republic from the same
state of suffering, gloom, and despair—while with proud
satisfaction we can reflect that no public ship of the kingdoms of Britain, France, or Spain, dare point a hostile gun
against American commerce or American citizens—while
with mingled sentiments of approbation and indignation we
behold our dignified government assuming a vindictive attitude against the buccaniers and pirates of the islands of
America—in the very depths of sorrow are we compelled
to utter forth the moans of anguish that the fearless " Naval
Heroes of the Revolution" have almost all "gone to their
long home, and the mourners go about the streets"—and
that during the year just closed, (1822) full one eighth of
the gallant, accomplished, patriotic, and matchless officers
of the present navy of the Republic, by death or retire-

ment have been snatched from the service, and are tenants of the tomb, the mansion, or the cottage. Those high minded men whose motto was

" Altius ibunt, qui ad summa nituntur"

are now either in the congregation of the dead, or in the promiscuous mass of the living.

But with a Roman civilian, let Americans exclaim, "Never despair of the Commonwealth"—let our surviving and remaining officers and seamen say, with the departed LAWRENCE, " Never give up the ship"—and let all, in the language of a favourite* of Washington,—" Thank God that we have constantly witnessed his protecting care of our beloved country; that we have seen the tree of Liberty, the emblem our Independence and Union, while it was a recumbent plant, fostered by vigilance, defended by toil, and not unfrequently watered with tears—and that, by his favour, we now behold it in the vigour of youthful maturity, standing protected from violation, by the sound heads, glowing hearts and strong arms of a new generation, elevating its majestic trunk towards heaven, striking its strong roots in every direction through our soil, and expanding its luxuriant branches over a powerful, united and prosperous nation."

* Oliver Wolcott, Governour of Connecticut, (1823) once Secretary of the Treasury, and successor to Alexander Hamilton.

T. Gimbrede s

JAMES MONROE
President of the United States.

APPENDIX.

As JAMES MONROE was the revolutionary comrade of ALEXANDER MURRAY, and his unvarying friend to the day of his death, the following hasty sketch of that GREAT MAN is attempted with deep solicitude, and inserted here with a diffidence which cannot be expressed.—

CHARACTER AND OFFICIAL SERVICES OF
JAMES MONROE,
A HERO OF THE AMERICAN REVOLUTION,
AND
FIFTH PRESIDENT OF THE AMERICAN REPUBLIC.

JAMES MONROE was born upon the soil which his ancestors acquired in the early settlements of Virginia. It was his beneficent destiny to have been born in the midst of great men ; and to have had the examples of the great, constantly within his aspiring view. That human pre-eminence, which, to human beings at a distance, assumes an inaccessible elevation, became familiar with him by being in contact with it, and almost imperceptibly rising as that ascended.

His was not a sudden flight from humble mediocrity to unrivalled eminence—but a regular gradation from minor stations, to the most elevated post occupied by living man.

In youth, he passed through the discipline of the schools, and acquired the honours of an academician. No sooner was he invested with these distinctions, than he assumed those of a character totally diverse—the insignia of a warrior.

47

As a young subaltern, he first faced the implacable foe of the rising Republic, at the Heights of Hærlem. At White Plains he met the same foe, clad in American armour.

At seventeen, when even hoary-headed veterans were desponding, and hoary-headed, and iron-hearted tories were exulting over the desperate emergencies of the strugling colonies, the lieutenant remained true to WASHINGTON, to AMERICA and to INDEPENDENCE.

At Trenton, in the midst of the warring elements, and the warring danger between Freemen and vassals, and at the moment of victory, he was prostrated by a wound, all but mortal. He survived—not to shew his shattered limb, or boast of a desperate wound, but to follow, to face and to fight the enemy, until they yielded, or until *he fell*.

As Aid-de-Camp to a superior officer, he fought in the sanguinary battles of Brandywine, Germantown and Monmouth. He entered the army of the Revolution as Lieutenant—he left it a Colonel—and left it with the unqualified approbation of his comrades and of Washington, the Father of his Country.

With a man who united in himself the qualities of a great jurist, a profound statesman and a sound philosopher, THOMAS JEFFERSON, he studied the science of law—the science of government, and the science of human nature. Deeply versed in them all, he commenced his civil, legislative, and diplomatic career; or rather he was propelled into these various and responsible situations, by the unsolicited suffrages of his discerning countrymen.

The motto that has governed his whole conduct, in every public station is found in his own official language—"FROM A JUST RESPONSIBILITY I SHALL NEVER SHRINK."

At the age of twenty-three years, he was a member of the highest branch of the legislature of Virginia.

At twenty-four, he was elected a member of the most profound body of men ever convened in the Western Hemisphere, and who had to discharge the most important and solemn duty ever devolved upon an human tribunal. It was no less than to govern three millions of high-minded people, in whom was awakened the slumbering spirit of Freedom which once glowed in the bosoms of Saxon Freemen in England. They were always English Freemen in America—they had now become Independent Americans.

They had dauntlessly hurled the gauntlet of defiance at the most potent empire on earth, and had tore asunder the ligament that bound them to it. Mr. Monroe had fought with them as a soldier—he had legislated with them as civilians—he knew them theoretically and practically. Although the youngest member of that august body, and although he had acquired by intuition, the maturity of age and the wisdom of experience, he was still " *Vir sapientiæ studiosus.*"

The course he pursued, pointed him out to the venerable, and gigantic statesmen of that unequalled assembly, as one of the rising hopes of the rising Republic. When, by the cautious limitation of civil power, he could no longer retain a seat in that body, he left it with the approbation of all.

He retired to the bosom of his native state, and found, in every citizen a warm friend. He was elected a member of the Virginia Convention, which was amongst the first to adopt the American Constitution. The year after its adoption, at the age of thirty-one, he was elected to the highest legislative branch of the government of the American Republic.

The first Congress, by this master compact of human wisdom, first found itself in the possession of efficient power. Mr. MONROE, as a Senator, was aware that he was invested with power, and that that power must be exercised consistently with the civil, moral, religious, and political rights of American Freemen.

It was in the Senate that the vast and comprehensive views of this Statesman were developed. The *natural* and geographical *divisions* of our vast Republic, vanished from his view. His mental grasp embraced the whole region from the Atlantic to the Mississippi—from the Canadas to the Mexican Gulph. He never could be brought to compromit the rights and privileges of one section of the Republic for the benefit of another. He had been in the Senate four years. He had been in the councils of WASHINGTON during that period, as he had been in his army during the War of the Revolution. His cool, collected, and regulated courage in the field, was equalled by his judgment, penetration and prescience in the Cabinet. He was an efficient actor in the establishment of the Judiciary and Financial System ; and aided essentially in organizing the Departments of State, the Treasury, the Army and the Navy. He was there the man of business and the practical Statesman.

If he was not one of those splendid luminaries that blind the beholders by excess of light, he was a mild and shining lamp, that guided the doubting, hesitating, and fearful, in the safe path of statistical experience. In the midst of the difficulties which encompassed the American Statesman who put the intricate machine of a Republic's government

into operation, Mr. MONROE was designated by WASHING-
TON to fill a station still more difficult—a station upon
which " shadows clouds and darkness rested."

He was appointed Ambassador to the French Republic.
Twenty-five millions of Frenchmen had disenthralled and
emancipated themselves from a monarchical despotism, and
an ecclesiastical tyranny, which had chained them to vassalage for thirteen centuries.

It was not like the American Revolution, in which Mr.
MONROE acted a conspicuous part—an unequalled design,
effected by unparalleled measures—it was a sudden convulsion, and revulsion, that transcended, and prostrated the
whole system of ordinary human operations. It showed
that the modern Gauls knew no medium between absolute
destruction, and systematic reformation. It was like the
suppressed fire of a volcanic mountain, gathering strength
by suppression and evincing its latent power by a devastating and irresistable eruption.

In the midst of this combustion, Mr. MONROE appeared
in the metropolis of the then French Republic, (the ally of
America in the War of the Revolution) as the mild and dignified representative, of a mild, dignified, and rising Republic in the New World.

His post was a post of duty and of danger. The unadorned majesty of his character, shone with a lustre, which,
while it conciliated the ardent leaders of the French Revo-
lutionists, maintained, unimpaired, the exalted administration of the exalted Washingron.

Recalled to the Cabinet of the American Republic, he
evinced to his government that in the land of FAYETTE,
ROCHAMBEAU, and MIRABEAU, and in the midst of the
Robespierres, *Marats*, and *Dantons*, of the French Revolu-

tion, he was still the cool, the firm, the unshaken, American Republican. The sentence of WASHINGTON, at this portentous period, is the best eulogy—" I believe JAMES MONROE to be an honest man."

The citizens of his native state, also the native state of WASHINGTON, JEFFERSON, MADISON and HENRY, deeply penetrated with, and fully conscious of his worth, placed him in the gubernatorial chair of Virginia, from which, after the expiration of the constitutional term, he carried an unanimous VOTE OF THANKS, for the faithful, dignified, and impartial manner in which he had discharged the duties of Chief Magistrate.

Retiring from the perpetual excitement and solicitude of public life, Mr. MONROE had scarcely began to enjoy the sweets of repose, before Mr. JEFFRSON, at the head of the Republic, designated him to assert and maintain the rights of America, before the Court of France.

The native expanse of his views, continued to expand with his expanding country. He viewed the waters of the Mississippi, and the Missouri, as of little less importance to his country than those of the Atlantic ; and the immense region of Louisiana a wild territory at the West, of a future value approximating to the invaluable worth of the cultivated region at the East.

His masterly penetration, as a diplomatist, secured them both for the Republic.

Devoted to his country from innate and acquired principle, and clothed with its authority, he repaired to the vascillating court of Spain, and left it as he found it, the sink of intrigue and corruption.

From thence he passed to the court of Britain. He there

found himself, surrounded by the imperious ministers of the most potent rival of the American Republic.

Serene, unmoved, and perfect master of himself, and of his business, he effected what *then* could be effected by negotiation—returned home, and left the event with his country.

The opinion formed of his services abroad, was evidenced by placing him again in the office of Chief Magistrate of Virginia.

But his character had become identified with the rights, the glory and the dignity of the whole Republic ; and MADISON, the successor of JEFFERSON, called him to fill the all-important Department of State.

In this station the Scholar, the Patriot, and the Statesman shone conspicuously, and perspicuously, in JAMES MONROE. No British subtilty could enthrall—no vapid promises allure—no menacing tone could deter the Secretary.

The firm language of remonstrance gave place to the sonorous notes of war ; and the insulted country was manfully told that protracted negotiation was ended by an appeal to arms.

Mr. MONROE, during the two first compaigns of the second war with Britain, sustained the dignity of the State Department, and, amidst the accumulated horrors of Vandal invasion, and Gothic devastation, was called also to head the Department of War.

Upon one day he had to act a significant part in the Cabinet—upon another to give official direction to the thunders of Plattsburgh, the Canadian Peninsula, and New-Orleans.

Upon the return of an honourable peace, after a glorious war, upon the land and on the ocean, the Secretary of State and of War enjoyed a temporary repose from the turmoil and agitation, of a vast accumulation of official duty.

The highest honour which man can claim in the nineteenth century, now awaited the acceptance of JAMES MONROE.

He had been virtually elected the Fifth President of the American Republic, by the spontaneous voice of the American People ; and needed only the Constitutional Formulæ to inaugurate him into that station—above all other temporal elevation—the Chief Ruler of the only genuine Republic on earth ; and made such by the election of TEN MILLIONS of the freest, happiest, and most intelligent people in the world.

The most impassioned language of eulogy would lag far behind reality, in speaking of his administration. It is found in the increasing happiness ; the augmenting wealth ; the moral and intellectual energy ; the rising glory, and impregnable defence of the great nation over which he presides.

This feeble sketch of the Character and Public Services of JAMES MONROE will be closed by a sketch still more imperfect, of his person.

He is a very little above the middle height of Americans, in his stature. Although he does not possess a robust frame, his presence would evince, to a close observer, that he was a man of very considerable muscular power.

There is not the least appearance of lassitude in his person ; but it exhibits a natural compactness, increased by bodily activity and vigorous exertion.

In the expression of his countenance, there is nothing that would attract attention, were it not for the character he has acquired, and the sphere in which he moves.

He seems to be a perfect novice in the art of *forcing* into his face, occular evidence of deep thought, wonderful acuteness, or the lineaments of wisdom ; and the *phisiognomist* would despair of gathering the qualities of his mind, from exterior indices. Nor would the *craniologist* succeed any better; for his head, like his face, in its exterior, is not strikingly different from other men's; and as he is sixty-three years of age, it does not exhibit more of the ravages of time than usually falls to the human lot.

When silent, his countenance indicates something like forbidding austerity ; but in familiar conversation, and when reciprocating civilities, it is often lighted up with a smile, beaming with benignity and benevolence.

When disengaged from official duties, his deportment is easy, unaffected, and unassuming. The disciples of *Stanhope*, although they would discover in the President a sufficiency of " modest assurance," they would look in vain for that artificial " *suavity of manners*" so captivating with superficial courtiers.

His manners are those of a plain, dignified gentleman. The graces, at his command, seem to have volunteered their services, conscious that into *his* service they never would have been impressed. His courtesies proceed from his native benignity, and his artless display of them would suffuse the cheek of affectation with the blush of shame.

If the President has any affectation, it is in his dress ; which though neat and rich, is so exceedingly plain, that, in a promiscuous assemblage, he could with difficulty be identified.

In his different Tours* through our vast Republic, for-

* The following elegant extract is from an address delivered to Mr. Monroe upon reaching the borders of the State of Maine in 1817.

48

eigners, and those who ape the *wardrobe* of foreigners,
wondered where he was ; and, when they saw him, wondered!!

Such, imperfectly drawn, is the person, the deportment,
and appearance of the MAN, whose CHARACTER is known in
the two hemispheres—duly appreciated in the East—admired, respected, and venerated in the West.

If he survives his Presidential Dignities, and, like his
great predecessors, WASHINGTON, ADAMS, JEFFERSON and
MADISON, seeks repose in retirement*—there, when appearing in native, unadorned majesty—" Nature may stand
up to all the world, and claim him as her own." From
this " private station," which to him will be " the post of
honour," he may in retrospect, (retiring into himself) contemplate upon a Life devoted to the great cause of the

The Committee who offered it consisted of the present Gov. Parris,
Hon. John Holmes, and W. P. Preble, (son of Com. Preble :)

" This journey, like the journey of your life, is commenced and pursued for the public good. Like that, its fatigues have been endured
with patience, its obstacles overcome with perseverance, its storms
encountered with firmness, and its refreshing sunshines relished with
equanimity and gratitude. In each, as you have advanced, you have
acquired additional honour, reverence, and love. In your future progress in both, may your health be preserved, your country's prosperity and glory secured ; and the affections, confidence, and union of the
people increased and confirmed. And when these respective journies
shall be ended, and you shall return home, may you at the close of
the one, be received in health and happiness to the embraces of an affectionate family, and of the other, to the favour and fruition of Him,
who will never fail to reward the great and the good."

* " It has ever been my proudest ambition from early youth to serve
my country, in such offices as my fellow-citizens have thought fit to
confide to me. It will be my most consoling reward, when I retire
from public life, to find, that my conduct has been such as to merit
and obtain their approbation." Tour of Monroe, p. 198, 3d edition.

Great Republic—upon the honours conferred upon him by his country—and patiently wait for that Order of his Supreme Commander, which will remove him from his temporal to his eternal honours.

The following " Familiar Letters," and opinions of the SECOND AND THIRD PRESIDENTS OF THE AMERICAN RE-PUBLIC, both of whom were the warm friends of Com. Murray, are annexed with undissembled delight.

The language of these " venerable octogenarians," the one labouring under years near half in number of those of Civilized New England, and the other of an age more than one third of that which is sometimes called the " Ancient Dominion" of the Republic, ought to be treasured up by the rising generation of American Patriots, with as much avidity, as were the " more last words," of an eminent divine in the 17th century, by the devotional professors of Christianity.

These " last words" of ADAMS and JEFFERSON, are almost like a " voice from the tomb," uttered by dead worthies, to their surviving posterity. " *Fortunatus Senex !*" may Americans exclaim to each of these venerated Patriots, Scholars, and Statesmen, You have lived for the Republic, and in the remembrance of that Republic you will never die. The motto of these great men may well be—

> " After my death, 1 wish no other herald,
> No other speaker of my living actions,
> To keep mine honour from corruption,
> But such an honest chronicler as Griffith."

This letter may be said to be " multum in parvo." This Doctor of Laws probes the wounds of the colonies to the bottom; as a Doctor of Medicine searches the remote cause of the disease of his patient. He does not try to remove the eruption upon the surface, but endeavours to extirpate the impurities of the blood which occasion it. It proves, in few words, the truth of Mr. Jefferson's remarks regarding Mr. Adams. " No one is better calculated than he, to give to the reader a correct impression of the earlier part of the contest." [The War of the Revolution.]

QUINCY, Feb. 13, 1818.

Mr. NILES—The American Revolution was not a common event. Its effects and consequences have already been awful over a great part of the globe. And when and where are they to cease ?

But what do we mean by the American Revolution ? Do we mean the American War ? The Revolution was effected before the War commenced. The Revolution was in the minds and hearts of the people. A change in their religious sentiments, of their duties and obligations. While the king, and all in authority under him, were believed to govern in justice and mercy according to the laws and constitution derived to them from the God of nature, and transmitted to them by their ancestors—they thought themselves bound to pray for the king and queen and all the royal family, and all in authority, under them ; as ministers ordained of God for their good. But when they saw those powers renouncing all the principles of authority, and bent upon the destruction of all the securities of their lives, liberties and properties, they thought it their duty to pray for the Continental Congress and all the thirteen state congresses, &c.

There might be, and there were others, who thoughtless about religion and conscience, but had certain habitual sentiments of allegiance and loyalty derived from their ed-

ucation ; but believing allegiance and protection to be reciprocal, when protection was withdrawn, they thought allegiance was dissolved.

Another alteration was common to all. The people of
America had been educated in an habitual affection for
England as their mother country ; and while they thought
her a kind and tender parent, (erroneously _enough, however, for she never was such a mother) no affection could
be more sincere. But when they found her a cruel Bel-
dam, willing like lady Macbeth, to " dash their brains out,"
it is no wonder if their filial affections ceased and were
changed into indignation and horror.

*This radical change in the principles, opinions, sentiments
and affections of the people, was the real American revolution.*

By what means, this great and important alteration in
the religious, moral, political and social character of the
people of thirteen colonies, all distinct, unconnected and
independent of each other, was begun, pursued and accomplished, it is, surely interesting to humanity to investigate,
and perpetuate to posterity.

The colonies had grown up under constitutions of government so different, there was so great a variety of reli-
gions, they were composed of so many different nations,
their customs, manners and habits had so little resemblance,
and their intercourse had been so rare and their knowledge
of each other so imperfect, that to unite them in the same
principles of theory and the same system of action, was
certainly a very difficult enterprize. The complete accomplishment of it, in so short a time and by such simple
means, was perhaps a singular example in the history of
mankind. Thirteen clocks were made to strike together ;
a perfection of machinery which no artist had ever before
effected.

In this research, the glorioroles of individual gentlemen and of separate states is of little consequence. The *means and the measures* are the proper objects of investigation. These may be of use to posterity, not only in this nation, but in South-America and all other countries. They may teach mankind that revolutions are not trifles ; that they ought never to be undertaken rashly ; nor without deliberate consideration and sober reflection ; nor without a solid, immutable, eternal foundation of justice and humanity ; nor without a people possessed of intelligence, fortitude and integrity sufficient to carry them with steadiness, patience, and perseverance, through all the vicissitudes of fortune, the fiery trials and melancholy disasters they may have to encounter.

The town of Boston early instituted an annual oration of the fourth of July, in commemoration of the principles and feelings which contributed to produce the revolution. Many of those orations I have heard, and all that I could obtain I have read. Much ingenuity and eloquence appears upon every subject, except those principles and feelings. That of my honest and amiable neighbour, Josiah Quincy, appeared to me the most directly to the purpose of the institution. Those principles and feelings ought to be traced back for two hundred years, and sought in the history of the country from the first plantations in America. Nor should the feelings of the English and Scots towards the colonies, through that whole period ever be forgotten. The perpetual discordance between British principles and feelings and of those of America, the next year after the suppression of the French power in America, came to a crisis, and produced an explosion.

It was not till after the annihilation of the French do-

minion in America, that any British ministry had dared to
gratify their own wishes, and the desire of the nation, by
projecting a formal plan for raising a national revenue from
America, by parliamentary taxation. The first great man-
ifestation of this design was by the order to carry into strict
executions those acts of parliament which were well known
by the appellation of the acts of trade, which had lain a
dead letter, for more than half a century, and some of them
I believe, for nearly a whole one.

This produced in 1760 and 1761, an awakening and a
revival of American principles and feelings, with an enthusiasm which went on increasing, till in 1775, it burst out in
open violence, hostility and fury.

The characters the most conspicuous, the most ardent
and influential in this revival, from 1760 to 1766, were—
first and foremost, before all and above all, JAMES OTIS ;*
next to him was OXENBRIDGE THATCHER ; next to him
SAMUEL ADAMS ; next to him, JOHN HANCOCK ; then Dr.
Mayhew, then Dr. Cooper and his brother. Of Mr. Hancock's life, character, generous nature, great and disinter-
ested sacrifices, and important services, if I had forces, I
should be glad to write a volume. But this I hope will be
done by some younger and abler hand. Mr. Thatcher,
because his name and merits are less known, must not be
wholly omitted. This gentleman was an excellent barris-
ter at law, in as large practice as any one in Boston. There
was not a citizen of that town more universally beloved
for his learning, ingenuity, every domestic and social vir-

---

* Tudor's life of James Otis may well occupy the same bureau as
Wirt's Life of Patrick Henry. The ancient dominion of Massachusetts has found an advocate as well as the ancient dominion of Virginia.

tue, and conscientious conduct in every relation of life. His patriotism was as ardent as his progenitors had been ancient and illustrious in this country. Hutchinson often said that " Thatcher was not born a plebeian, but he was determined to die one." In May, 1763, I believe he was chosen by the town of Boston one of their representatives in the legislature, a colleague with Mr. Otis, who had been a member from May 1761, and he continued to be re-elected annually till his death in 1765, when Mr. Samuel Adams was elected to fill his place, in the absence of Mr. Otis, then attending the congress at New-York. Thatcher had long been jealous of the unbounded ambition of Mr. Hutchinson, but when he found him not content with the office of Lieutenant-Governor, the command of the castle and its emoluments, of judge of probate for the county of Suffolk, a seat in his majesty's council in the legislature, his brother-in-law secretary of state by the king's commission, a brother of that secretary of State, a judge of the Supreme Court, and a member of council, now in 1760 and 1761, soliciting and accepting the office of chief justice of the superier court of judicature, he concluded, as Mr. Otis did, and as every other enlightened friend of his country did, that he sought that office with the determined purpose of determining all causes in favour of the ministry at St. James's and their servile parliament.

His indignation against him henceforward, to 1765, when he died, knew no bounds but truth. I speak from personal knowledge.—For, from 1758 to 1765, I attended every superior and inferior court in Boston, and recollect not one in which he did not invite me home to spend evenings with him, when he made me converse with him as well as I could, on all subjects of religion, morals, law, politics, his-

tory, philosophy, belles-lettres, theology, mythology, cosmo-
gany, metaphysics.—Locke, Clark, Leibnitz, Bolingbroke,
Berckley,—the pre-established harmony of the universe,
the nature of matter and of spirit, and the eternal establishment of coincidences between their operations, fate,
foreknowledge, absolute—and we reasoned on such un-
fathomable subjects as high as Milton's gentry in pandemonium ; and we understood them as well as they did, and
no better.—To such mighty mysteries he added the news
of the day, and the tittle-tattle of the town. But his favorite subject was politics, and the impending threatening
system of parliamentary taxation and universal government
over the colonies. On this subject he was so anxious and
agitated that I have no doubt it occasioned his premature
death. From the time when he argued the question of
writs of assistance to his death, he considered the king,
ministry, parliament and nation of Great-Britain as determined to new model the colonies from the foundation ; to
annul all their charters, to constitute them all royal governments ; to raise a revenue in America by parliamentary
taxation ; to apply that revenue to pay the salaries of gov-
ernors, judges and all other crown officers ; and, after all
this, to raise as large a revenue as they pleased, to be applied to national purposes at the exchequer in England ;
and further to establish bishops and the whole system of the
church of England, tythes and all, throughout all British
America. This system, he said, if it was suffered to prevail would extinguish the flame of liberty all over the
world ; that America would be employed as an engine to
batter down all the miserable remains of liberty in Great-
Britain and Ireland, where only any semblance of it was
left in the world. To this system he considered Hutchin-

son, the Olivers' and all their connections, dependants, adherents, shoe-lickers—as entirely devoted. He asserted that they were all engaged with all the crown officers in America and the understrappers of the ministry in England, in a deep and treasonable conspiracy to betray the liberties of their country, for their own private personal and family aggrandizement. His phillippicks against the unprincipled ambition and avarice of all of them, but especially of Hutchinson, were unbridled; not only in private, confidential conversations, but in all companies and on all occasions. He gave Hutchinson the sobriquet of "Summa Protestatis," and rarely mentioned him but by the name of "Summa." His liberties of speech were no secrets to his enemies. I have sometimes wondered that they did not throw him over the bar, as they did soon afterwards major Hawley. For they hated him worse than they did James Otis, or Samuel Adams, and they feared him more—because they had no revenge for a father's disappointment of a seat on the superior bench to impute to him as they did to Otis; and Thatcher's character through life had been so modest, decent, unassuming—his morals so pure, and his religion so venerated, that they dared not attack him. In his office were educated to the bar, two eminent characters, the late judge Lowell, and Josiah Quincy, aptly called the Boston Cicero.

Mr. Thatcher's frame was slender, his constitution delicate; whether his physicians overstrained his vessels with mercury, when he had the small pox by inoculation at the castle, or whether he was overplyed by public anxieties and exertions, the small pox left him in a decline from which he never recovered. Not long before his death he sent for me to commit to my care some of his business at the bar.

I asked him whether he had seen the Virginia resolves :
" O yes—they are men ! they are noble spirits ! It kills
me to think of the lethargy and stupidity that prevail here.
I long to be out. I will go out. I will go out. I will go
into court, and make a speech which shall be read after my
death as my dying testimony against this infernal tyranny
which they are bringing upon us." Seeing the violent agitation into which it threw him, I changed the subject as soon
as possible, and retired. Had he been confined for some
time. Had he been abroad among the people, he would
not have complained so pathetically of the " lethargy and
stupidity that prevailed," for town and country were all
alive ; and in August became active enough, and some of
the people proceeded to unwarrantable excesses, which
were more lamented by the patriots than their enemies.—
Mr. Thatcher soon died, deeply lamented by all the friends
of their country.

Another gentleman who had great influence in the commencement of the revolution, was Dr. Jonathan Mayhew,
a descendant of the ancient governor of Martha's Vineyard.
This divine had raised a great reputation both in Europe
and America, by the publication of a volume of seven ser-
mons in the reign of king George the second, 1749, and by
many other writings, particularly a sermon in 1750, on the
thirtieth of January, on the subject of passive obedience
and non-resistance ; in which the saintship and martyrdom
of king Charles the first are considered, seasoned with wit
and satire superior to any in Swift and Franklin. It was
read by every body ; celebrated by friends and abused by
enemies.—During the reigns of king George the first and
king George the second, the reigns of the Stuarts, the two
Jameses and the two Charleses, were in general disgrace

in England. In America they had always been held in abhorrence.--The persecutions and cruelties suffered by their
ancestors under those reigns had been transmitted by history and tradition, and Mayhew seemed to be raised up to
revive all their animosities against tyranny, in church and
state, and at the same time to destroy their bigotry, fanati-
cism and inconsistency. David Hume's plausible, elegant,
fascinating and fallacious apology, in which he varnished
over the crimes of the Stuarts, had not then appeared. To
draw the character of Mayhew would be to transcribe a
dozen volumes. This transcendant genius threw all the
weight of his great fame into the scale of his country in
1751, and maintained it there with zeal and ardour till his
death in 1766. In 1763 appeared the controversy between
him and Mr. Apthorp, Mr. Caner, Dr. Johnson and Arch-
bishop Secker, on the charter and conduct of the society
for propagating the gospel in foreign parts. To form a
judgment of this debate, I beg leave to refer to a review
of the whole, printed at the time and written by Samuel
Adams, though by some, very absurdly and erroneously,
ascribed to Mr. Apthorp. If I am not mistaken, it will be
found a model of candor, sagacity, impartiality, and close,
correct reasoning.

If any gentleman supposes this controversy to be nothing
to the present purpose, he is grossly mistaken. It spread
an universal alarm against the authority of parliament. It
excited a general and just apprehension that bishops, and
dioceses, and churches, and priests and tythes, were to be
imposed on us by parliament. It was known that neither
king nor ministry, nor archbishops, could appoint bishops in
America without an act of parliament; and if parliament
could tax us, they could establish the church of England,

with all its creeds, articles, tests, ceremonies and tythes, and prohibit all other churches as conventicles and schism shops.

Nor must Mr. Cushing be forgotten. His good sense and sound judgment, the urbanity of his manners, his universal good character, his numerous friends and connexions, and his continual intercourse with all sorts of people, added to his constant attachment to the liberties of his country, gave him a great and salutary influence from the beginning in 1760.

Let me recommend these hints to the consideration of Mr. Wirt, whose life of Mr. Henry I have read with great delight. I think, that after mature investigation, he will be convinced that Mr. Henry did not "give the first impulse to the ball of independence"—and that Otis, Thatcher, Samuel Adams, Mayhew, Hancock, Cushing, and thousands of others were labouring for several years at the wheel before the name of Henry was heard beyond the limits of Virginia.

If you print this, I will endeavor to send you something concerning Samuel Adams, who was destined to a longer career, and to act a more conspicuous and, perhaps, a more important part than any other man. But his life would require a volume. If you decline printing this letter, I pray you to return it, as soon as possible, to,

Sir, your humble servant,

JOHN ADAMS."

The following letter is a *precious morceau ;* as it evinces the exalted magnanimity of Mr. JEFFERSON, in giving to his once great political rival, Mr. ADAMS the rank he de serves amongst that matchless constellation of Statesmen who composed the Old Congress.—

"*Monticello, February* 19, 1813.

SIR—Your favour of the 13th has been duly received, together with the papers it covered, and particularly Mr. Barralet's sketch of the ornaments proposed to accompany the publication of the Declaration of Independence, contemplated by Mr. Murray and yourself. I am too little versed in the art of design, to be able to offer any suggestions to the artist. As far as I am a judge, the composition appears to be judicious and well imagined. Were I to hazard a suggestion, it should be, that Mr. Hancock, as president of Congress, should occupy the middle and principal place.

No man better merited than Mr. John Adams to hold a most conspicuous place in the design.—He was the Pillar of its support on the Floor of Congress, its ablest advocate and Defender against the multifarious assaults it encountered; for many excellent persons opposed it on doubts whether we were provided sufficiently with the means of supporting it, whether the minds of our constituents were yet prepared to receive it, &c. who, after it was decided, united zealously in the measures it called for.

I must ask permission to become a subscriber for a copy when published, which, if rolled on a wooden roller, and sent by mail, will come safely.

Accept the assurance of my respect and best wishes.

TH: JEFFERSON.

Mr. Wm. P. Gardner, Washington."

This extract from one of the late letters of the venerable ADAMS, shows his anxiety to rescue from oblivion the memories of the distinguished fathers of NEW-ENGLAND. He has lived himself for posterity, and *sees posterity* while he *yet lives* :—

"I have no disposition to vilify the character of the illustrious William Penn, or to depreciate his merits, so celebrated for his wisdom, toleration, and humanity to the Indians ; but I think that New-England furnishes the biography of several characters, who, more than half a century before him, had exerted equal talents, equal exertions, greater sacrifices, and severer sufferings, in the same pious and virtuous cause. Mr. Penn was very fortunate in having to choose his own companions, and in meeting with Indians of a very mild and pacific character ; but the first settlers in New-England had spies and emissaries sent out with the express purpose of counteracting and destroying their puritanical establishments. The character of Sir Christopher Gardiner, of Weston, the heart of the establishment of Wessaguscus, and Thomas Morton, of Mount Wallaston, ought to be minutely investigated. They were all in the confidence of Arch-bishop Laud, as appears explicitly, by the writings of Thomas Morton, in his New Canaan. This Thomas Morton was as great a plague to our Forefathers, as Tom Paine has been to us in our day. His writings, conduct, and character, ought to be examined, and stated at full length. He and those other emisaries furnished the Indians with arms, and other ammunition, and taught them the use of them ; and, what was worse, gave them spirituous liquors, and commenced their habits of intoxication."

Of the writers of the two following letters, who talk away in all the charming playfulness of a "green old age," we may say—

"They are men—take them all in all,
"We ne'er shall look upon their like again."

From Mr. Jefferson to Mr. Adams.

" *Monticello, June* 1, 1822.

" It is very long, my dear sir, since I have written to you. My dislocated wrist is now become so stiff that I write slowly and with pain ; and, therefore, write as little as I can. Yet it is due to mutual friendship to ask once in a while how we do ? The papers tell us that Gen. Stark is off at the age of ninety-three.—***** still lives, at about the same age, cheerful, slender as a grasshopper, and so much without memory that he scarcely recognizes the members of his household. An intimate friend of his called on him not long since. It was difficult to make him recollect who he was, and sitting one hour, he told him the same story four times over. Is this life ?—with lab'ring step

> To tread our former footsteps ? pace the round
> Eternal ?—to beat and beat
> The beaten track—to see what we have seen—
> To taste the tasted—o'er our palates to descant
> Another vintage?

" It is, at most, but the life of a cabbage, surely not worth a wish. When all our faculties have left, or are leaving us one by one, sight, hearing, memory, every avenue of pleasing sensation is closed, and athumy, debility, and mal aise left in their places, when the friends of our youth are all gone, and a generation is risen around us, whom we know not, is death an evil ?

> When one by one our ties are torn,
> And friend from friend is snatch'd forlorn ;
> When man is left alone to mourn,
>   Oh, then, how sweet it is to die !
>
> When trembling limbs refuse their weight,
> And films slow gathering dim the sight ;
> When clouds secure the mental light,
>   'Tis nature's kindest boon to die !

" I really think so. I have ever dreaded a doating old age ; and my health has been generally so good and is now so good, that I dread it still. The rapid decline of my strength during the last winter has made me hope sometimes that I see land. During summer, I enjoy its temperature, but I shudder at the approach of winter, and wish I could sleep through it with the dormouse, and only wake with him in spring, if ever. They say that Starke could walk about his room. I am told you walk well and firmly. I can only reach my garden, and that with sensible fatigue. I ride, however, daily ; but reading is my delight. I should wish never to put pen to paper; and the more because of the treacherous practice some people have of publishing one's letters without leave. Lord Mansfield declared it a breach of trust, and punishable at law. I think it should be a penitentiary felony ; yet you will have seen that they have drawn me out into the arena of the newspapers. Although I know it is too late for me to buckle on the armour of youth, yet my indignation would not permit me passively to receive the kick of an ass.

" To turn to the news of the day, it seems that the cannibals of Europe are going to eating one another again. A war between Russia and Turkey is like the battle of the kite and snake ; whichever destroys the other, leaves a destroyer the less for the world. This pugnacious humour of mankind seems to be the law of his nature, one of the obstacles to too great multiplication provided in the mechanism of the Universe. The cocks of the hen yard kill one another ; bears, bulls, rams, do the same, and a horse in his wild state, kills all the young males, until worn down with age and war, some vigorous youth kills him.*** ** I hope we shall prove how much happier for man the

50

Quaker policy is, and that the life of the feeder is better than that of the fighter ; and it is some consolation that the desolation by these maniacs of one part of the earth, is the means of improving it in other parts. Let the latter be our office ; and let us milk the cow, while the Russian holds her by the horns, and the Turk by the tail.* God bless you, and give you health, strength, good spirits, and as much of life as you think worth having.

THO'S. JEFFERSON.

Mr. Adams' Reply.

Montezillo, June 11, 1822.

Dear Sir.—Half an hour ago I received, and this moment have heard read for the third or fourth time, the best letter that ever was written by an Octogenarian, dated June 1st.

*   *   *   *   *   *

I have not sprained my wrist; but both my arms and hands are so overstrained that I cannot write a line.—Poor Starke remembered nothing and could talk of nothing but the battle of Bennington. ***** is not quite so reduced. I cannot mount my horse but I can walk three miles over a rugged rocky mountain, and have done it within a month ; yet I feel when sitting in my chair as if I could not rise out of it ; and when risen, as if I could not walk across the room ; my sight is very dim, hearing pretty good, memory poor enough.

I answer your question—is death an evil ?—It is not an evil. It is a blessing to the individual and to the world ;

---

* In the War of the Revolution, when Gen. Putnam commanded at Philadelphia, and Sir Wm. Howe at New-York, the general was asked how much he could depend upon N. Jersey. " She is true," said he, " but what can she do when Pennsylvania has her by the horns, and New-York by the tail ?"

yet we ought not to wish for it till life becomes insupportable. We must wait the pleasure and convenience of the 'Great Teacher.' Winter is as terrible to me as to you. I am almost reduced in it to the life of a bear or a torpid swallow. I cannot read, but my delight is to hear others read ; and I tax all my friends most unmercifully and tyrannically against their consent.

The ass has kicked in vain ; all men say the dull animal has missed the mark.

This globe is a theatre of war—its inhabitants are all heroes. . The little eels in vinegar and the animalcules in pepper-water, I believe are quarrelsome. The bees are as warlike as the Romans, Russians, Britons or Frenchmen. Ants, caterpillars and canker-worms, are the only tribes among whom I have not seen battles ; and heaven itself, if we believe Hindoos, Jews, Christians and Mahometans, has not always been at peace. We need not trouble ourselves about these things, nor fret ourselves because of evildoers ; but safely trust the 'Ruler with his skies.' Nor need we dread the approach of dotage ; let it come, if it must. *****, it seems, still delights in his four stories ; and Starke remembered to the last his Bennington, and exulted in his glory : the worst of the evil is, that our friends will suffer more by our imbecility than we ourselves.

*   *   *   *   *   *

In wishing for your health and happiness, I am very selfish ; for I hope for more letters ; this is worth more than five hundred dollars to me, for it has already given me, and it will continue to give more pleasure than a thousand. Mr. Jay, who is about your age, I am told experiences more decay than you do.   I am your old friend.

JOHN ADAMS.

President JEFFERSON.

The following is from the pen of a distinguished scholar who visited President Adams in 1822.

" The residence of the venerable patriot stands in a beautiful retired spot, shaded with trees, and every thing within and without the premises, wears an air of neatness, comfort and genuine republican simplicity, that charms one. A modern fashionable, about visiting those whom the world calls great, would expect to find the vestibules, the drawing rooms, and boudoirs choked up with fiery dragons and serpents as decorations to their costly Parisian furniture. But not so with this veteran father of our Republic. With him, extravagance has not superseded convenience, nor fashion banished comfort and good taste from his dwelling. This distinguished benefactor of his country, whose life was for a time embittered by injustice and persecution, is now 87 years old. He may be said " fairly to have outlived the prejudices which party animosity excited against him ; in his own time the storm has passed by, and the last hours of his course are unclouded and serene." We found him in tolerable health, cheerful, and in good spirits. In conversation he was quick and sprightly ; and I was pleased to find that his faculties, apparently, were not benumbed by age. Upon every subject he was perfectly at home. Indeed I never saw the man of whom, notwithstanding the imperceptible ravages of time, it might more truly be said, in the language of Shakspeare—

> " He is a scholar, and a ripe and good one ;
> Hear him but reason in divinity,
> And, all admiring, with an inward wish,
> You would suppose him the most learned prelate.
> Hear him debate of Commonwealth affairs,
> You'd say it hath been all-in-all, his study.
> List his discourse of war, and you shall hear

A fearful battle rendered you in music.
Turn him to any cause of policy,
The Gordian Knot of it he will unloose,
Familiar as his garter."

His knowledge of the ever-varying politics of the several
states, is perfect up to the present time; and I found that
he was as thoroughly acquainted with all the political
squabbles of New York, their causes and consequences,
with the proceedings of the late convention in that state,
and with every point of the new constitution, as though he
had attended and written down the journals and arguments
himself. I have seldom seen the man who appeared so
perfectly happy."

The following elegant remarks upon the two last preceding letters are from the pen of a distinguished American
writer.

" The following Letters have been obtained by solicita-
tion ; and are sent to the press by the permission of their
venerable authors. The character, standing, and age of
the writers, the one in his eightieth, the other in his eighty-
seventh year, give them peculiar interest, and they cannot
fail to be read with great pleasure. It is delightful to witness this kind of correspondence between these two distinguished men, the asperities of party by which they were
at one time separated, worn down, and nothing remaining
but the interchange of sentiments of unfeigned kindness
and respect. It is charming to see an old age like this,
retaining, even under its decays and infirmities, the intellectual vigour unimpaired ; and displaying amidst its snows,
the greenness and freshness of the summer of life. It is an
enviable and privileged height to which these great men
have attained ; from which they are permitted to look

down upon an extensive and eminently happy country, enjoying the fruit of their labours and sacrifices, more than realizing their boldest anticipations ; and regarding them with that gratitude and respect to which their magnanimity and distinguished patriotism so emphatically entitle them.

The letter of Mr. Jefferson was written soon after an attack upon him by the " Native Virginian ;" and when there was a strong expectation of a war between Russia and Turkey ; this will explain some allusions in them."

The following remarks of the distinguished Editor of " The London Morning Chronicle" must have been " wormwood" to " the miserable beings who fill the thrones of the Continent." The Editor may be asked whether he considers the " fast anchor'd isle" of Britain as belonging to " the Continent ?" Whether in the " absence of pure monarchy" *there*, he can help " despising the idols he worships ?" But he is undoubtedly a loyal Englishman : and although he scatters the " paper bullets of the brain" he can readily adopt the language of the British knight in Shakespeare, " *No abuse, Hal ! no abuse 'pon honor, Hal !*" " *The Lion will not touch the true Prince.*"

" *America and Europe.*—What a contrast the following Correspondence of the two Rival Presidents of the greatest Republic of the world, reflecting on old age dedicated to virtue, temperance and philosophy, presents to the heartsickening details occasionally disclosed to us of the miserable beings who fill the Thrones of the Continent. There is not, perhaps, one Sovereign of the Continent who in any sense of the word can be said to honour nature, while many make us almost ashamed of it. The curtain is seldom drawn aside without exhibiting to us beings worn out with vicious indulgence, diseased in mind, if not in body, the creature of caprice and insensibility. On the other hand, since the foundation of the American Republic, the Chair has never been filled by a man, for whose life (to say the least) any American need once to blush. It must, therefore, be some compensation to the Ameri_ cans for the absence of pure Monarchy, that when they look upwards their eyes are not always met by vice and meanness, and often idiocy ; as it is a deduction from the advantage of those who possess not Kings that they cannot help despising the idols they worship."

The following authentic document must extort from every reader the most unqualified admiration. It goes to confirm the declaration of the energetic Adams in one of the preceding letters, that in New England—"thousands were labouring for several years at the wheel before the name of Henry was heard beyond the limits of Virginia."

The writer of the preceding sketches, acknowledges the rapturous delight with which he perused and still peruses " Wirt's Life of Henry." In that master-piece of American Biography, the author is no longer " The British Spy" —he is the whole-souled Virginian in Virginia. Virginia, in his hands is " all in all" in the " old thirteen colonies," and Patrick Henry is all in all in Virginia. Like a song of enchantment, his harmonious " concord of sweet sounds," allures his New-England reader from Fanueil Hall, where the cradle of Independance was first rocked ; where Hancock, the Adamses, Otis, &c. " raised such a flame in Massachusetts as expelled all royal rule in America ;"—yes, he ravishes him away from the land of his ancestors,—places him in the " House of Burgesses in Virginia," and makes him forget the descendants of the pilgrims in the sonorous notes of Henry, and the fascinating tones of Lee, who, he almost makes him believe—" gave the first impulse to the ball of Independence."

" In the year 1813, I paid a visit to Mr. Jefferson, in his retirement to Monticello. During the visit, the credibility of history became a topic of conversation, and we naturally adverted to that of our own country. He spoke with great freedom of the heroes and patriots of our Revolution, and of its gloomy and brilliant periods. I will give the substance of a part of his remarks. " No correct history of that arduous struggle, has yet been or ever will be written. The actors in important and busy scenes are too much absorbed in their immediate duty, to record events, or the motives and causes which produced them. Many secret springs, concealed even from those upon whom they operate, give an impulse to measures which are supposed to be the result of chance ; and an accidental occurrence of causes is often attributed to the connected plan of leaders, who are themselves as much astonished as others at the events they witness. They who took an active part in these important transactions can hardly recognize them as they are related in the histories of our Revolution. That of Botta, an Italian, is the best. In all of them events are misrepresented, wrong motives are assigned, and justice is seldom done to individuals, some having too much, and some too little praise. The private correspondence of three or four persons in different official stations at that time, would form the best history. I have heard that Mr. Adams is writing something on the subject.—No one is better qualified than he to give to the reader a correct impression of the earlier part of the contest. No history has done him justice, for no historian was present to witness the Continental Congress. In his zeal for independence he was ardent; in contriving expedients and originating measures, he was always busy; in disastrous times, when gloom sat on the countenances of most of us, his courage and fortitude continued unabated, and his animated exhortations restored confidence to those who had wavered. He seemed to forget every thing but his country, and the cause which he had espoused.

" In a journey to the southward, I fell in company with an aged and highly respected gentleman, a native of one of the middle states, who in our revolutionary war espoused the cause of the King, and held an important post in the royal army. He conversed with great frankness of his principles and motives, and appeared to have been well acquainted with the events of that period. " It has been disputed," said I, " where the Revolution originated, in Massachusetts or Virginia. What was the opinion of the Royalists of that period, and what is yours? " That it originated in Massachusetts," was his reply, " and if I was to state *who, in my opinion, contributed most to bring on the contest,* I should name JOHN ADAMS, who was afterwards your President. Concerning him I will relate an anecdote. He came into notice during the administration of Governor Bernard, and distinguished himself by his resolute opposition to many of his measures. The Attorney General, Sewell, was however his bosom friend. At that time the office of a Justice of the Peace was, on many accounts, advantageous to a young man; and with the knowledge of Adams, the Attorney General requested Bernard to appoint his friend to that office. The Governor expressed his desire to oblige Mr. Sewell, but observed,

" This young man has ranked himself with my opponents. He denounces and endeavours to thwart my measures and those of the ministry. I could not justify it to my sovereign to bestow a favour on such a person. And I wish you to tell him from me, that *so long as he continues to oppose me and the ministry, he must expect no promotion.*" Sewell conveyed the message to Adams. " *Then tell the Governor from me,*" replied the latter, " THAT I WILL NOT CHANGE MY COURSE, BUT WILL RAISE SUCH A FLAME IN THE PROVINCE AS SHALL EXPEL HIM FROM IT, AND ALL ROYAL RULE FROM AMERICA." The truth of this anecdote has been confirmed to me by another respectable gentleman, who was then a student in the office of Mr. Sewell."

The following Letter from Mr. JEFFERSON to Lieut. Gov. BARRY of Kentucky, evinces the unaffected modesty of the writer. While his countrymen are literally saturating him with eulogy, he shrinks from it, not as *Cesar* did from a *crown*, that he might grasp it the stronger, but that he may give place to the superlative merits of his compatriots. His whole life has been a practical comment upon this language. Witness his generous applause of his immediate predecessor, and his potent rival, the ex-President ADAMS ! Witness his invariable courtesy to his successors the ex-President MADISON, and the present Executive MONROE. And, notwithstanding the baleful and blasting anathemas of ascetic and frigid malice, witness his veneration for the Father of the Republic—the departed WASHINGTON.

The political axioms in this *little letter,* so *truly great,* ought to become the *text-book* of American Statesmen ; and be appended to Washington's Farewell Address. This idea forces upon the mind the melancholy consideration that ADAMS, JEFFERSON and MADISON, await only the

" Great Teacher's" summons, to join the immortalized
WASHINGTON in eternity.   Then may we say with the
Bard—

> " While others hail the *rising Sun*,
> " We'll bow to those whose race is run."

" *Monticello, July* 2d, 1822.

" SIR—Your favour of the 15th June is received, and I
am very thankful for the kindness of its expressions respecting myself; but it ascribes to me merit which I do not
claim.   I was one only of the band devoted to the cause of
Independence, all of whom exerted equally their best endeavours for its success, and have a common right to the
merits of its acquisition.   So also in the civil revolution of
1801, very many and very meritorious were the worthy
patriots who assisted in bringing back our government to its
republican tack.   To preserve it in that, will require unremitting vigilance.   Whether the surrender of our opponents, their reception into our camp, their assumption of our
name, and apparent accession to our objects, may strength-
en or weaken the genuine principles of republicanism—may
be a good or an evil, is yet to be seen.   I consider the party
divisions of whig and tory, the most wholesome which can
exist in any government; and well worthy of being nour-
ished to keep out those of a more dangerous character.
We already see the power, installed for life, responsible to
no authority, (for impeachment is not even a scare crow)
advancing with a noiseless and steady pace to the great object of consolidation; the foundations are already deeply
laid, by their decisions, for the annihilation of constitutional state rights, and the removal of every check, every coun-
terpoize to the ingulfing power of which themselves are to
make a sovereign part.   If ever this vast country is brought

under a single government, it will be one of the most extensive corruption, indifferent and incapable of a wholesome care over so wide a spread of surface. This will not be borne, and you will have to choose between reformation and revolution. If I know the spirit of this country, the one or the other is inevitable. Before the canker is become inveterate, before its venom has reached so much of the body politic as to get beyond control, remedy should be applied. Let the future appointments of Judges be for 4 or 6 years and renewable by the President and Senate.— This will bring their conduct at regular periods, under revision and probation, and may keep them in equipoise between the general and special governments. We have erred in this point by copying England where certainly it is a good thing to have the Judges independent of the King ; but we have omitted to copy their caution also, which makes a judge removeable on the address of both legislative houses. That there should be public functionaries independent of the union, whatever may be their demerit is a solecism in a republic of the first order of absurdity and inconsistence.

THOMAS JEFFERSON."